THREE STRIKES AND YOU'RE OUT
VENGEANCE AS PUBLIC POLICY

DAVID SHICHOR & DALE K. SECHREST
editors

SAGE Publications
International Educational and Professional Publisher
Thousand Oaks   London   New Delhi

For information address:

SAGE Publications, Inc.
2455 Teller Road
Thousand Oaks, California 91320
E-mail: order@sagepub.com

SAGE Publications Ltd.
6 Bonhill Street
London EC2A 4PU
United Kingdom

SAGE Publications India Pvt. Ltd.
M-32 Market
Greater Kailash I
New Delhi 110 048 India

Printed in the United States of America

Library of Congress Cataloging-in-Publication Data

Main entry under title:

Three strikes and you're out: Vengeance as public policy / David Shichor, Dale K. Sechrest.
    p. cm.
  Includes bibliographical references and index.
  ISBN 0-7619-0004-7 (acid-free paper).—ISBN 0-7619-0005-5
(pbk.: acid-free paper).
    1. Criminal justice, Administration of—United States. 2. Criminal
law—United States. 3. Recidivism—United States—Prevention.
4. Prison sentences—United States. 5. Mandatory sentences—
United States. I. Sechrest, Dale K. II. Title.
HV9950.S55 1996
364.973—dc20   *SC 1*   96-10039

This book is printed on alkaline paper.

96 97 98 99 10 9 8 7 6 5 4 3 2 1

Sage Production Editor: Gillian Dickens   Sage Typesetter: Marion Warren

Contents

Acknowledgments

|||| This book evolved out of a conference of the Association for Criminal Justice Research (California) at two sessions on "Three Strikes and You're Out" held in October 1994. Participants included Mike Reynolds, who was the chief citizen architect of the California law and the ballot initiative that was passed in November 1994 (Proposition 184) in which the voters approved a new three-strikes law by a 72% to 28% margin. Mr. Reynolds's daughter had been murdered in a senseless purse theft by a repeat felon in 1992, a case that is reaching trial as this book goes to press. Other participants included two authors in this book, a deputy district attorney, a deputy director of the California Department of Corrections, the director of California's Legislative Analyst's Office, and columnist Dan Walters of the *Sacramento Bee*.

The authors produced chapters in this national area of great social and legal change for which it is difficult to know the eventual outcome of events. In this sense, they were required to speculate in areas where the outcome is uncertain at this time, much like the early innings of the game for which these laws are nicknamed.

The authors wish to thank their respective families for the support and encouragement involved in putting together this volume. The staff of Sage Publications, particularly C. Terry Hendrix, was especially helpful in seeing the book through to completion.

Introduction

Public concern with violent crime, the inability of the criminal justice system to curb violence, and the widespread perception of leniency toward repeat criminals—fueled by political rhetoric—have led to a wide range of legislation aimed at dealing with habitual offenders. The most notable of these laws are generally grouped under the rubric of "three strikes and you're out." Arguments surrounding these laws range from beliefs that they will control persistent, serious, and violent offenders to concerns about their ultimate effectiveness and high cost. It is often felt that these laws will reduce crime and save taxpayers money (see American Society of Criminology, National Policy Committee, 1995, p. 15).

Debate over the constitutionality, propriety, utility, and efficiency of such laws appears destined to continue for some time. As this book goes to press the California Supreme Court ruled on June 20, 1996 that judges have the power to overlook prior convictions in three-strikes cases, a power which belonged to prosecutors under the 1994 law (Dolan & Perry, 1996). The elimination of discretion by judges was seen by the Court as unconstitutional. This decision has brought the governor, the legislature, prosecutors, and other concerned parties into conflict with the judiciary and will generate legislative attemps to stregthen the law in California. It is likely that similiar challenges will be raised in the 36 other jurisdictions which have comparable laws (Turner et al., 1995).

The chapters in this book represent a broad range of issues relevant to three-strikes laws, including local and national variations of habitual offender, career criminal, and recidivist statutes. Historical, legal, economic, and social issues are addressed along with specific information on the application of these types of laws nationally. The effects of such laws are difficult to measure due to the dearth of research on earlier, often weaker, laws and because many "true" three-strikes laws have been passed only in the past few years, as indicated by several authors. Current information is offered on the problems of implementation of three-strikes and mandatory minimum laws at the state and local levels, their potential for crime reduction, and their effect on correctional systems. Furthermore, the effect of the media on the development of three-strikes laws is reviewed, as are issues related to law enforcement in an era of increasingly harsh penalties for repeat offenders. Perspectives are offered that relate to offenders generally and to female offenders and street gang members specifically. A separate chapter explores the relevance of three-strikes laws for white-collar crime. The conclusion summarizes many of the relevant issues and provides some direction for future research in the area of this kind of punishment and its use in American society.

Part 1 of the book deals with legal and historical issues. Zeigler and del Carmen examine, through decisions of the U.S. Supreme Court, the constitutional conflict presented when habitual offender statutes are challenged on Eighth Amendment grounds as being cruel and unusual. They provide a brief historical background on the origins of repeat offender provisions and the term *cruel and unusual punishment* and track their ultimate collision in the 1980 landmark case of *Rummel v. Estelle.* A trilogy of cases is analyzed for the decade that followed *Rummel,* which found the Supreme Court clearly divided on the constitutionality of three-strikes measures with respect to issues of disproportionate punishments. In essence, the proportionality doctrine prohibits a punishment more severe than that deserved by the offender for the harm caused or the acts committed. Another section of this chapter summarizes current applications of proportionality laws. A final section discusses the emerging constitutional challenge under the doctrine of separation of powers, which in our system of checks and balances separates the power to punish the offender within the three branches of government: legislative, which has inherent power to define and provide punishment for crime; executive, which has the power to prosecute criminal conduct; and judiciary, which has the duty to provide a remedy for legislative and executive excesses. The authors indicate that the Supreme Court is struggling with these new sentencing laws within the framework of a proportionality standard, although they do not envision many reversals of three-strikes laws.

The history of the habitual offender within the broader framework of the development of the field of criminology and penology is explored by Jonathan Simon. As part of a volume interpreting and analyzing the three-strikes laws, the author offers a brief survey of the history of the relationship between criminology, penology, and laws against recidivists, focusing on the habitual offender and the career criminal. His conclusion considers the criminological basis of three-strikes laws and what it suggests about the relationship of penal strategies, criminological theory, and social control policies.

Part 2 addresses issues surrounding the implementation of three-strikes laws. Greenwood et al. discuss the future effect of three-strikes legislation based on an analysis of the implications of the law for California. They provide a detailed summary of the alternative measures they considered in evaluating the California law, including a previous legislative initiative considered for adoption by the California legislature. They describe how they used different models to forecast the outcome of three-strikes measures. The findings include reductions in crime and increases in costs projected for the previous law, the new law, and the various alternatives, along with anticipated trends in benefits and costs. Finally, costs are placed in budgetary perspective, including the various state services that may be affected to fund the different scenarios. They conclude that only time and the workings of the criminal justice system will determine the ultimate benefits and drawbacks of the new law.

Continuing the section on implementation, Cushman describes the effect of the California three-strikes law on justice systems operating at the county government level in California, often a neglected topic because state and national levels receive more attention. The author's intention is to prepare the reader—and officials of local government in other states where similar legislation may be enacted—to anticipate the challenges this law will present. Analysis focuses on Santa Clara County (a large county south of San Francisco), where the three-strikes law is assessed for system effect using a database of prior offenders to see how many would have been candidates for being processed by the new law. The most likely scenario depicting expected systemwide changes based on the law is presented. A discussion of the implications for other local jurisdictions is provided. A particular concern is with increases in local jail populations requiring higher security levels as jury trials increase due to the decline in plea bargained settlements of three-strikes cases, a theme echoed by Austin in this volume. Sadly, Cushman notes that empirical evidence will not necessarily make a difference in changing public opinion, a problem that "puzzles practitioners, and it is heretical to academics and researchers." Equally disconcerting is the concern that these types of laws may indeed aggravate the very conditions they wish to mitigate (i.e., a degradation in public safety caused by a deterioration of the justice apparatus).

Part 3 addresses the effect of three-strikes laws on the various agencies of the criminal justice system. Wiatrowski explores the implications of three-strikes laws for law enforcement, with particular concern for their role in crime control. He notes that the law is premised on the deterrence notion that if there are certain and serious consequences to crime, individuals confronted with the third crime will choose not to offend. In the past, the police have been at the forefront of crime control strategies, but these strategies have not been effective in having the police achieve the objective of controlling crime. Although the police will not be involved directly in three-strikes policies, this legislation has significant implications for policing, especially as offenders react to being arrested for a second or third strike that may place them in prison for 25 or more years. Wiatrowski explores the relationship of this legislation to the police role in crime control. He suggests that police reactions may vary widely, and questions may be raised about the effect of the law on police structure and organization.

Feeley and Kamin address the effect of three-strikes laws on the courts. They suggest that such laws are best understood within the context of a "moral panic" or symbolic crusade. It is suggested that these laws represent an effort at social change that may have marginal instrumental value in improving the effectiveness and efficiency of crime control. As such, they are not unique to the history of social policy in the area of criminal justice. The chapter explores similar legislation, such as the consequences of the Rockefeller drug law of 1972, state and federal mandatory minimum laws, and California's recent Victim's Bill of Rights. Standard patterns of response to law embraced in the midst of moral panic are identified and elaborated on, which include the judicial response, problems of injustice, efforts to reinstitute long-standing procedures, and legal steps taken to ameliorate the effects of these laws and rectify various problems. Finally, preliminary evidence is provided that these processes may have already begun.

The effect of three-strikes laws and mandatory minimums on prison populations is addressed by Austin, as mentioned earlier. Current initiatives pose enormous potential challenges to jail and prison administrators at all governmental levels. The degree of effect felt by each state will depend in great measure on how laws are worded and how they are implemented by the courts. Austin reviews the merits of such laws in application based on the initial experiences of states that have adopted three-strikes or mandatory minimum laws. He notes that in many cases the concerns raised by such laws were overstated; however, the truth-in-sentencing proposals, which are calculated to increase time served, have far more serious implications than three-strikes laws. The analysis indicates that three-strikes laws may have less effect on jail and prison systems than truth-in-sentencing laws, which require inmates to serve higher proportions of their sentences as a result of second-strike offenses (80% of the original sentence in California), not third strikes.

Part IV encompasses several specific issues that are relevant to the application of three-strikes laws. The chain of events that results in the three-strikes phenomenon is examined by Surette. He examines the effects of the media in developing the three-strikes concept, with particular reference to the California law that evolved out of the abduction and murder of a young girl (Polly Klaas) by a repeat felon. He finds that the effects of the media as an influence on social and criminal justice policy are difficult to discern and do not operate in direct or simple ways. Actual events, media coverage, and resulting criminal justice policy are difficult to assess independently or in combination. He uses a "social construction of crime and justice reality" approach to assist in developing an understanding of the relationship between the media and the formulation of policy in criminal justice organizations. A final concern is that emotionally driven opinion generated by the media will result in the passage of additional anticrime legislation without rational dialogue and without an objective assessment of the effect of various types of three-strikes laws.

Issues of suppression legislation are addressed by Klein from the perspective of the street gang, how it is defined, and how the law relates to the behavior of gangs and gang members. He makes the point that issues of definition of gang membership are no longer matters of scholarly interest, if that was ever the case. How gang behavior is defined has consequences in the law, just as the definitions found in three-strikes law have serious consequences for criminal offenders, especially in light of the fact that some three-strikes laws (e.g., in California) may count certain juvenile offenses as previous strikes. Criminological definitions, which favor neither prosecution nor defense, are given little weight due to the legalistic nature of the new laws. He suggests two possible approaches for criminologists to consider regarding the legislative validity of new laws and their applicability in the courts.

Casey and Wiatrowski discuss the potential effect of three-strikes legislation on women and present several substantive arguments opposing the use of this legislation for women offenders. They note that women are not the type of offenders at which the legislation is directed because they do not tend to be violent, predatory repeat offenders. They provide a historical perspective on female offenders, indicating their crimes, sentences, and imprisonment rates, with a particular emphasis on their demographics and their social circumstances. Variations in sentencing based on gender are discussed in relation to habitual offender legislation. They find that assessing the effect of three-strikes laws on women is difficult in light of evidence that women often commit violent crimes in response to physical and emotional abuse. They suggest a "differing needs" approach to the sentencing of female offenders, for whatever sentencing structure used.

Geis takes a unique view of the application of three-strikes laws. He notes that the failure to extend the three-strikes policy to white-collar offenders provides persuasive evidence of the class bias that fuels a viciously punitive policy. He documents a select segment of crimes of lethal white-collar violence perpetrated by people who run the country's corporate giants and the economic and social loss they have produced. He is concerned about our reluctance as a society to pursue these individuals with the same fervor we pursue common criminals. As a general deterrent, is it likely that this law would also deter more white-collar crime than street crime, and if so, why is it not used in that arena? His concluding remarks suggest some fundamental problems with the overall application of the law.

A concluding chapter by the authors summarizes several points of the book and raises some new issues, particularly with respect to the future of three-strikes laws. Concerns are expressed that three-strikes laws may miss their real targets—repeat violent offenders. This question was raised even by the father and grandfather of one of the victims in whose memory the California law was fashioned. Concern is also expressed for the long-term implications of these types of measures based on the inability of the judicial and correctional systems to manage the population increases accompanying these laws. An appellate court in California has now determined that defendants in three-strikes cases may challenge old convictions, a decision that if upheld, will again add to the problems of implementing these types of laws. In the final analysis, sheer lack of resources may dictate the future of three-strikes laws, or other types of adaptations may occur such as those suggested by Feeley and Kamin. The recent decision by the California Supreme Court to return discretion to judges in three-strikes cases is a clear example of the types of problems and adaptations that may arise. Moreover, and aside from questions about proportionality of punishment and equity, the idea of laws fashioned in an emotional political climate as quick fixes for social ills does not seem sensible or acceptable for American society.

References

American Society of Criminology, National Policy Committee. (1995, November/December). Task force reports. *The Criminologist, 20*(6), 4-16.

Dolan, M., & Perry, T. (1996). Justice deal blow to '3 strikes,' lower courts allowed discretion in sentencing. L.A. Times, 6-21-96, p. A1.

Rummel v. Estelle, 445 U.S. 263, 100 S. Ct. 1133 (1980).

Turner, M.G., Sundt, J.L., Applegate, B.K., & Cullen, F. (1995). "Three strikes and you're out" legislation: A national assesment. Federal Probation 59(3):16-35.

Postscript

The California Supreme Court ruled on June 20, 1996 that judges have the power to overlook prior convictions in three-strikes cases, a power which belonged to prosecutors under the 1994 law (*San Diego Co. v. Romero*, S. Ct. S045097). While this decision occurred as the book was going to press, it does not affect significantly the analysis of three-strikes and habitual offender laws and their consequences for the law and society generally. Researchers of California's three-strikes law predict that the ruling may not have a significant impact on the implementation of the law. Meanwhile, supporters attempt to change the wording of the law to preserve its original intent of limiting the discretion of judges.

PART

1

Legal and Historical Issues

Chapter One

Constitutional Issues Arising From "Three Strikes and You're Out" Legislation

FRANK A. ZEIGLER
ROLANDO V. DEL CARMEN

Seated at counsel table after an adverse jury verdict, the lawyer turned to the defendant to offer consolation. The client, realizing that all that could be done had been done, gave a wan smile and said, "You do the crime, you do the time." With that, the sheriff escorted the convicted felon away to serve a life sentence.

Over the years, that scenario has become familiar and is replayed daily in courts throughout the country. In contemporary language, the above aphorism might be more aptly stated: "You do the third crime, you do a lifetime." This reformulation is derived from the "three strikes and you're out" legislation passed in 1994 in California that is gaining momentum across the United States ("Recent Legislation," 1994).[1] The constitutional limits on these mandatory minimum sentencing schemes are left for the courts to resolve primarily by interpreting the "cruel and unusual punishments" clause of the Eighth Amendment and similar state constitutional provisions.

How the words *cruel and unusual* are defined by the courts reflects an evolving standard based on a developing societal view on punishment for crime. In *People v. Romero* (1995), the first constitutional test of California's new statute, the appellate court's decision reflects this public view in upholding three-strikes punishment. The opinion states that the ultimate test whether the statute is cruel and unusual or disproportionate can be determined by the results of California's initiative referendum (Proposition 184) conducted November 1994, in which the voters approved the new three-strikes law by a 72% to 28% margin. The judicial attitudes appear to be that the public has spoken; the appellate court defers to the will of the public. It is not always that simple, however.

This chapter examines, through decisions of the U.S. Supreme Court, the constitutional conflict presented when habitual offender statutes are challenged on Eighth Amendment grounds as being cruel and unusual. First, a brief historical background traces the origins of repeat offender provisions and the term *cruel and unusual punishment* and tracks their ultimate collision in the landmark case of *Rummel v. Estelle* (1980). Next, the chapter analyzes a trilogy of cases in the decade that followed that found the Supreme Court clearly divided on the constitutionality of three-strikes measures. Another section summarizes current applications of proportionality laws. A final section discusses the emerging constitutional challenge under the doctrine of separation of powers.

It must be noted at the outset that the legislative power to enact habitual offender laws similar to current three-strikes statutes has rarely been rejected by the courts on a constitutional basis, but when they have, it has been on disproportionality grounds. Given this, the main thrust of this chapter is on the proportionality doctrine as it relates to the cruel and unusual punishments clause of the Eighth Amendment. In essence, the proportionality doctrine prohibits a punishment more severe than that deserved by the offender for the harm caused or the acts committed. Over the years, the Supreme Court has woven an uneven tapestry of standards for evaluating three-strikes provisions, as the cases discussed below illustrate.

Background

James Madison borrowed the phrase "cruel and unusual" from the English Bill of Rights of 1689 and incorporated these words into the Eighth Amendment to the U.S. Constitution in 1791. It is essentially a term of enlightenment—that government is obliged to respect the human dignity of its citizens. Traditionally, the framers were thought to have been concerned only with torturous punishment methods. The accepted view today, however, is that the framers' intention was to create a right to be free from excessive punishment ("The Effectiveness," 1961). Despite its importance as a constitutional protection, the debate on the inclusion of the phrase "cruel and unusual" at the Constitutional Convention involved just two speakers and featured fewer than 200 words.[2] From such inauspicious beginnings, this clause has evolved to become the major constitutional limitation on today's three-strikes legislation.

Serving as backdrop to the constitutional conflict between cruel and unusual punishment and the enhancement of the length of sentences for repeat offenders are two cases decided by the U.S. Supreme Court almost nine decades ago but whose effect is felt up to the present. These cases are seminal on the issue of cruel and unusual punishment.

Cruel and Unusual Punishment: Weems v. United States

The constitutional principle that the punishment should fit the crime was first articulated by the Supreme Court in *Weems v. United States* (1910). As sometimes happens in developing law, unusual circumstances gave birth to precedent. William Weems was convicted of falsifying a public document and was sentenced to 15 years of hard labor. His punishment included shackling at the ankle and wrist and permanent loss of a multitude of civil rights, including parental authority, property ownership, and permanent surveillance for life (*Weems*, 1910, p. 364).

The majority opinion began with unusual candor by admitting that there was no precedent, and little commentary, on the meaning of the words cruel and unusual from which to fashion an interpretation of the Eighth Amendment. Nevertheless, the Court went on to say that justice required that punishment for crime be graduated and proportioned to the offense (*Weems*, 1910, p. 367). Reasoning that the Constitution must be read in light of contemporary social needs, the Court took the course of a broad interpretation of the Eighth Amendment. Thus, the doctrine of proportionality was born. The test used to reverse the conviction was an objective comparison of punishments of similar crimes in other jurisdictions and a comparison with punishments for more serious crimes within the same jurisdiction (*Weems*, 1910, p. 380).

The decision can be read as the first pronouncement by the Supreme Court on the basic conflict between legislative enactment of punishment measures and judicial interpretation of their constitutionality. The power of the legislature to define crime and punishment is vast, but not absolute; therefore, constitutional limits exist. The Court, in sweeping language, recognized the evolutionary potential for humaneness in a broad application of the cruel and unusual punishments clause. *Weems* was a landmark holding in Eighth Amendment law; most scholars commenting on the decision were surprised by the ruling (Fredman, 1910). There had been little prior indication that the Court was inclined to expand the cruel and unusual punishments clause into the area of sentencing—using the proportionality rationale.

The proportionality doctrine enunciated in *Weems* must be viewed as the most important limitation on present three-strikes legislation. This Eighth Amendment protection, however, had to wait more than 50 years to be held applicable to state criminal proceedings. This came about in *Robinson v. California* (1962), where the defendant was given a 90-day sentence by the trial court for narcotics addiction. The Supreme Court nullified the sentence, saying that any imprisonment for merely being addicted, as opposed to being found in personal possession or selling a specific controlled narcotic, was disproportionate. The importance of *Robinson* is twofold: First, it placed limitations on the states to criminalize a person's status (e.g., addiction to drugs or vagrancy, having no money); second, for purposes of this chapter, it made proportionality review of criminal sentences applicable to the states through the due process clause of the Fourteenth Amendment. Prior to this, an Eighth Amendment analysis was used only for federal crimes.

Graham v. West Virginia and Early Habitual Offender Statutes

The Supreme Court's first review of habitual offender laws came in *Graham v. West Virginia* (1912). In that case, the Court traced their beginnings to English statutes that "inflicted severer punishment upon old offenders" (*Graham*, 1912, p. 625). The record does not disclose how "old" John H. Graham was. It does indicate he had previously been convicted of grand larceny and burglary before his final grand larceny conviction resulted in a life sentence under a forerunner three-strikes provision enacted in Virginia in 1796 and later codified when West Virginia was partitioned and entered statehood in 1863.

In the 19th century, a majority of states had statutes that enhanced punishment for previous felons (*Graham*, 1912, p. 622). The Court in *Graham* first disposed of the former jeopardy argument of twice being punished for the same crime (using the former convictions) before indicating that habitual offender laws did not constitute cruel and unusual punishment.

Early repeat offender statutes were cumbersome, requiring the warden of the receiving penitentiary to investigate a person's criminal history and return him for a second indictment and jury trial on his previous convictions. The sole issue at this trial was whether the "convict is the same person mentioned in several records."[3] With the Baumes Act (1926)[4] passed by New York and adopted by other states, the procedure was simplified into one proceeding with the defendant's prior record determined at his initial trial and his sentence enhanced accordingly.

California enacted a forerunner three-strikes provision in 1927.[5] Its purpose was more remedial than deterrent. The theory that a small number of offenders committed a majority of crimes was yet to be known and was not the rationale for the statute. Eleven other states in that era had similar statutes in effect that were designed to sentence nonviolent third offenders to life imprisonment. Criminal punishment at that time did not reflect the public frustration that currently drives three-strikes legislation, hence these early statutes were seldom used to incapacitate a certain category of offenders. California repealed its early version in 1935. By 1980, when the Supreme Court first fully examined the conflict between three-strikes laws and cruel and unusual punishment, only West Virginia, Washington, and Texas still had nonviolent three-strikes statutes in their penal codes (*Rummel,* 1980, p. 296, n. 13).

The Collision: Proportionality and Three Strikes

Rummel v. Estelle (1980) was the first of four Supreme Court cases between 1980 and 1991 that yield seemingly inconsistent holdings on proportionality review. These decisions exemplify the struggle within the Court to clarify the parameters of punishment under three-strikes provisions and cruel and unusual punishment. This collision between criminal and constitutional law is discussed in the cases that follow.

Rummel v. Estelle: The Turning Point

William Rummel was convicted in Texas in 1964 of credit card fraud to obtain $80.00 worth of goods; was convicted in 1969 of passing a forged check for $28.36; and, in 1973, was convicted of obtaining money ($120.75) by false pretenses. All three nonviolent offenses were classified as felonies under Texas law. Rummel was prosecuted for his third "strike" offense under the Texas equivalent three-strikes provision. Within the statute, a third-strike conviction would result in a mandatory life imprisonment. Pursuant to the statute, the trial judge imposed the obligatory life sentence (*Rummel,* 1980, pp. 264-266).

Thereafter, an intense constitutional debate ensued within the appellate courts on the proportionality of Rummel's sentence. The Texas Court of Criminal Appeals affirmed his conviction in *Rummel v. State* (1974). A divided panel of the Fifth Circuit reversed his conviction as disproportionate in *Rummel v. Estelle* (1978). On rehearing, the circuit court, sitting en banc, rejected the panel's ruling and affirmed the conviction in *Rummel v. Estelle* (1978). On appeal, the Supreme Court, Justice Rehnquist writing for a 5-4 majority, held that the state of Texas could constitutionally impose a sentence of life imprisonment for three sequential nonviolent felonies.

The Court justified the *Rummel* (1980) result by distancing it from the precedent of proportionality in *Weems* (1910), stressing that recent applications had been limited to death penalty cases such as *Coker v. Georgia* (1977) because of their finality. A "bright line" was thereby drawn between death and imprisonment. The majority reasoned that to do otherwise would invite imprecision in future cases in attempting to draw a clear line on different lengths of imprisonment (*Rummel*, 1980, p. 275). *Weems* was characterized as limited by its particular facts (shackling at the wrist and ankles); the Court emphasized the highly subjective character of legal analysis used in establishing constitutional limits on amounts of punishment. The Court concluded that punishment is traditionally a state instead of a federal concern and is purely a matter of legislative judgment (*Rummel*, 1980, p. 282).

In a dissent, premised on *Weems* and the humanitarian intent of the framers of the Constitution, Justice Powell opined that proportionality analysis is an inherent aspect of the cruel and unusual punishments clause. He felt a constitutional obligation to measure "the relationship between the nature and number of offenses committed and the severity of the punishment inflicted upon the offender" (*Rummel*, 1980, p. 288). Justice Powell laid out three objective criteria, earlier announced in *Weems*, for reviewing proportionality challenges to the length of criminal sentences: (a) the nature of the offense, (b) comparison with sentences imposed in other jurisdictions for commission of the same crime, and (c) comparison with sentences imposed in the same jurisdiction of commission of other crimes (*Rummel*, 1980, p. 295).

Applying these criteria, the dissent concluded that Rummel's sentence violated the Constitution. First, the strike offense of false pretenses was found to be nonviolent. Next, the dissent established that Texas punished repeat offenders dramatically harsher than other jurisdictions. Finally, within the Texas statutory equivalent three-strikes scheme, Rummel's sentence for three nonviolent felonies was harsher than for those first and second offenders who committed more serious crimes, such as murder or rape (*Rummel*, 1980, pp. 295-303). The majority conceded in a footnote that one could imagine extreme examples when the doctrine of proportionality would be an issue (*Rummel*, 1980, p. 274, n. 11).

The *Rummel* decision is best understood in the context of Justice Rehnquist's statement that defendant Rummel had been well informed of the consequences of repeated criminal conduct (two prior prison sentences) and given every opportunity to reform. Therefore, the early three-strikes statute was nothing more than a "societal decision that when such a person commits yet another felony, he should be subjected to the admittedly serious penalty of incarceration for life, subject only to the state's judgment as to whether to grant him parole" (*Rummel*, 1980, p. 278). To the dissenters, however, evolving standards of decency necessitated the Court's exercise of its historic role as the final interpreter of the cruel and unusual punishments clause and felt that under the circumstances of this case, the Court ought to have rejected the punishment as unconstitutional.

The battle to delineate the precise contours of proportionality was fought again 2 years later in *Hutto v. Davis* (1982). The decision exemplifies the intensity of the continuing debate over the three-strikes legislation.

Hutto v. Davis: Anarchy in the Fourth Circuit

In *Hutto v. Davis* (1982), the Supreme Court upheld the power of the states to punish repeat offenders with severe sentences, including first offenders. Although not a three-strikes decision, *Davis* (1982) is instructive because it set the stage for a reversal of *Rummel* (1980) a year later in *Solem v. Helm* (1983).

Roger Davis's first offense in 1976 resulted in conviction on two counts of both possessing with intent and distributing 9 ounces of marijuana. A Virginia jury set his sentences at 20 years on each charge to run consecutively, or a 40-year prison term. *Davis's* procedural history resulted in the Fourth Circuit reversing his conviction on proportionality grounds in 1979 (*Davis v. Davis,* 1979). Two weeks after issuing its mandate in *Rummel* (1980), the Supreme Court ordered *Davis* (1979) vacated and remanded for further consideration in light of *Rummel*.

On remand, the Fourth Circuit reaffirmed its earlier reversal, reasoning that Davis's sentence fell within that narrow group of "rare" cases the majority in *Rummel* had conceded in a footnote that the doctrine of proportionality might apply (*Davis v. Davis,* 1981). In the protocol of the Supreme Court's supervisory powers over the circuit courts, this rejection of *Rummel* was almost unprecedented, prompting the Court to again grant review and state that "unless we want anarchy to prevail within the federal judiciary, a precedent of this Court must be followed by the lower federal courts no matter how misguided the judges of those courts may think it to be" (*Hutto v. Davis,* 1982, p. 375).

In affirming Davis's punishment, Justice Burger defended the bright line drawn in *Rummel* between death penalty cases and varying lengths of imprisonment. *Davis's* major premise was that an Eighth Amendment review should not be subjective; the Court also concluded that the 40-year sentence was beyond the constitutional range of the federal courts (*Davis*, 1982, p. 373). Once again, the Court stressed that federal courts should be reluctant to review legislatively mandated terms of imprisonment, be it within a habitual offender scheme or otherwise. This reluctance is based on the Tenth Amendment, which reserves to each state the power to determine varying lengths of sentences for the same criminal violation. (Using this approach, grand larceny may carry a 10-year maximum for a first offense in one state and 2 years in another.)

Justice Powell concurred and followed the precedent of *Rummel*, perhaps in an effort to quell the uprising in the Fourth Circuit. He pointed out, however, that neither the majority in *Rummel* nor the majority in *Davis* had laid the doctrine of proportionality to rest (*Davis*, 1982, p. 277). In retrospect, Justice Powell's concurrence was the fulcrum for his opinion 1 year later in *Solem v. Helm* (1983), which would reverse an almost identical three-strikes provision in South Dakota.

Three justices dissented in *Davis*, distinguishing *Rummel* as a three-strikes case that was not applicable to the first offense before the Court. The dissent also refused to go along with the Court's criticism of the mischief of the Fourth Circuit Court of Appeals. Moreover, the dissent argued that this was one of those exceedingly rare cases where the disparity of Davis's punishment, in comparison to other sentences in Virginia for marijuana offenders, required reversal on proportionality grounds. To support this, the dissent alluded to an unusual letter from Davis's trial prosecutor, included in the record, which characterized the sentence as "grossly unjust" (*Davis*, 1982, p. 385).

The *Davis* decision resulted in uncertainty in the Eighth Amendment analysis of the length of legislative sentences for both repeat and first offenders. With the majority of the Court demanding objective criteria (while rejecting all proffered criteria as too subjective), the two leading opinions in *Rummel* and *Davis* resulted in legal confusion within various circles regarding the applicability and scope of proportionality review ("The Eighth Amendment," 1982). State courts were equally confused; some chose to disregard Supreme Court interpretation and proceeded instead to decide similar cases under their parallel state constitution's cruel and unusual punishments clause.[6]

Solem v. Helm: Three-Factor Proportionality for Three Strikes

Just three terms after *Rummel,* the Supreme Court, by a 5-4 majority in *Solem v. Helm* (1983), demonstrated that no constitutional precedent is safe from revision. In a dramatic departure, the Court reversed a three-strikes life imprisonment sentence.

Jerry Helm had spent much of his life in the penitentiary and had six previous nonviolent felony convictions. In 1979, he pleaded guilty to writing a bad check for $100. Instead of asking the trial court to sentence Helm under the South Dakota general criminal statute, which carried 5 years for the offense charged, the prosecutor proceeded under an equivalent three-strikes provision. This resulted in a life sentence (*Helm,* 1983, p. 280).

The trial court record reveals that the sentencing judge indicated to Helm that it would be up to him and the parole board when he would be released. Unknown to the judge, a buried provision in the statute provided that Helm was not eligible for parole.[7] This proved crucial to the reversal of the sentence by the Eighth Circuit in *Helm v. Solem* (1982) and provided the rationale for the majority decision in the Supreme Court.

Justice Powell, who dissented in *Rummel* (1980), began the majority opinion by tracing the origin of the cruel and unusual punishments clause and proportionality back to English common law and *Weems* (1910). The opinion stressed the need for deference to both the legislature and the sentencing courts. Such deference meant that successful proportionality challenges would be rare, but no sentence was beyond constitutional scrutiny. As he did in dissent in *Rummel,* Justice Powell opined that when sentences are reviewed under the Eighth Amendment, courts should be guided by three objective factors or the "Helm test": (a) a comparison of the gravity of the offense and the harshness of the penalty, (b) a comparison with sentences imposed for other crimes in the same jurisdiction, and (c) a comparison with sentences imposed for the same crime in other jurisdictions (*Helm,* 1983, pp. 291-292). Although these factors are relative, they are not purely subjective. Judges are assumed competent to make broad comparisons of crime, relative harm, and culpability; moreover, legal line-drawing has always been a standard technique of the judicial art.

Applying the *Helm* test to the facts, the majority concluded that the three-strikes sentence was cruel and unusual. The strike crime of writing a $100 check was nonviolent and involved a small amount. The statute carried heavy penalties for two prior convictions that the court also viewed as nonviolent, minor offenses. Life imprisonment without possibility of parole was the most severe punishment available in South Dakota, hence the first factor suggested an imbalance between crime and punishment. Second, the court reviewed punishment for other crimes in the state and found that only a few much more serious crimes were mandatorily punished by life imprisonment without parole. Thus, the Court concluded that Helm's life sentence was more severe than sentences that South Dakota imposed for far more serious crimes. Finally, the majority considered the sentence in the national context and concluded that Helm would have been punished less severely for his third offense in every other state (*Helm,* 1983, pp. 298-300).

Because *Rummel* (1980) and *Helm* (1983) were essentially the same case (involving three-strikes life imprisonment punishment for nonviolent offenders), Justice Powell distinguished the facts by emphasizing the difference between life imprisonment with and life imprisonment without parole. Parole is a regular part of the rehabilitative process, is governed by legal standards, and assuming good behavior, is the normal expectation of a defendant like Rummel. On the other hand, Helm's only possibility of release was executive clemency, which lacked articulable standards (*Helm,* 1983, p. 303).

The dissenters were outraged that the majority would apply the three-factor test that *Rummel* had categorically rejected as imprecise while rejecting the bright-line rule of *Rummel* (proportionality review only for death sentences). Chief Justice Burger's dissent further highlighted the intra-Court dissonance that mandatory minimum sentencing evokes and that would reoccur in *Harmelin v. Michigan* (1991). In conclusion, the dissent reiterated its concern that proportionality review of length of sentences would open the floodgates to lower courts making subjective determinations of excessive sentences.

This prediction proved to be false, however, in the 8 years that followed. Lower courts had little difficulty in applying Eighth Amendment proportionality to cases involving legislative determinations.

During this period, only four state cases were reversed on the basis of the *Helm* three-factor test and none in the federal courts. These cases were *Clowers v. State* (1988), in which there was a reduction of a 15-year sentence without parole for a forged check; *Ashley v. State* (1989), in which there was a reduction of sentence for a defendant who burgled a home of $4.00 to pay for food eaten in a store; *Gilham v. State* (1988), in which the court struck down a felony conviction for using a vehicle in a criminal endeavor when the defendant had engaged in the lesser crime of prostitution; and *Naovarath v. State* (1989), in which the court set aside a life sentence without parole for an adolescent who killed an individual who repeatedly molested him.

The Eighth Amendment balance between crime and punishment in *Helm* would again change 8 years later when a divided Supreme Court issued a decision that would result in another reversal of precedent and a narrowing of the constitutional principle of proportionality review.

Harmelin v. Michigan: Proportionality "Strikes Out"

The war on drugs served as the catalyst for a third 5-4 Supreme Court decision on the constitutionality of three-strikes measures and similar mandatory minimum sentencing schemes. In *Harmelin v. Michigan* (1991), the Court again reversed itself on when proportionality review can be applied and returned full circle to principles announced a decade earlier in *Rummel.* The disagreement over the contours of the Eighth Amendment, as applied to legislative punishment, is evidenced by the five separate opinions the decision generated.

Ronald Harmelin was stopped for a routine traffic violation. A search of his vehicle revealed 672 grams of cocaine. Michigan's statute required that Harmelin be sentenced to life imprisonment (for possession of more than 650 grams) with no possibility of parole even though he had no prior felony record. Review was granted by the Supreme Court to consider the issue of whether a mandatory life sentence constitutes cruel and unusual punishment.

Justice Scalia rejected the principle that the Eighth Amendment requires a proportionality review for non-death penalty cases and called for the overruling of *Helm* (1983). Only Chief Justice Rehnquist, however, shared this view. The other three members of the plurality, led by Justice Kennedy, discerned a narrow proportionality doctrine in the Eighth Amendment, even though they agreed with Justice Scalia that there was nothing unconstitutional about Harmelin's sentence (*Harmelin*, 1991, p. 1008). The four dissenting justices argued, in three separate opinions, that mandatory sentences or three-strikes provisions like *Helm* called for more searching analysis.[8]

The decision's balance tilted in the direction of Justice Kennedy's concurrence. It began with a recognition of *Helm's* three-factor test and a narrow proportionality doctrine. To provide guidance in limiting appellate review of sentences, the concurring opinion rejected Harmelin's contention that full comparative analysis under *Helm's* three factors was required. Justice Kennedy stated that under the first prong—severity of the crime and harshness of penalty—Harmelin's sentence was proportionate. With that threshold determination, an analysis of the second and third prongs of *Helm* became unnecessary. This conclusion was rested on the three-part severity of Harmelin's drug offense: (a) A drug user may commit crime because of drug-induced changes in cognitive ability, (b) a drug user may commit crime to buy drugs, and (c) a violent crime may occur as part of the drug culture (*Harmelin*, 1991, p. 1002).

To support its position, the plurality cited results from *Drug Use Forecasting* (National Institute of Justice, 1990), in which a vast majority of arrestees had tested positive for illegal drugs. Therefore, Justice Kennedy reasoned that the Michigan legislature could conclude that because of the link between drugs, violence, and crime, the possession of large amounts of cocaine warranted the deterrence and retribution of a life sentence.

The decision in *Harmelin* (1991) represents a subtle shift in the balance between severity of crime and harshness of punishment from one of disproportionality to that of gross disproportionality. In conceding the harmful effects of drug trafficking on the nation, the Court failed to take into account defendant Harmelin's low position in the drug hierarchy or his first-offense status. In *Rummel* (1980), *Davis* (1982), and *Helm* (1983), the Court examined the nature of the crimes and the history of the individual defendants. In *Harmelin* (1991) the focus was on the abhorrent nature of the drug problem and its current status as "one of the greatest problems affecting the health and welfare of our population" (p. 1002).

The Implications of *Harmelin*: Current Applications of Proportionality to Three-Strikes Legislation

Federal Courts

The four cases analyzed above constitute a roller-coaster ride in Supreme Court proportionality review. Seldom has a constitutional amendment generated such closely split decisions as the cruel and unusual punishments clause has in defining the legislative parameters of three-strikes laws and mandatory sentences. Using the antidrug justification in *Harmelin,* the Court stripped the Eighth Amendment of much of its potential to prohibit the lifelong imprisonment of individuals for one offense and, correspondingly, of three-strikes offenders (see, generally, Vandy, 1993).

Under the last-decided-best-decided theory of legal precedent, only the extremely rare case wherein the punishment is grossly disproportionate to the crime will the threshold of *Harmelin* be crossed. Although the Court has not completely retreated to the bright-line rule of applying the Eighth Amendment only to death penalty cases, three-strikes measures similar to the California statute appear well poised to withstand constitutional challenges. Federal courts have cited *Harmelin* as the dispositive case in Eighth Amendment challenges, and three recent circuit court opinions appear to have settled the issue at the federal level at least for now.[9]

California's Three-Strikes Statute and Proportionality

The preceding discussion has highlighted the Supreme Court's view of proportionality under the Eighth Amendment of the U.S. Constitution. The California three-strikes statute has prompted other jurisdictions to implement similar legislation that will likely result in legal challenges.

As proportionality challenges develop, each state must chose between the holding of *Harmelin* under federal law or interpret its three-strikes measure under its own state constitution's cruel and unusual punishments clause. In *Romero* (1995), mentioned earlier, the California Court of Appeals looked to the California Constitution in holding the statute constitutional (*Romero,* 1995, p. 378). In a departure from *Harmelin,* the court applied the three-factor *Helm* test while mandating defendant Romero's sentence of 25 years to life for his third conviction.

In another departure, the Michigan Supreme Court, a year after *Harmelin,* reconsidered its 650-gram "lifer" law and held in *People v. Bullock* (1992) that such sentences for simple possession for first offenders were disproportionate to the crime under the Michigan state constitutional provision against cruel and unusual punishment. The decision used the three-objective criteria of *Helm* to examine the individual circumstances of defendant Bullock and concluded that it would be unfair to impute full responsibility of the defendant for any unintended consequences that might be later committed by others in connection with the seized cocaine (*Bullock,* 1992, p. 876). The decision applied only to those convicted of simple possession, which meant Ronald Harmelin's earlier sentence was reduced to life, with eligibility for parole in 10 years.

Summary of Current Varying Interpretations of the Proportionality Review

In general, federal courts are currently in accord with the "grossly disproportionate" approach announced in *Harmelin* (1991). In contrast, at the state level, *Romero* (1995) retains the objective comparison criteria of *Helm* (1983) in applying a somewhat cursory proportionality review. Finally, *Bullock* (1992) totally rejects *Harmelin* by engaging in extended proportionality review using the three factors of *Helm,* along with the individual circumstances of the defendant, to find Michigan's 650-gram life statute cruel and unusual. *Bullock* represents that rare situation where in-depth analysis favors the defendant (*Helm,* 1983, p. 285).

The difference in the above approaches is central to determining the balance between crime and punishment and the constitutionality of three-strikes laws. Proportionality of the length of sentence is determined by each court's application of the three-step sequence of objective criteria of *Helm* to Eighth Amendment review. As with most balancing analyses, the difficulty remains in identifying important variables, assigning them a weight, and deciding their cumulative effect (*Helm*, 1983, pp. 292-295).

Although *Harmelin* appears to severely limit the three criteria in *Helm*, chances are that most initial state court decisions will follow the extended analysis of *Helm* in reviewing their respective three-strikes legislation. This is evident in the *Romero* and *Bullock* state court decisions. The fact that *Harmelin* was divided on a 5-4 plurality lessens its precedential value. A comparison between the gravity of the offense and the harshness of the penalty is a matter of judicial determination. The other two factors in *Helm*—comparison of sentences for other crimes in the same jurisdiction and comparison with sentences for the same crime in other jurisdictions—induce a deference to preferences expressed by the state legislature. It is within this framework that three-strikes statutes will likely be decided. Rare, then, will be a case that will favor the defendant. Even in that case, a successful proportionality challenge does not set the defendant free; instead, it merely obliges the state to resentence within broad constitutional limits.

Perspective: Mandatory Sentencing and the Emerging Constitutional Issue of Separation of Powers

It is evident from court decisions that currently the Eighth Amendment is a limited source for invalidating three-strikes statutes. *Solem v. Helm* (1983) stands as the only Supreme Court decision declaring a criminal sentence disproportionate. The opinion, however, was based on the nonviolent nature of Helm's three offenses coupled with a no-parole provision within the early South Dakota three-strikes statute.[10]

The new California law,[11] learning well the lesson of *Helm*, requires that prior strike crimes be "violent" or "serious"[12] (the current offense can be any felony). The statute also provides for parole release, but increases the length of imprisonment for offenders with one prior by reducing the "good time" credits prisoners can earn from one half to only one fifth of the total sentence and mandating a minimum of 25 years for those with two or more prior convictions.

At first glance, the California law appears to comport with the essentials of *Helm*. A closer examination, however, reveals an important distinction. The South Dakota trial judge who sentenced defendant Helm had the option to dismiss from the record Helm's previous nonviolent crimes, thereby avoiding the imposition of a life sentence without parole if the court was persuaded that such punishment was not proportionate to the offense of writing a $100 bad check. Under the California three-strikes scheme, this individualized, proportionate review does not exist. Only the prosecution is vested with the power to dismiss a prior strike conviction(s).[13] This legislative change in the balance of power in the sentencing process is emerging as a second constitutional challenge to three-strikes legislation.

In the context of criminal punishments, our system of checks and balances separates the power to punish the offender within three constitutional functions. The legislature has inherent power to define and provide punishment for crime, the executive has the power to prosecute criminal conduct, and the judiciary has the duty to provide a remedy for legislative and executive excesses (*People v. Tenono,* 1970).

Other three-strikes laws in various states include statutory provisions, similar to those in the California law, that abrogate the long-standing historical power of judges to discretionarily impose criminal punishments. Not unexpectedly, Proposition 184 represents the public's displeasure with the judicial system's "revolving door" and "soft on crime" judges, who use loopholes to reduce punishment (*Romero,* 1995, p. 377).

The emerging separation-of-powers constitutional challenge is exemplified in *Romero* (1995), the first appellate decision on California's three-strikes statute. Jesus Romero had five previous felony convictions when he was arrested for possession of one tenth of a gram of cocaine. Two of the prior convictions were for residential burglary, qualifying Romero with two strikes ("life priors") and a mandatory sentence of 25 years to life imprisonment. The trial judge dismissed from the record Romero's two strikes and imposed a sentence of 6 years, reasoning that the mandatory sentence constituted cruel and unusual punishment under the California Constitution. The trial court further opined that the three-strikes provision that allowed only the executive (prosecutor) to dismiss prior convictions violated separation of powers (*Romero,* 1995, p. 371).

On review, the California Court of Appeals rejected the trial court's determinations and returned the case with instructions to sen-

tence Romero in accordance with three strikes (25 years to life imprisonment). Addressing the issue of separation of powers, the court
found the narrowing of judicial discretion to dismiss strike convictions as consistent with the public's pronouncement in Proposition
184 that the judiciary keep its "hands off three strikes" and the certainty of the statute's punishment for repeat offenders (*Romero*, 1995,
p. 377).

The decision was also premised on a narrowing of prosecutorial
discretion contained within the law. Whereas three strikes grants the
prosecutor sole authority to dismiss strike convictions "in the interest
of justice," other provisions[14] require the executive to plead and prove
all prior convictions available on a defendant, thus eliminating a
valuable tool from a prosecutor's plea bargaining arsenal. The appellate court found a balance in the statute because the legislature had
placed limitations on the use of discretion on both the judicial and
executive branches of government (*Romero*, 1995, p. 373). As this
chapter goes to press, *Romero* is pending before the California Supreme
Court.

The U.S. Supreme Court has yet to determine the constitutionality
of state statutes that curtail the traditional authority of judges in the
sentencing process. Interestingly, the Court has previously affirmed
prosecutorial discretion on the use of prior convictions in the plea
bargaining process. In *Bordenkircher v. Hayes* (1978), the defendant was
offered a 5-year sentence by the prosecutor in exchange for a plea of
guilty. Hayes did not plead guilty and was charged with being a habitual
offender under Kentucky law. He was convicted and sentenced to life
imprisonment. The Supreme Court upheld Hayes's conviction and
concluded, in a 5-4 decision, that the prosecutor's alleged vindictive-
ness was within the sound discretion of prosecutorial authority (*Hayes*,
1978, p. 358).

Hayes would appear to be inconsistent with three-strikes limitations
on a prosecutor's discretion to use prior strike convictions in the plea
bargaining process. The narrowing of both judicial and executive
authorities in three strikes, therefore, may result in legal challenges
from both branches of government as state legislatures across the
nation expand their power to punish offenders who "strike out" for the
third time.

Conclusion

Over the years, the Supreme Court has struggled with the concept of cruel and unusual punishment as applied to sentencing. The standard is proportionality. The Court has shown deference to punishment choices made by state legislatures, sometimes bowing to political realities when resolving constitutional dilemmas. In *Rummel* (1980), the majority sought to develop havens behind which to retreat. In *Davis* (1982), the majority had difficulty implementing its policy decision. In *Helm* (1983), a new majority of those present at *Rummel* recognized the inability of some state criminal justice systems to guard constitutional rights under the Eighth Amendment. In reaffirming principles of proportionality in sentencing, the *Helm* majority reasserted its role as final arbiter of the Constitution. The emergence of the drug wars brought with it the *Harmelin* (1991) plurality and ushered in three-strikes legislation and a return to legislative deference.

These four Court decisions first clarified and then confused proportionality review. Even if the states retain the objective criteria of the three-factor test of *Helm* after *Harmelin*, it is unlikely that there will be many three-strikes reversals. With mandatory sentencing severely hampering judicial discretion, the appellate courts might assert their authority and reject, under the doctrine of separation of powers, legislative provisions within three-strikes statutes that transfer sentencing discretion to the executive branch. Because the contest is being played in their ballpark and because they make the crucial calls, courts may ultimately find a way to limit three-strikes punishments and the courts' assumption that prior convictions contain all the information needed for justice to be served. Should that happen, the judiciary will then have redefined its role in society's continuing search for a system of justice where the punishment truly fits the crime.

Notes

1. Seventeen other states have implemented similar three-strikes measures in which the third strike results in a calculated low end (usually 25 years) to life imprisonment, with differing parole restrictions. Five other states are debating similar measures. See also *People v. Romero*, 37 Cal. Rptr.2d 364, 381 (1995) for a list of states with three-strikes laws.

2. *Annals of the Congress of the United States* (J. Bales, Ed., Vol. 1), 754 (1789).

3. Code of West Virginia, chap. 165, sec. 4 (1863).

4. New York Penal Laws, para. 1941 et seq. (1926).

5. California Statutes, chap. 634, para. 1, p. 1066 (1927).

6. See, for example, *State v. MuLally,* 127 Ariz. 92, 618 P.2d 586 (1980); *State v. Fain,* 94 Wash.2d. 387, 517 P.2d 720 (1980).

7. South Dakota Codified Laws, para. 24-15-4 (1979). See also Aked (1984).

8. Justice White dissented, joined by Justices Blackmun and Stevens. Justice Marshall filed a separate dissenting opinion. Justice Stevens also filed a dissenting opinion in which Justice Blackmun also joined.

9. See *United States v. Kramer,* 955 F.2d 479 (7th Cir. 1992); *United States v. Lowden,* 955 F.2d 128 (1st Cir. 1992); *United States v. Hopper,* 941 F.2d 419 (6th Cir. 1991). But compare in *Austin v. United States,* 113 S. Ct. 2801 (1993), the Court reversed a civil forfeiture as disproportionate under the excessive fines clause of the Eighth Amendment.

10. South Dakota Comp. Laws Ann., para. 22-6-1 (1969).

11. California Penal Code, sec. 667(b)-(i).

12. California Penal Code, sec. 667(d).

13. California Penal Code, sec. 667(f)(2).

14. California Penal Code, sec. 667(f)(1) and (g)(1).

Cases

Ashley v. State, 538 So.2d 762 (Miss. 1989).
Bordenkircher v. Hayes, 434 U.S. 357 (1978).
Clowers v. State, 522 So.2d 762 (Miss. 1988).
Coker v. Georgia, 433 U.S. 584 (1977).
Davis v. Davis, 601 F.2d 153 (4th Cir. 1979) (en banc).
Davis v. Davis, 646 F.2d 123 (4th Cir. 1981).
Gilham v. State, 549 N.E.2d 555 (Oh. 1988).
Graham v. West Virginia, 224 U.S. 616 (1912).
Harmelin v. Michigan, 501 U.S. 957 (1991).
Helm v. Solem, 684 F.2d 582 (8th Cir. 1982).
Hutto v. Davis, 454 U.S. 370 (1982).
Naovarath v. State, 779 P.2d 944 (Nev. 1989).
People v. Bullock, 485 N.W.2d 866 (Mich. 1992).
People v. Romero, 37 Cal. Rptr.2d 364 (1995).
People v. Tenono, 473 P.2d 933 (Cal. 1970).
Robinson v. California, 370 U.S. 660 (1962).
Rummel v. Estelle, 568 F.2d 1193 (5th Cir. 1978).
Rummel v. Estelle, 587 F.2d 651 (5th Cir. 1978) (en banc).
Rummel v. Estelle, 445 U.S. 263 (1980).
Rummel v. State, 509 S.W.2d 630 (Tex. Crim. App. 1974).
Solem v. Helm, 463 U.S. 277 (1983).
Weems v. United States, 217 U.S. 349 (1910).

References

Aked, J. (1984). Solem v. Helm: The Supreme Court extends the proportionality requirement to sentences of imprisonment. *Wisconsin Law Review,* pp. 1401-1430.

The effectiveness of the Eighth Amendment: An appraisal of cruel and unusual punishment [Note]. (1961). *New York University Law Review, 36,* 846.

The Eighth Amendment: Judicial self-restraint and legislative power [Note]. (1982). *Marquette Law Review, 65,* 434-443.

Fredman. (1910). Comment on recent judicial decisions—Cruel and unusual punishment. *Journal of Criminal Law, 1,* 612.

National Institute of Justice. (1990, June). *Drug use forecasting annual report* (Vol. 9). Washington, DC: Author.

Recent legislation: California enacts enhancement for prior felony convictions [Note]. (1994). *Harvard Law Review, 107,* 2123.

Vandy, K. (1993). Mandatory life sentences with no possibility of parole for first time drug possessors is not cruel and unusual punishment, *Harmelin v. Michigan,* 501 U.S. 957 (1991) [Note]. *Rutgers Law Review, 23,* 883.

Chapter Two

Criminology and the Recidivist

JONATHAN SIMON

In modern life government has little prestige. The prestige which it derived originally from its supposed connection with divinity has been lost. The earlier prestige continued, by force of custom, through the period when government was relatively simple because the problems of life were relatively simple. But government has been quite inadequate in dealing with the complex problems of modern life, and consequently the popular loss of faith in government is becoming constantly more general. Some people are trying to revive the faith by appeals to symbols such as the flag and the "Star-Spangled Banner." But apparently nothing except science can be substituted for divinity as a reason for faith in government. Government must stand on scientific efficiency or it cannot stand at all.

Edwin H. Sutherland (1934, p. 593)

As the great Edwin Sutherland saw so clearly, criminology has long been an essential element in the task of governing modern societies.[1] Even before the discipline of criminology was born, the new science of statistics focused heavily on crime and even on problems generated by the numerology of juries and sentences (Hacking, 1990, pp. 87-104).[2] The penal philosophers whose works defined classical criminology such as Cesare Beccaria and Jeremy Bentham were broadly interested in the problem of adequate government of the population (Beirne, 1991). They focused on crime as a key feature of this task but did not think of themselves a specialists on criminality. The transformations in penal practices that they helped encourage, however, especially the prison, created a concentrated flow of knowledge about crime and a special population subject to penal governance, both of which formed the surface for a science peculiarly dedicated to crime and punishment, but one that never lost its link to government[3] (Garland, 1985, p. 79). As political and social changes have periodically raised anew the problem of how to govern modern society, criminology has been a pivotal site for testing new technologies and strategies as well as sounding out new articulations of the rationality of rule.

This does not mean, to be sure, that criminologists are always persons of political influence, or that criminological ideas move freely into practical legislation. Even in times when criminology has enjoyed considerable political prestige, its influence on legislation has always been mediated by a number of factors, including the play of contending political forces, the resistance of embedded ideologies, and the pull of specific institutional establishments (Garland, 1985; Rothman, 1980). What it does mean is that criminology always exists in a tense proximity to power that operates both as a stimulus to research and a constant challenge to scientific legitimacy.

Criminology in its quest to constitute itself as a scientific discipline has been haunted by the fear that its objects, crimes and criminals, are conventional and thus dependent on cultural formations that are themselves malleable and contingent (Sutherland, 1934, pp. 17-18). Criminologists have frequently sought refuge in one or more of the broader sciences of the human subject, including economics, biology, and sociology. But this quest for a broader framework has consistently been limited by the recognition that much of the political and social appeal of criminology has always been its potential to solve the social problems that most concern the public. As a consequence, criminology can never stray far from highly politicized conceptions of crime as a social problem.

The recent rash of laws mandating lengthy imprisonment sentences for recidivists under the slogan "three strikes and you're out" (so called because most of them mandate a life sentence after a third serious or violent felony) is an example of criminology's ambivalent relationship to penal policy. Such laws, and these are only the latest in a long history of recidivist measures, have rarely had the unqualified support of the criminological community (three-strikes laws have been noteworthy for the absence of vocal criminological supporters; Greenwood et al., 1994). Yet the public support for these measures, at a time when government spending is generally in deep disrepute, reflects the ongoing influence of criminological ideas over our political efforts to govern society.

Known by diverse names at different times (habitual offender, professional criminal, career criminal, high-rate offenders, violent predators, etc.), the recidivist has long interested both criminological researchers and politicans (Morris, 1951, pp. 3-4). Criminologists of various schools, and in various eras, have been wary of the lack of scientific precision in the concept of the recidivist, but they have also recognized the importance to criminology as a discipline in being able to offer effective tools to handle this figure, which embodies what the public fears most (Maltz, 1984).

Behind this figure of the persistent criminal is the closely related idea that determinable and relatively small populations of recidivists are responsible for a large portion of crimes. This idea has periodically preoccupied penal policy for well over a century. It has survived changing theoretical fashions in criminology and previous cycles of optimism and defeat. What accounts for this robustness? This chapter argues that it stems from the relationship between government and criminology. This is a relationship of conscience and convenience (Rothman, 1980), but it is also a relationship of mutual constitution.

Although criminology did not invent the recidivist, it has found in this popularly invested subject something very dear to its own heart, the belief that understanding and differentiating among offenders systematically could yield major efficiencies in the burdensome task of controlling crime. That there is a special subpopulation of dangerous offenders whose identification and neutralization would result in dramatic reductions in the overall crime rate without resulting in a massive increase in the portion of that population undergoing incarceration is a solution that is deeply compatible with the ambitions of modern governments. Its reproduction in a number of different legislative programs, deploying different technologies and shaped by a variety of different theoretical enterprises, reflects this compatibility.

The failure of particular efforts has not dulled it because whenever one attempts to think penal strategies within the rationality of governing through science all roads lead to the recidivist.[4]

As part of a volume contextualizing the three-strikes laws, this chapter offers a brief survey of the history of the relationship between criminology and laws against recidivists. Historians of modern penality have identified a number of major and minor transformation points since the 18th century (Foucault, 1977; Garland, 1985; Rothman, 1971, 1980, 1983). For purposes of tracking the recidivist concept, this history may be broken down into three more or less stable regimes through which the power to punish has been exercised in modernizing societies since the middle of the 18th century. Not all of these have been equally reflected in all modern societies, nor has each been of necessarily equal significance.

Jacksonian penality.[5] In the first half of the 19th century, the penitentiary prison emerged as a leading technology for punishing serious crimes. Although never driving out corporal punishments or alternatives like transportation, the penitentiary clearly dominated the penal imagination and facilitated the rapid growth of a whole set of governmental and scientific formations around the penitentiary regime, the management of the prison, and the fate of the released prisoner.

Progressive penality. The turn of the 19th century witnessed a profusion of new penal techniques in both North America and Europe aimed at a range of pathological types including juvenile delinquents, "inebriates," "defectives," and "the insane." The penitentiary, which had long remained largely invisible to the law, received explicit recognition as new laws transformed the rational penal code bequeathed by the revolutionary generation.

The new penality. Since the late 1960s, penal systems in the United States particularly (but also Europe) have moved away from explicit reliance on normalization. The same practices of imprisonment and community supervision remain but with a focus on incapacitating dangerous offenders.

The Recidivist in Jacksonian Penality

The recidivist as a subject of concern predates the emergence of a genuinely scientific criminology. As early as the late 18th century, urban elites became concerned with the accumulation of a "dangerous class" of poor in the great preindustrial cities. Presumed to have no productive role in the economy, this ill-defined population was thought to live habitually through vagrancy, prostitution, and crime. By the middle of the century, this group stigma had begun to give way to a focus on a large but more defined group of habitual criminals, who came to be seen as a fundamental problem for liberal strategies of government in general and its penal strategies in particular.

Jacksonian penality in the United States was centered on the individual but largely as a black box of presumptively rational and moral responses to environmental incentives. If crime represented something like an accidental failure of communication between penal code and legal subject (Pasquino, 1980, p. 17), the task of government was to clarify the message. The penitentiary became the central instrument of this government in the United States (Rothman, 1971). Its appropriateness was at first premised on its ability to neutrally conduct the deterrent message of the penal code. The prison could extract time with a banker's precision and with none of the features of monarchical excess (atrocity, publicity, capriciousness). The prison rapidly generated its own forms of knowledge and new purposes for its existence, especially the goal of reforming the offender through isolation, silence, work, and religious exhortation (Dumm, 1987; Foucault, 1977; Ignatieff, 1978).

This new penal strategy was a key component of the broad reformation in the strategies of governing society at the end of the 18th century. The mercantilist policies of the 18th century stressed the police power and the expansion of state administration. In contrast to this, liberal political economists conceived of laissez-faire as an alternative strategy for government based on treating the economy as an autonomous and self-regulating mechanism. Although contemporaries talked about restricting the state and expanding the space of individual freedom, from the perspective of government what was emerging was a set of new strategies for regulating the population without directly coercing individuals. Jacksonian penality in the United States (and its

Victorian contemporary in Great Britain) was a key site of both contradiction and realization for this new liberal strategy of government. The development by midcentury of professional police and penal establishments powered a grid of deterrent signals designed to regulate the conduct of the population from afar (Garland, 1985, pp. 36-70).

The term *habitual criminal,* as it began to be used in the general discourse on the dangerous classes, was largely irrelevant to the penal strategies of liberal government. To be sure, classical penal philosophy could imagine variation among offenders in their criminal activity, but it understood such habitual offending as a possible outcome of what David Garland (1988, p. 7) has called a "general anthropology" of the human subject, that is, one that treated crime as a possible response of all citizens who are inadequately directed by the deterrent and incentive signals of proper government, rather than treating it as an endemic feature of certain subgroups and types. Thus, far from being a boon to the prestige of the penal system, the new concern with habitual offenders always threatened to become a potent source of "problematization" (Garland, 1985, p. 61).

The rapidly growing urban populations in the early 19th century outstripped the apparent demand for their labor in the commercial economy that characterized cities like London and Paris (Chevalier, 1973). The market for alarmist descriptions of impoverished neighborhoods and their denizens that grew in the middle of the century reflects at least the perception that this was so. Crime, intermittently and highly imperfectly measured by reports to the newly created London police, was a major focus of this fear of what was taking place in the wretched precincts so graphically described.

These discourses (e.g., Fregier, 1838; Mayhew, 1865) were not yet criminological as that concept would be understood later. Their authors were learned men and literate members of the elite linked to both police and social work. The publication of statistical data on crime (although of dubious value) offered quantitative texture to the disturbing images of the urban poor and became a potent source of complaint for parliamentary oppositions (Leps, 1992, p. 25; Radzinowicz & Hood, 1980, p. 1309).

The image of the habitual criminal in this discourse was not yet that of the "individual delinquent"; it was still an instance of a whole class (or perhaps even race although the term did not yet have the solidity it would later). Anticipating (or perhaps laying down the tracks for) the functionalism of criminal anthropology and sociology, they imagined these swarms of prostitutes, vagrants, and robbers to be a kind of parasitic infection of the social body or perhaps an excrescence of it (Porter, 1986, pp. 28-30; Radzinowicz & Hood, 1980, pp. 1310-1311).

In Great Britain, these fears were almost certainly intensified by the end of transportation, in the 1850s, at the demand of eastern Australia (Radzinowicz & Hood, 1980). Great Britain had relied heavily on transportation to rid itself of serious felons by shipping them to the other side of the globe, where they could participate in a separate society altogether. This method had permitted strong use of the criminal law against the dangerous classes without the provocation of many executions and with less investment in prisons. Without extensive use of prisons, the whole problem of what to do about the released prisoner, let alone the recidivist, never came up (Garland, 1985, p. 7; Morris, 1951, p. 23; Radzinowicz & Hood, 1980, p. 1308).[6]

Between 1869 and 1885, Great Britain and a handful of U.S. states adopted habitual offender laws that provided for mandatory extensions of confinement for the repeat offenders.[7] The stimulus to these laws was not so much criminological theory as public concern stoked by the end of transportation and the increased reliance for social control on the reformative and deterrent power of the penitentiary. These laws seemed to mark the failures of the Jacksonian penality rather than revitalizing it. But this was not a period of major innovation, and these laws remained largely ignored and isolated from spreading. Then, after 1895 in Britain and 1900 in the United States, a great number of laws were passed establishing extended and often life terms for multiple offenders (Elliott, 1931, p. 187).

The dangerous classes and the habitual criminal that were crystallizing out of the crowd at the end of the 19th century brought both opportunity and challenge to the task of governing. These notions clearly undermined an approach to liberal governmentality, which presumed the self-regulating capacities of the population if provided sufficiently clear incentives. They also undermined the claims of a penality based on deterring or reforming individuals through the application of a general and uniform discipline. But the habitual offender also provided a key reason for expanding government and penal agencies in particular.

The Recidivist in Progressive Penality

Scholars of the history of penality have recognized an important transformation at the end of the 19th century (Garland, 1985; Radzinowicz & Hood, 1980, 1990; Rothman, 1980, 1983). The basic component of 19th-century penal practice, the prison, remained, but a plethora of new techniques and distinctions emerged, including the indeterminate sentence, parole, probation, juvenile justice, and specialized corrective regimes for inebriates, the insane, and habitual offenders.[8]

The causes of this great wave of penal reforms are multiple and complex. The failures of the penitentiary system were becoming more visible to the public through the focus of newly developed mass newspapers (Rothman, 1980, p. 18), which found in crime a major motivator for sales (Leps, 1992). Rothman and Garland have both emphasized the links between the transformation in penality and the larger problematization of government brought on by the massive expansion in the industrial economy and its social by-products during this period, particularly in Britain and the United States. The liberal governmentality, of which the prison had been such a central instrument, found itself challenged by the visibly social nature of late 19th-century problems and thus the decreasing plausibility of strategies aimed at communicating incentives to individuals. Penality was a privileged site for developing rationality of rule that would bolster the governability of industrial society without knocking out the legal underpinnings of a capitalist economy.

Examining the English case, Garland (1985) argues that the penal system was important because it fell right on the intersection of the major issues fueling the crisis of liberal government.

> At the end of the nineteenth century, then, there was a period of crisis and transformation produced by a complex series of intersecting events and developments. This crisis centered around two related issues: the proper role and function of the state in relation to the economic and social spheres, and the condition and regulation of the lower classes. The penal complex, being a series of state agencies dealing overwhelmingly with the poor, was clearly implicated in this crisis—its ideological foundations and strategic position being undermined by the breakdown of market society and its political balances. Moreover, penality was simultaneously undergo-

ing a serious crisis of operation and of public legitimacy, which provided an additional force of transformation. (p. 65)

By the end of this period of governmental reform, the state had taken on major new commitments to intervene in the social life of the poor in the name of stabilizing the conditions of the working class and of urban life generally. Both Garland and Rothman suggest that these changes achieved new entitlements for the working classes in both the United States and Great Britain but that they also represented efforts to protect political power from the expansion of democratic liberties (especially in Great Britain, where the working class had only achieved suffrage). A new welfare approach to governmental rationality replaced the liberal emphasis on creating general incentive structures with strategies targeted directly at the social order itself through mechanisms like insurance, public health, public education, and social work. The new techniques of Progressive penality carried this welfare theme in their emphasis on addressing the roots of crime in the biological, economic, and social pathologies of specific populations.

The emergence of criminology as a self-consciously positivist science played a critical role in shaping this new penality. But criminology had competitors with which it shared enough common goals for a great many coalitions but also significant differences. These included eugenics, which focused on isolating and containing defective humans and preventing their reproduction, and social work, which sought to create a direct normative supervision over the lives of immigrants, defectives, and others (Garland, 1985).

In both countries, habitual offender laws became a central feature of the new regime. In Great Britain, the Habitual Criminals Bill of 1869 represented one of the first major changes to the Victorian penal regime (Radzinowicz & Hood, 1990, p. 245). The law made a minimum term of 7 years' imprisonment mandatory on conviction of a third offense. Complaints that the severity of the law was being diluted due to court tactics encouraged a whole series of adjustments over the next couple of decades as legislators wrangled with how to define a habitual offender (just by numbers of convictions or by evidence regarding the offender's lifestyle?) and how to prevent judges from finding loopholes in the mandatory rules. The Crime Prevention Act of 1908 has been widely recognized by historians as the pivotal act in the turn-of-the-century transformation of British penality. The law recognized the importance of individualizing penal strategies to particular problems of criminality. Special procedures and institutions were designated for juveniles, with the aim of reducing exposure to prison and intensifying reform influences. On the other end of criminality, the habitual offender was to receive a special sentence, not exceeding 15 years, of preventive detention on top of his sentence of penal servitude in punishment of his current offense. A special prison with a regime deemed less severe was established to hold such offenders after the completion of the penal portion of their sentence (Garland, 1985, p. 219; Radzinowicz & Hood, 1990, p. 268 ff.).

From the very beginnings, positivist criminology was wary of the habitual offender concept. If the habitual offender was too specific for classical criminology with its highly abstract conception of human subjectivity, it was already too general for the positivist criminology with its emphasis on developing scientific typologies of offenders. Still, habitual offenders were what the public feared, and criminologists recognized both social duty and opportunity in invoking this figure.

Perhaps the most influential work of 19th-century criminology, Lombroso's *L'Uomo Delinquente* (1876/1912),[9] included the habitual criminal in its typology of criminal populations but in a somewhat obscure location. The book's most famous subject was "the born criminals," whose innate criminality, a kind of evolutionary regression, was revealed in distinctive morphological irregularities—stigmata—and who made up a large proportion of the criminal population. They were distinguished in Lombroso's schema from "occasional criminals," by which Lombroso meant not persons who commit crimes only occasionally but those persons who are constitutionally "normal" and whose criminal propensities (which Lombroso took to be a general feature of early childhood) are only realized in the occasional bearer due to child-rearing and environmental factors. The habitual criminal is relegated in Lombroso's schema to the main subgroup of occasional criminals, whose criminality, unarrested by proper environmental factors, becomes a matter of habit.

The American and British reception of Lombroso involved the implicit transformation of this schema in which the central role of the born criminal was elided by his habitual cousin (Rothman, 1980, pp. 58-59).[10] Excited by the possibilities for successful interventions in the social reproduction of criminality that Lombroso's work invoked, but put off by the seeming determinism of his biological speculations, Anglophone criminologists emphasized the most ecumenical of Lombroso's later writings while they mimicked his insistence that a scientific expertise could ultimately identify and deal with dangerous criminals. The famous studies of English convicts by Charles Goring (1913) demonstrated statistically that morphological irregularities of the type identified by Lombrosans were no more likely to be found among convicts than among other populations. At the same time, Goring concluded that the causes of crime were social and biological factors acting on the individual offender, which could be demonstrated and disaggregated through a statistically rigorous science of the criminal (Garland, 1988, p. 11).

In his 1893 work, *Introduction to the Study of the Dependent, Defective and Delinquent Classes,* Charles Henderson (1893/1908), Professor of Sociology at the University of Chicago, described habitualisation in terms readily assimilable to the emerging general account of social control. His schema comes directly from Lombroso.

> These persons have not striking marks of the instinctive criminal, and apparently not innate tendency to antisocial conduct. There may be a hidden moral weakness which easily yields to the impulses of circumstances and corrupting environment. Impunity at the first lapses increases the tendency to secure the objects of desire without labor. The forbidden acts, going without detection and punishment, form the links in a chain of habits which ever grows heavier. (Henderson, 1893/1908, p. 222)

American criminologists shared Lombroso's ambivalence about the habitual offender. Lombroso's "born criminal" might be the wrong theory, but at least it pointed in the direction of what a scientific account of criminality might look like. Maurice Parmelee, in his 1917 textbook *Criminology,* noted that the habitual offender lacked scientificity; indeed, it had a kind of simplicity that questioned the need for a science of crime at all.[11]

> It is likewise psychologically erroneous in most if not all cases to speak of a habitual criminal. Habit exists only when through constant repetition a person acquires great facility in performing a particular action. By habitual criminal is ordinarily meant a person who commits criminal acts fre-

quently, but not owing to inherited traits as in the case of the so-called born criminal. This person is therefore said to have acquired the habit of crime. But in many cases the habitual criminal commits many different kinds of crime. At one time he may commit a crime against the person, such as assault; at another time he may commit a crime against property, such as burglary. It is evident that he must employ different actions in these two types of crime. And even if he always commits the same type of crime, as, for example, larceny, he will under different circumstances commit the crime in different ways. (Parmelee, 1917, p. 196)

Still, there was an obvious point of intellectual convergence between criminology program and the habitual offender concept. The growing popularity of sociological and psychological explanations of crime made it possible to conceive of habits less mechanistically as the more or less durable associations forged between the individual delinquent and criminogenic neighborhoods and friendship networks. Describing the best knowledge about reformation, for example, Sutherland (1934) pointed toward strategies of manipulating the stimulation of tendencies toward delinquency and, second, by "sublimation" of these tendencies toward socially positive outcomes. "Both processes," Sutherland (1934) argued, "really consist in the modification of habits" (p. 555).[12]

Moreover, the existence of habitual offenders as a widely and popularly recognized category of criminal enhanced the promise of criminology to solve mysteries underlying society's most-feared criminal threats (Garland, 1985, p. 187). As late as the 1940s, law professor John Barker Waite (1943) could characterize the existence of "repetition of crime" as evidence that the treatment of convicted criminals, even under Progressive indeterminate sentence laws, remained in practice punitive and lacking in real treatment alternatives (p. 86).

If the idea of the habitual offender could be accommodated to the criminological program in the early 20th century, habitual offender laws were a good deal less attractive (Sutherland, 1934, pp. 495-496). The standard critique was that such laws left the determination of habitualness to the arbitrariness of past record. By imposing a life sentence on a third or fourth offense, the laws arbitrarily threw together the professional criminal, whose long record reflects crime as a serious career, and the marginal petty offender, who manages to create a long record by persisting in minor offenses and not being clever enough to elude capture and conviction.

Most criminologists would have preferred laws that provided complete discretion to scientifically informed agents in determining what penal measures to bring to bear on offenders. The indeterminate sentence was the legislative proposal that most perfectly represented this vision. It would in principle permit those offenders most readily amenable to treatment to be released on parole back to the community very early while providing lifetime incapacitation for those who could not be broken from the criminal life.

The centrality of the habitual offender and habitual offender laws in Progressive penality was not so much a reflection of their significance for criminological research (although they appeared there) as it was a point of balance. The habitual offender represented a place of intersection between criminology and its reform rivals, on the one hand, and reform and defenders of the established penal strategies, principally the prison establishment and its government allies, on the other (Garland, 1985; Rothman, 1980). The anchoring of the new British system around habitual offender laws rather than an indeterminate sentence for all offenders constituted what Garland calls a pragmatic compromise between criminology and its competitors.

Rothman and Garland both emphasize the logic of individualization as the major theme of criminology in this era. Whether they focused more on clinical observations, ethnographic description, or statistical analysis, criminologists assumed that uncovering more and more distinct variations among criminals would lead to progress in both science and treatment. Penal strategies appropriate to welfare conceptions of government needed to be capable of responding to the social dimensions of crime. Paradoxically, this required a deeper knowledge of the individual, which could permit the truly dangerous offender to be pulled from the crowd that no longer constituted the unruly mass of a dangerous class.

In Britain, the habitual offender acts became integrated with the procedures favored directly by criminologists. Linked to separate regimes for juveniles, inebriates, and the insane, the habitual offender laws could be seen as marking the extreme of a continuum of sanctions aimed at the specific features of different types of offenders. In the American case, the habitual offender laws were often passed to act as brakes on already-adopted indeterminate-sentencing laws. These measures were supported by law enforcement and conservative opponents of the reform process. They effectively served to set a limit on the discretion of parole authorities. This was mediated by the fact that the laws did not kick in until a number of felony convictions (and thus parole failures presumably) and by the ability of district attorneys to charge bargain around the provisions (Rothman, 1980, p. 199).

In both countries, the compromise was made easier by the ability of supporters to characterize the laws in terms that made them sound very much like the vision of penality coming out of criminological circles (Garland, 1985, p. 175; Rothman, 1980, p. 199). Supporters of the criminological program, like sociologist Mabel Elliott (1931, p. 186), viewed the laws as a lagging indicator of change in the right direction.

The capstone of this compromise was the separation of the habitual offender from the dangerous classes in general and to its status as a criminological object. The program of preventive detention for habituals was undoubtedly aimed at improving the security of the law-abiding population, but it was also intended to improve the prospects of the less severely deviant offenders who would be given a better chance at normalization through the removal of these most infected criminals (Garland, 1985, p. 242).

The Recidivist in the New Penality

Scholars have suggested that penality is once again undergoing a change comparable in scope to the earlier moments of rupture that produced Progressive and Jacksonian penalties (Cohen, 1985; Ericson & Carriere, 1994; Feeley & Simon 1992, 1994; Nelken, 1994; Rothman, 1983; Simon & Feeley, 1995). The decades after World War II were in many respects a continuation and a reinvigoration of Progressive welfarist strategies of government, which had been stalled by the Great Depression and then jump-started by the vigorous need for labor during the war.

The 1950s and 1960s represented a peak for the penal side of welfare government, with most states leaning in the direction of highly individualized sentences and explicity reformative goals (Friedman, 1993, p. 305). Since the mid-1970s, the system has been rocked by a continuing series of transformations that has shattered this posture. The major elements of this include (a) a widespread legislative turn away from reformative justifications for punishment and individualization in sentencing, (b) the movement of narcotics crimes and sanctions against them from the periphery of crime control to the center, and (c) a dramatic increase in the overall rate of incarceration.

This is not the place for a sustained analysis of this transformation, which we are still undergoing. Like earlier ruptures, its causes were both internal to the penal realm and external. The rapid deindustrialization of the United States beginning in the 1960s and accelerating greatly in the 1970s and 1980s destabilized the social anchors of welfare governmentality generally. Advances in the rigor of criminological methods during the 1950s and 1960s made the failures of reformative penal methods more visible than they had been in the past. The politicization of crime, beginning with the 1964 presidential election and the due process revolution (from opposite sides of the political spectrum), placed a heavy burden of public oversight on the penal system just as its practice was being undermined by social and economic changes.

As during earlier periods of transformation in penality, criminology has played an important but complex role. Criminological research on incapacitation and its popularization has been especially influential in justifying if not initiating the massive expansion of incarceration that has taken place since the end of the 1970s. Even more important has been the consolidation of a number of practices of long standing into a fundamentally new surface for criminological intervention. One critical element has been the emergence of the criminal experience of the population as a "real" object. Despite the long history of criminal statistics, it was not until the first national victimization surveys were conducted in the 1960s in the United States that something approaching what criminologists had always meant as the "crime rate" became a visible object of public discourse. Closely related has been the rapid accumulation of a statistical knowledge of how the institutions that carry out criminal policy function as a system. The phrase "criminal justice system" has often been criticized as unrealistic, but in a certain sense the plethora of research numbers about the functioning and interaction of different agencies has assured that the system has a material existence.

The recidivist once again played a central part in the construction of a new penality. Most of these changes have intensified the significance of the recidivist in the law. Perhaps the most important has been the effort of the federal government over the past three decades to encourage the states through grants and knowledge dissemination to focus resources on recidivists at all levels of the criminal justice system, but especially police and prosecution functions (Moore, 1986, p. 354; Rhodes, Tyson, Weekly, Conly, & Powell, 1982).

Recidivism has also received recognition in the new determinate sentencing laws around the United States that routinely limit the judge's discretion to allow recidivists to escape imprisonment and set terms to increase on formula reflecting the past record. Parole and probation, once charged with completing rehabilitation and helping keep offenders safely within the community, have in recent years become major engines of incarceration, sending two thirds and sometimes more of their caseloads back to prison (Simon, 1993, pp. 205-229).

Ironically, this incarceration machine has been slowed some by the sheer inability of states to pay for prisons fast enough. In many states, the new ultra-tough laws are reduced in fact by the necessity of meeting judicially enforced population caps on prisons in the form of automatically credited "good time" that can reduce a sentence by as much as a third or a half. Old recidivist laws, which remained on the books (although often unused), have in recent years been revitalized by prosecutors seeking to avoid automatic sentence reductions, and new laws have been passed by popular initiatives creating mandatory term extensions for recidivists (Dubber, 1990, p. 195). Three-strikes laws passed recently resemble in many respects their predecessors from the 1920s, but whereas then they represented a limit on what was perceived as an ascendant rehabilitative penality, today they represent a goad to a punitive, incapacitation-oriented penality that is perceived as too slow.

As before, the recidivist and antirecidivism laws have been important sites for the articulation of criminological discourses on the emerging crisis of government. Since the early 1970s, a burgeoning field of criminological research has redoubled past efforts to document the effects of such offenders (Blumstein, Cohen, Roth, & Visher, 1986, pp. 188-189). The study of "criminal careers" had its origins in Progressive Era criminology if not earlier, but since the 1970s it has expanded to become the dominant theme in the criminological research program. As early as the 1920s, criminologists like Ernest Burgess at Chicago and Sheldon and Eleanor Glueck at Harvard were studying the fates of the individuals in particular cohorts of people released from prison to identify different paths of success and failure and their correlates. This early program of criminal careers research was over-shadowed by the tremendous success of the sociological paradigm represented by the likes of Sutherland, which stressed the failures of normative reproduction in individual life circumstances (Laub & Sampson, 1991). Since the 1970s, however, the sociological paradigm over criminology has waned, and the criminal careers model has flourished and with it a different way of conceptualizing the recidivist.

A crucial text in this transformation was the modern classic, *Delinquency in a Birth Cohort* (1972) by Marvin Wolfgang, Robert Figlio, and Thorsten Sellin. Taking an entire cohort of boys born in Philadelphia in the year of 1945 who remained in the city between the ages of 10 and 18, the authors assembled a database of criminal activity from official records and used it to construct a statistical picture of crime in a birth cohort. First was the cohort itself. Criminologists had always been interested in the distribution of crime within the population but had never before been able to present the criminality of a "natural" population (in contrast to an institutional sample). The population became a "real" object that could be grasped by criminology. Second, the authors found that "chronic offenders" (defined as those who committed five or more delinquent acts) represented only 6% of the entire cohort but accounted for more than half of reported crimes of the entire group. The obvious conclusion that the authors drew was that intervention aimed at suppressing this subpopulation could be highly efficient (Wolfgang et al., 1972, p. 105). Third, the authors constructed a matrix of events that expressed the passage of the entire cohort through their criminal careers as a set of contingencies whose actual probabilities could be specified, including arrests, convictions, and imprisonment.

Delinquency in a Birth Cohort has been widely criticized for many specific failings (perhaps most important is its reliance on official records), but its influence as a model for relevant criminological research cannot be underestimated. It is within this new paradigm that most significant research on recidivists has been conducted during the past 25 years. As the Panel on Research on Criminal Careers reported,

The basic finding—that a small number of extraordinarily active offenders account for a disproportionately large share of total arrests—attracted the interest of scholars and practitioners and stimulated efforts to understand offenders' termination patterns. This problem has often been pursued by examining persistence probabilities of at least one more event after each event in a criminal history. (Blumstein et al., 1986, p. 89)

A good example of the complex transformation of the recidivist in the new criminal careers research program is a 1978 report by Joan Petersilia, Peter W. Greenwood, and Marvin Lavin, titled *Criminal Careers of Habitual Felons*. The authors, particularly the first two, have gone on to become leading figures in contemporary criminology. The study, conducted under a grant from the Law Enforcement Assistance Administration, involved intensive qualitative interviews with 49 habitual offenders who were serving time for armed robbery at a medium-security prison. This methodology was admittedly weak by the usual standards of quantitative analysis, but was offered as useful for deriving testable hypotheses and was supported by reference to the Progressive tradition of detailed case studies, in particular, Sutherland's *The Professional Thief.*

We sought to illuminate the development of serious criminal careers in the hope of identifying vulnerable times when appropriate interventions by the criminal justice system might best have reduced the offenders' threat to the community. Initially we were optimistic that such points could be identified, for earlier research had suggested that habitual offenders tend to follow a common maturation process. We expected the interview data to reveal systematic development patterns in which juvenile offenders were transformed into adult professional criminals. Moreover, we expected the adult professionals to pursue crime as a preferred occupation, continually developing their skills, increasing their profits, and becoming more specialized. It is now clear that this is too simplistic a notion. The reality of criminal career development is much more complex and diverse. (Petersilia et al., 1978, p. vi)

Although the focus on criminal "types" was reminiscent of Progressive criminology, their subjective features turned out to be rather thin vessels for the more important discernment of quantitative differences in individual crime rates. The real goal of the report was not to explain the development of "intensive" offenders or what keeps the "intermittent" offenders intermittent (indeed, the authors acknowledged that most correlations in this regard are marginal) but to identify high-rate offenders who would be the most efficient targets for imprisonment. Although rehabilitation and deterrence were mentioned as research concerns, largely to show how they failed, incapacitation was given pride of place (Petersilia et al., 1978, pp. v, xii).

Since the publication of *Delinquency in a Birth Cohort,* researchers have continued to build support for the proposition that a small group of offenders with high individual rates of offending under a variety of different rubrics accounts for the majority of crime (see citations in Dubber, 1990, pp. 193-194; Weis, 1986, p. 27). This notion of individual frequency, or *lambda* as it is technically known, has become the crucial handle that contemporary criminology can offer crime policy. By distinguishing between participation and frequency, the criminal careers research program has opened up an entirely different way of representing the problem of crime for criminal justice practitioners and researchers. It is not that earlier criminologists did not think about the frequency with which certain criminals, recidivists, committed crimes, but their research methods and ultimately their theoretical ideas made it nearly impossible to separate frequency from the thicker picture of the offender's life history and community circumstances. Today's criminal careers research makes it possible to isolate the problem of frequency through the mix of high-frequency offenders in the pool of criminal participants at any one time.

Perhaps the best known and most controversial of the subsequent studies was Peter Greenwood's 1982 report for RAND (with Allan Abrahamse), *Selective Incapacitation.* Drawing on self-report data from incarcerated robbers and burglars (as well as official criminal records), the researchers estimated individual frequencies and sought to correlate these with a range of variables thought to be predictive. The report found that the worst 10% of the inmates, with respect to reported frequency of criminal activity during their periods of freedom, accounted for a majority of the crimes committed by the entire group. The resulting scheme proposed a series of seven factors, including age at first arrest and first drug use and the regularity of employment and incarceration, but excluding factors like race and age, and claimed to be an efficient predictor of high-rate offenders. The RAND proposal drew mixed responses and has been expressly adopted by no jurisdiction (Visher, 1986). But the idea of the high-rate offender as a pivotal target of criminal policy has only grown and dispersed to less visible issues like the preventive detention of drug offenders (Wish & Johnson, 1986, pp. 70-75).

Although the criminal careers research program in criminology has helped make the recidivist once again a crucial target of criminal policy, its relationship to traditional habitual offender laws has been more ambivalent. As the Criminal Careers Panel pointed out, the older habitual offender laws may, in fact, have been counterproductive:

> From the perspective of incapacitation, prison capacity is used inefficiently if offenders are imprisoned beyond the time at which their criminal activity would have terminated if they were free on the street. Therefore, it is reasonable to ask whether "habitual-offender" laws, which mandate very long sentences, may result in incarceration of offenders well after they have ceased to be serious risks. (Blumstein et al., 1986, p. 15)

At the same time the new research points toward an alternative model of incapacitation based on selectivity:

> Selective treatment of offenders in the criminal justice system is one way to direct criminal justice discretion more effectively toward reducing the level of crime. Recent research findings have rekindled interest in basing selection explicitly on classifications derived from empirically demonstrated relationships between specific variables and criminal career dimensions, especially the frequency of serious criminal activity. In various ways, such information has long been used as a selection criterion: in formal ways in parole release decisions and in structuring prosecution priorities for "career criminal units" and more often informally in setting pretrial release conditions and sentencing. The recently discussed crime control strategy of "selective incapacitation" at sentencing . . . is based on selection rules defined explicitly in terms of frequency classifications. (Blumstein et al., 1986, p. 15)

Although few criminologists have vocally supported the three-strikes wave of legislation, the proponents of these measures have drawn on the criminal careers paradigm to make their case. The most frequently mentioned criminological idea in the debate has been (often badly distorted) the finding by Wolfgang and his colleagues (1972) on the chronic offenders in the Philadelphia birth cohort. Proponents have continually cited some version of the figure that 6% of the offenders in the cohort committed 70% of the crimes (Butterfield, 1995). The discussion rarely goes back to incorporate the context of the study (juvenile delinquents born 50 years ago). Nor has any effort been made on the part of proponents to incorporate the kind of implementing considerations that the criminal careers research program has foregrounded in its own policy aimed pronouncements (Blumstein et al., 1986). For example, no real effort is made to argue that the definitions of strikes used in the laws has a strong relationship to individual offense rate, or lambda. Neither has attention been paid to the essential insight that incapacitative effect may be estimated by past conduct but that it really depends on hypothetical future conduct. Lifetime incarceration for a person whose offending career is on a predicted downswing due to age is a relatively inefficient way to achieve crime prevention.

Conclusion

The survival of the recidivist as an object of concern for criminology over more than a century and through three important revolutions in penality demonstrates its importance in the relationship between crime and the task of governing modern society. From the dangerous classes to the habitual offender to the career criminal, there has been a consistent search for a selected target through which the challenge of crime might be mastered. Criminology, which has grown with the need for government to deploy rational strategies aimed at ameliorating crime, has never fully embraced the recidivist in any of his guises (although the most recent one is closest). At the same time, recidivists remain a figure that criminology must comprehend for criminology to be as relevant as possible.

In conclusion, I want to focus on three important points of comparison between the place of the recidivist in Progressive penality and in the new penality: the locus of the individual, the claims of expertise, and what each form of penality offers government.

Knowing the Individual

It is interesting that criminology now and at the beginning of the century claimed to be improving on its predecessors by finally bringing the individual criminal into focus.[13] Progressive Era criminologists complained that the Jacksonian penal regime treated every individual offender largely the same. They promised to get inside the subject and reveal the causal dynamics of criminality, whether biological, psychological, or sociological. Depending on the approach, methods included clinical observation or interview, observation in the community, and statistical analysis of correlates of recidivism. Many of the new criminal careers criminologists have criticized Progressive criminology for failing to develop adequate individual-level data on crime (Blumstein et al., 1986, p. 29). Earlier research had often fallen into the so-called ecological fallacy of generalizing from geographically organized data, say, the crime rate for a neighborhood, to making inferences about the individuals in that set—for example, they are more involved in crime than people in other neighborhoods (Weis, 1986, p. 5). The new research distinguishes the participation rate (the portion of a population that participates in crime) and the frequency (the rate at which members of that participant group commit crimes). The latter, as noted above, has become of vital importance to the large strategy of incapacitation.

Thus, the individual is important to both research programs but in utterly different ways. The individual habitual offender was seized on by Progressive criminality as a route into the genealogy, child rearing, and community life that produced him. The individual offender in the criminal careers model is a kind of one-person population whose conduct contributes to the crime of an aggregation of other populations and who can be known only in and as a population. The community exists but only as a set of interactions that do or do not alter the rate at which the offender commits crimes (Blumstein et al., 1986, p. 29).

Expertise and Power

Criminology has always sought to enhance the significance of its own expertise to the exercise of governmental power. The indeterminate

sentence, for example, which for nearly a century defined the aspira-
tions of enlightened penal practice, made the ability to interpret an
individual's life history and conduct in prison essential to the meaning
of a just sentence. Deciding whom to parole and when rarely fell to
criminologists, but its authority required the presumption of the kind
of knowledge of the individual that criminology boasted and sometimes produced. The new sentencing systems, like the U.S. sentencing
guidelines, emphasize automatic or semiautomatic rules of decision
that make it possible to individualize sentences based on "objective"
features of criminal conduct, but not on the basis of clinical judgments
about criminality. The reform sentencing systems all disparage the
kind of clinical judgments made by parole authorities in the past.
Criminal careers research on recidivism offers expertise in setting up
systems that are just as much automatic rule systems as current guidelines. Indeed, subsequent research has suggested that selectivity in
incapacitation could be achieved without looking beyond criminal
record items that the current systems already include (Cohen, 1983).

How Are We Governed?

The historiography of modern punishment suggests that major
transformations in penal practices, especially those focused against
recidivists, have been keyed to broader crises of government. At the
turn of the century, criminology helped formulate a model of government that addressed the security of populations through a knowledge
of the individual. By bridging the gap between an old fear of the
dangerous classes and the emerging realities of mature industrial cities,
the criminological discourse on the habitual offender helped legitimize the expansion of welfare strategies of government. The new
criminology of recidivism offers a picture of individuals as distinct
crime rates that influence the crime rate of the whole population. In
this sense, and despite the formal neutrality of criminal careers research to specific goals of punishment, the career criminal has helped
legitimize a massive expansion of segregative strategies, mainly, more
use of incarceration.

The overwhelming pressure for antirecidivism laws has, as in the
past, come largely from the political field rather than from criminology. But the history too briefly sketched above suggests that crimi-

nology has a great if indirect effect on the formation of public under-standing. In periodically reconstructing the figure of the recidivist, criminology has also reinvented its relationship to the task of govern-ing. The new penality with its emphasis identifying and tracking high-risk offenders has helped to prepare the ground for three-strikes laws by reinforcing the belief that little can be done to prevent or correct an offender's criminality and undermining the belief that individual strategies of corrections can help reduce crime.

Notes

1. Michel Foucault (1991) coined the term *governmentality* to describe the ascendance of the idea that the human population with its biological, social, and economic forces was the major subject and object of governing. This seems obvious to us, but for centuries the task of governing as understood by rulers had as much or more to do with territories, military strength, and revenue collection than with the human beings who made up the population of a country.

2. As early as the 16th century, political theorists responding to the legacy of Machiavelli began to describe the good prince in terms that reflected the new discourses about economics, demography, and other indicators of social health. By the middle of the 19th century, the "blizzard of numbers" (Hacking, 1990) produced by government officials and social scientists had made the population a concrete and compelling reality. Government policy from that point increasingly addressed itself to the population, seeking to address social ills by treating parts of the population and measuring success and failure by changes in the condition of the population as reflected in statistics.

3. Government here does not simply mean the state, but rather the capacity to rule at all levels of society in which the state has become more and more involved in the 19th and 20th centuries.

4. It is perhaps for this reason that criminologists have returned to reflectively examine the criminological treatment of the habitual offender (see Elliott, 1931; Morris, 1951). Norval Morris's 1951 volume in particular remains a classic of legal, scientific, and philosophical analysis. The topic has been particularly interesting to historians of criminal justice, including Rothman (1980), Radzinowicz and Hood (1980, 1990), and Garland (1985).

5. British historians describe this same regime as Victorian and the following one as Edwardian (Garland, 1985; Radzinowicz & Hood, 1990).

6. A smaller stream continued to western Australia until 1868. The French continued to deploy transportation as a significant penal measure into the 20th century.

7. Some date back even farther. Virginia had a habitual offender law on the books in 1849, and Massachusetts had a similar law in 1817 (Elliott, 1931, p. 187).

8. Between the publication of the Gladstone Report in 1895 and the outbreak of World War I, Great Britain, for example, adopted more than 20 major penal statutes effecting practices of sentencing, the organization of penal institutions, the length and regimen of incarceration, and the conduct of aftercare (Garland, 1985, pp. 277-278). The United States underwent comparable changes, which, due to the federal basis of American

criminal justice, are far more difficult to enumerate. From the turn of the century through the 1920s, a large number of American states adopted separate juvenile procedures and institutions, some clinically oriented prison techniques, and most important, indeterminate sentence systems that permitted prison sentences to be individualized to reflect the reformability or incorrigibility of the offender (Rothman, 1980).

Both Garland (1985) and Rothman (1980) have argued that new penal strategies are best seen as part of much larger movements for reforming how government worked. Rothman attributes penal reform to the interest taken in crime by the dynamic elements of the new, urban, educated classes in the United States, which have been known to history as the Progressives. These actors sought change along a broad set of governmental fronts, including the organization of elections, the regulation of markets, and expansion of education and public health.

9. A somewhat popularized and translated version was published by Lombroso's daughter, Gina Lombroso-Ferrero: *Criminal Man According to the Classification of Cesare Lombroso* (New York: 1911).

10. The French aggressively opposed Lombrosan criminology and focused on his earlier and most biological writings to characterize him as an enemy of reform.

11. Sutherland was just as dismissive in the 1934 edition of his *Principles of Criminology* (p. 548).

12. Sutherland (1934) quotes Dewey as the "best statement of the method of modification of habits" (p. 548).

13. Laub and Sampson (1991) offer a fascinating analysis of the contextual factors that led the supremacy of the sociological criminology focused on Sutherland's differential association theory over the promising early variant of criminal careers research carried out by Sheldon and Eleanor Glueck. The Gluecks shared the contemporary concern with representing the habitual offender against a data field of aggregated individual careers. They differ from today's dominant approach through their psychological focus in variables.

References

Beirne, P. (1991). Inventing criminology: The "science of man" in Cesare Beccaria's *Dei Delitti e Delle Pene* (1764). *Criminology, 29,* 777-820.

Blumstein, A., Cohen, J., Roth, J. A., & Visher, C. (Eds.). (1986). *Criminal careers and "career criminals."* Washington, DC: National Academy Press.

Butterfield, F. (1995, September 11). First federal three strikes conviction ends a criminal's 25-year career. *New York Times,* pp. A1, A9.

Chevalier, L. (1973). *Laboring classes and dangerous classes in Paris during the first half of the nineteenth century.* Princeton, NJ: Princeton University Press.

Cohen, J. (1983). Incapacitation as a strategy for crime control: Possibilities and pitfalls. In M. Tonry & N. Morris (Eds.), *Crime and justice: An annual review of research* (Vol. 5, pp. 1-84). Chicago: University of Chicago Press.

Cohen, S. (1985). *Visions of social control.* New York: Polity.

Dubber, M. D. (1990). The unprincipled punishment of repeat offenders: A critique of California's habitual criminal statute [Note]. *Stanford Law Review, 43,* 193-240.

Dumm, T. (1987). *Democracy and punishment: Disciplinary origins of the United States.* Madison: University of Wisconsin Press.

Elliott, M. A. (1931). *Conflicting penal theories in statutory criminal law.* Chicago: University of Chicago Press.

Ericson, R., & Carriere, K. (1994). The fragmentation of criminology. In D. Nelken (Ed.), *The futures of criminology* (pp. 89-109). London: Sage.

Feeley, M., & Simon, J. (1992). The new penology: Notes on the emerging strategy of corrections and its implications. *Criminology, 30,* 449-474.

Feeley, M., & Simon, J. (1994). Actuarial justice: The emerging new criminal law. In D. Nelken (Ed.), *The futures of criminology* (pp. 173-201). London: Sage.

Foucault, M. (1977). *Discipline and punish: The birth of the prison.* New York: Pantheon.

Foucault, M. (1991). Governmentality. In G. Burchell, C. Gordon, & P. Miller (Eds.), *The Foucault effect: Studies in governmentality* (pp. 87-105). Chicago: University of Chicago Press.

Fregier, H.-A. (1840). *Des Classes Dangereuses de la Population dans les grandes Villes, et des Moyens de les Rendre Meilleurs* (2 vols.). Paris: Bailliere.

Friedman, L. M. (1993). *Crime and punishment in American history.* New York: Basic Books.

Garland, D. (1985). *Punishment and welfare: A history of penal strategies.* Brookfield, VT: Gower.

Garland, D. (1988). British criminology before 1935. *British Journal of Criminology, 28,* 1-17.

Goring, C. (1913). *The English convict: A statistical study.* London: His Majesty's Stationery Office.

Greenwood, P. W., with Abrahamse, A. (1982). *Selective incapacitation* (Report prepared for the National Institute of Justice). Santa Monica, CA: RAND.

Greenwood, P. W., Rydell, C. P., Abrahamse, A. F., Caulkins, J. P., Chiesa, J., Model, K. E., & Klein, S. P. (1994). *Three strikes and you're out: Estimated benefits and costs of California's new mandatory-sentencing law* (Report No. MR-509-RC). Santa Monica, CA: RAND.

Hacking, I. (1990). *The taming of chance.* Cambridge, UK: Cambridge University Press.

Henderson, C. R. (1908). *Introduction to the study of the dependent, defective and delinquent classes.* Boston: D. C. Heath. (Original work published 1893)

Ignatieff, M. (1978). *A just measure of pain: The penintentiary in the Industrial Revolution.* London: Penguin.

Laub, J. H., & Sampson, R. J. (1991). The Sutherland-Glueck debate: On the sociology of criminological knowledge. *American Journal of Sociology, 96,* 1402-1440.

Leps, M.-C. (1992). *Apprehending the criminal: The production of deviance in nineteenth-century discourse.* Durham, NC: Duke University Press.

Lombroso, C. (1912). *Crime, its causes and remedies.* Chicago: American Law Institute. (Original work published as *L'Uomo Delinquente* in 1876; revised edition published as *L'Homme Criminel* in 1887 in Paris)

Maltz, M. (1984). *Recidivism.* Orlando, FL: Academic Press.

Mayhew, H. (1865). *London labour and the London poor: The condition and earnings of those that will work, cannot work, and will not work* (4 vols.). London: Charles Griffin.

Moore, M. (1986). Purblind justice: Normative issues in the use of prediction in the criminal justice system. In A. Blumstein, J. Cohen, J. A. Roth, & C. Visher (Eds.), *Criminal careers and "career criminals"* (Vol. 2, pp. 314-355). Washington, DC: National Academy Press.

Morris, N. (1951). *The habitual criminal.* Cambridge, MA: Harvard University Press.

Nelken, D. (Ed.). (1994). *The futures of criminology.* London: Sage.

Parmelee, M. (1917). *Criminology.* New York: Macmillan.

Pasquino, P. (1980). Criminology: The birth of a special savior. *Ideology and Consciousness, 7,* 17-32.

Petersilia, J., Greenwood, P. W., & Lavin, M. (1978). *Criminal careers of habitual felons.* Washington, DC: National Institute of Law Enforcement and Criminal Justice.

Porter, T. (1986). *The rise of statistical thinking, 1820-1900.* Princeton, NJ: Princeton University Press.

Radzinowicz, L., & Hood, R. (1980). Incapacitating the habitual criminal: The English experience. *Michigan Law Review, 78,* 1305-1385.

Radzinowicz, L., & Hood, R. (1990). *The emergence of penal policy in Victorian and Edwardian England.* Oxford: Clarendon.

Rhodes, W., Tyson, H., Weekly, J., Conly, C., & Powell, G. (1982). *Developing criteria for identifying career criminals.* Washington, DC: U.S. Department of Justice.

Rothman, D. J. (1971). *The discovery of the asylum: Social order and disorder in the new republic.* Boston: Little, Brown.

Rothman, D. J. (1980). *Conscience and convenience: The asylum and its alternatives in Progressive America.* Boston: Little, Brown.

Rothman, D. J. (1983). Sentencing reforms in historical perspective. *Crime & Delinquency, 29.*

Simon, J. (1993). *Poor discipline: Parole and the social control of the underclass, 1890-1990.* Chicago: University of Chicago Press.

Simon, J., with Feeley, M. (1995). True crime: The new penology and public discourse on crime. In T. G. Blomberg & S. Cohen (Eds.), *Punishment and social control: Essays in honor of Sheldon Messinger* (pp. 147-180). New York: Aldine de Gruyter.

Sutherland, E. H. (1934). *Principles of criminology.* Chicago: J. B. Lippincott.

Visher, C. A. (1986). The Rand Inmate Survey: A reanalysis. In A. Blumstein, J. Cohen, J. A. Roth, & C. Visher (Eds.), *Criminal careers and "career criminals"* (Vol. 2, pp. 161-211). Washington, DC: National Academy Press.

Waite, J. B. (1943). *The prevention of repeated crime.* Chicago: Callaghan.

Weis, J. G. (1986). Issues in the measurement of criminal careers. In A. Blumstein, J. Cohen, J. A. Roth, & C. Visher (Eds.), *Criminal careers and "career criminals"* (Vol. 2, pp. 1-51). Washington, DC: National Academy Press.

Wish, E. D., & Johnson, B. D. (1986). The impact of substance abuse on criminal careers. In A. Blumstein, J. Cohen, J. A. Roth, & C. Visher (Eds.), *Criminal careers and "career criminals"* (Vol. 2, pp. 52-88). Washington, DC: National Academy Press.

Wolfgang, M. E., Figlio, R. M., & Sellin, T. (1972). *Delinquency in a birth cohort.* Chicago: University of Chicago Press.

PART 2

Implementing the Law

⋈⋈⋈
Chapter Three

Estimated Benefits and Costs of California's New Mandatory-Sentencing Law

PETER GREENWOOD
C. PETER RYDELL
ALLAN F. ABRAHAMSE
JONATHAN P. CAULKINS
JAMES CHIESA
KARYN E. MODEL
STEPHEN P. KLEIN

In recent years, public outrage over crime has found political expression in the proposal and enactment of various laws mandating very long sentences for repeat felons. Laws of this type, often termed "three strikes and you're out," have been passed by overwhelming margins in the states of Washington and California, and more than 30 other states have similar statutes under active consideration (Rohter, 1994).

This chapter originally appeared as *Three Strikes and You're Out: Estimated Benefits and Costs of California's New Mandatory-Sentencing Law* (Report No. MR-509-RC), by P. W. Greenwood, C. P. Rydell, A. F. Abrahamse, J. P. Caulkins, J. Chiesa, K. E. Model, and S. P. Klein, 1994, Santa Monica, CA: RAND.

Although all the proposed statutes would increase sentences substantially, they differ in the number and types of offenders they would affect. The new federal crime law, for example, would affect only the small number of defendants in federal courts who have accumulated three convictions for crimes involving serious injuries to their victims. Others would affect a large percentage of all defendants. The California law mandates 25 years to life in prison for an offender convicted of any felony following two prior convictions for serious crimes. It also doubles sentences on the second "strike," requires consecutive sentences for multiple counts, and limits "good time" credits.

The basic arguments advanced by proponents of the three-strikes concept are the following:

- It will protect the public by incapacitating (removing from society) those chronic offenders who have demonstrated by their acts that they are both dangerous and unwilling to reform.
- It will deter repeat offenders still on the street from committing further felonies.
- It will save money by cutting down on the number of times that career criminals need to be processed by the system.
- It is the "right thing to do." Aside from the savings and other effects, justice demands that those who repeatedly cause injury and loss to others have their freedom revoked.

Critics of the concept argue that

- Substantial increases in the use of imprisonment over the past decade have had little, if any, effect on violent crime rates.
- Life terms for three-time losers will require the allotment of expensive prison space to offenders who are well past their peak ages of criminal activity.
- The demand for jury trials, caused by the law's restrictions on plea bargaining, will actually raise the costs of the criminal justice system and cause further delays in resolving criminal cases.
- The same amount of money applied to measures other than three strikes would reduce crime by a greater amount.
- The third-strike penalty is an unduly harsh one for criminals convicted of certain felonies such as drug possession.

Thus, although some of the debate is cast in moral terms, most of the disagreements are over questions that lend themselves to quantitative analysis. Little such analysis has appeared. To the average citizen, of course, increased punishment for serious crimes has intuitive appeal. But citizens may want to know just how much crime reduction they are getting for their money. Could they do as well for less money? And just what is the total cost of the law? Citizens are not getting much information on that from the law itself, the media, or their elected representatives. The law bears no explicit price tag; the media are better at depicting crime's human tragedy than at drawing up balance sheets; and politicians have at last found a cause that will offend no powerful interest group.

The analysis described in this chapter is designed to help clarify the ongoing debate over this issue by providing unbiased estimates of the likely effects of the proposed laws. These estimates are based on a mathematical model that tracks the flow of criminals through the justice system, calculates the costs of running the system, and predicts the number of crimes criminals commit when on the street. The model permits us to explore the extent to which these estimates change with changes in critical assumptions regarding the behavior of offenders and the response of the criminal justice system to the various provisions of the law.

It was our hope that this analysis would inform voter reaction in California to Proposition 184 on the November 1994 ballot, which was almost identical to the law passed by the legislature earlier that year.[1] Our analysis includes different versions of the three-strikes law, including an alternative considered by the legislature. Although these were not on the ballot, we hoped the legislature might review them as possible substitutes for the current law if voters rejected the three-strikes ballot initiative. We also hoped our analysis would enlighten the ongoing debate over three-strikes proposals in other states.

We begin with a detailed summary of the alternative measures we consider. We then describe how we modeled crime and imprisonment and present the results of our analysis. The findings include reductions in crime and increases in costs projected for the previous law, the new law, and the various alternatives, along with anticipated trends in benefits and costs. Finally, we place the costs in budgetary perspective.

Sentencing Alternatives for Repeat Offenders

California, along with the rest of the nation, experienced a general rise in reported crime rates in the 1970s and 1980s, but both the reported rates and victimization surveys show crime rates steady or declining over the past 15 years (see Figure 3.1). Reported crime rates peaked around 1980 and declined steadily through 1985 when they again began to advance, although very slowly (California Department of Justice, 1992).

Violent crime (murders, rapes, and some robberies and assaults), on the other hand, rose more swiftly after the early 1980s decline (see Figure 3.2). Although still only one sixth of the total crime rate, violent crime has doubled over the past 20 years.

Like many states, California began toughening its sentencing policies and adding prison capacity in the early 1980s, just as crime rates began a modest 5-year decline. In fact, California was the leader among states in this trend, tripling its prison population in the decade since 1982. Between 1984 and 1991, more than 1,000 bills were passed by the California legislature to change felony and misdemeanor statutes. Virtually none of these bills decreased sentences. Many lengthened them. This trend culminated in the introduction of several bills in this past legislative session, all of which required imprisonment of repeat felons for 25 years to life.

However, although the alternative measures' overall thrust was similar, they varied significantly in the offenders they targeted and in some of the sanctions they imposed. We evaluate two of those proposed laws (including the new three-strikes law) and three other alternative policies for increasing sentences of repeat offenders. We compare each of those with the previous law. To understand the differences among the various alternatives, one must understand what is meant by "serious" and "violent" felonies in California.[2]

The exact definition of serious and violent requires detailed lists of penal code violations. Generally speaking, violent crimes involve injuries to victims or, in some cases, threat with a deadly weapon. Serious crimes include virtually all violent crimes,[3] plus others where there is a potential for injury to victims. To understand the distinction between serious and violent, it may be helpful to compare these California categories with the FBI Uniform Crime Reports (UCR) index catego-

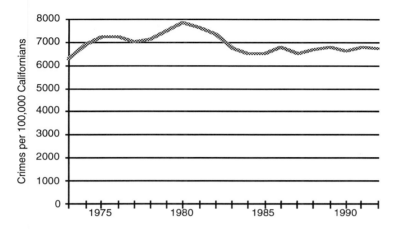

Figure 3.1. California Crime Rate, 1973-1992
SOURCE: California Department of Justice (1992).

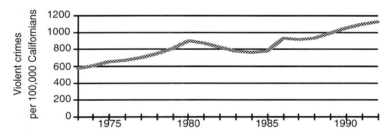

Figure 3.2. California Violent Crime Rate, 1973-1992
SOURCE: California Department of Justice (1992).

ries (Federal Bureau of Investigation, 1993). Crimes that are serious but not violent include almost all arsons and about half of robberies, assaults, and burglaries. Violent crimes include all murders, most rapes, and about half of robberies and assaults.[4] (Details of this comparison are presented with an explanation of the breakdown between serious and violent for each FBI crime category.)

In addition to violent and serious but not violent, we also define in our analysis a "minor" category that consists of all felonies that are not serious. These include such FBI index crimes as thefts and nonresidential burglaries, along with crimes not on the index, such as forgery, fraud, and drug offenses. With these definitions in mind, let us now identify the provisions of the alternatives we evaluate. (The provisions are summarized in Table 3.1. Key provisions serving as inputs to our quantitative analysis are presented comparatively.)

Previous Law

California is a determinate-sentencing state: Judges have few choices in sentencing. Instead, the legislature specifies prison terms for particular categories of crime, as well as additions to those sentences for specified circumstances, for example, prior record. There were several repeat offender provisions in effect before passage of the new three-strikes law. For example, a person convicted of a serious felony could be sentenced to 5 additional years in prison for each previous serious felony conviction. Other prior laws included third- and fourth-strike provisions triggered by the infliction of great bodily injury or use of force likely to produce such injury. Those convicted of such crimes after having two prior prison terms for violent felonies could get 20 years to life. Those with three prior prison terms could get life without parole. However, previous law also reduced the length of prison sentences by allowing credit for work time and good behavior up to 50% of the sentence. It also permitted probation as a sentence for a person convicted of a felony unless probation was specifically proscribed for that crime.

In actual practice, the tough repeat offender provisions have been partially vitiated by the lenient good-time credits and by plea bargaining. Even after the increase in sentence severity of recent years, many felony convictions—even violent felony convictions—do not result in a prison term. In our analysis, we used both the sentencing rules and the average actual sentences to estimate time served for violent, serious but not violent, and minor crimes.

Jones Three Strikes

We refer to the three-strikes bill (AB 971) signed into law by Governor Wilson in March 1994 as the Jones law, after one of the legislation's

TABLE 3.1   Alternatives Evaluated

Alternative	Second-Strike Sentence	Third-Strike Sentence	Is Prison Required?	Good Time Allowed
Previous law	Extra 5 years[a]	Extra 10 years for third serious conviction; 20 years to life for third violent felony incarceration	No	Up to 50% of sentence
Jones three-strikes law	Double the nominal sentence[b]	25 years to life	Yes, if sentence is enhanced	Limited to 20% after first strike
Jones second-strike only	Double the nominal sentence	Double the nominal sentence	Yes, if sentence is enhanced	Limited to 20% after first strike
Jones violent only	Double the nominal sentence if violent	25 years to life if violent	Yes, for violent second or third strike	Limited to 20% for violent second or third strike
Rainey three strikes	Extra 10 years for second violent felony incarceration	25 years to life	Yes, for serious second or third strike	None, if violent or third strike
Guaranteed full term	Same as previous law	Same as previous law	Yes, if serious[c]	None, if serious

NOTE: Serious incorporates violent. For all alternatives, a strike accrues on conviction of a serious felony; for Jones three-strikes law, the third strike accrues on conviction of any felony. A nominal sentence is that provided by law for the crime for which the offender is convicted (no enhancements); treated as actual average sentence under previous law in quantitative analysis. For excluded cases, present law applies (e.g., if table text says, "for violent second or third strike," present law applies for serious nonviolent).
a. Sentences for previous law are as given by statute. In quantitative analysis, sentences input are actual averages.
b. This also applies to minor felony following one strike (although no second strike accrues in this case).
c. This alternative also provides that half of all minor felons are not sentenced to prison.

sponsors. First and second strikes are convictions for serious felonies
(whether violent or not). The third strike is a conviction for any felony.
All persons receiving a second or third strike go to prison.

Because good-time credits of 20% are still allowed, we assume for
our analysis that the average time served is 80% of the nominal
sentence. For conviction of any felony with one prior strike, the
nominal sentence is double the nominal sentence under the previous
law, plus the previous law's enhancements. So, to calculate the total
actual prison sentence for a second strike, we used 80% of double the
average nominal sentence (specific to the nature of the crime) under
the previous law. Persons convicted of any felony with two prior strikes
receive a nominal sentence of at least 25 years to life. The 20%
good-time provision makes the actual sentence at least 20 years to life.
In our analysis, we treat this as 20 years in prison.[5]

It is worth noting that neither the Jones three-strikes law nor any of
the alternatives changes sentencing policies for juveniles, who are
responsible for at least one sixth of serious crime in California.

Jones Second-Strike Only

As the name "three strikes" emphasizes, public discussion of the
Jones three-strikes law focuses on the third strike. However, as just
noted, the law provides for a doubling of nominal sentences for
second-strike offenders—and mandates prison time for all such offenders. How much of the effect of the Jones law will come from the
second-strike provisions? Or, to put it another way, what does the
third-strike provision add? To find out, we constructed an alternative
law with the same provisions as the Jones law except that conviction
of any felony with one or more prior strikes results in a doubling of the
nominal sentence for the latest crime (in other words, no automatic
20-year term for a third strike).

Jones Violent Only

The crimes that have driven the three-strikes movement are largely
violent (e.g., the Klaas and Reynolds murders). Violent crimes, however, occur much less frequently than do such crimes as residential
burglary and unarmed robbery, which, although serious, are not vio-

lent. Does the Jones law cast too wide a net in imposing repeat offender penalties on persons convicted of crimes that are serious but not violent? We created an alternative formulation of the Jones law that allows serious, nonviolent crimes to count as strikes, but does not invoke the Jones law's penalties unless a conviction is for a violent crime. For example, an offender with two serious, nonviolent convictions and a violent third conviction would get 25 years to life. An offender with the same prior convictions and a serious, nonviolent third conviction would receive the same sentence as he would have under the previous law (including 50% good-time credit).

Rainey Three-Strikes

Among the three-strikes bills considered by the legislature was AB 1568, known as the Rainey bill after its author. The Rainey bill maintained the previous law's 5-year-per-strike sanctions for serious, nonviolent convictions, but raises the violent conviction sanction to 10 years per previous incarceration. Like the Jones law, Rainey imposed a third-strike penalty of 25 years to life, but it required that the third strike be a serious felony and allowed no good time at all for violent felons on any strike.

Guaranteed Full Term

For the final alternative, we made a significant departure from the three-strikes variants in an attempt to come up with an option that would reduce serious crime as much as possible at less cost. We believed we might achieve this goal with an alternative containing only three provisions. First, all convictions for serious or violent felonies (even those with no prior strikes) result in a prison term. Second, no good time is allowed for people sent to prison for serious crimes. Third, to reduce costs while minimizing the effect on crime, we cut in half the proportion of people convicted of minor crimes who receive prison terms (proportionately increasing the fractions who are sent to jail only as opposed to prison—or who are not incarcerated at all). For convenience, we refer to this as the "guaranteed full term" alternative but note that that applies only to convictions for serious felonies.

How the Analysis Was Done

In this section, we review the approach we took in conducting our analysis. We begin with a general overview of the way we modeled offender populations. We then describe how we simulated the different aspects of offenders and offenses. We conclude with a presentation of the factors underlying our cost estimates and some key limitations in our analytic approach.

Projecting Offender Populations

Our analysis has two principal policy-relevant outputs—crime and criminal justice system costs. We want to know how much the felony crime rate is reduced by keeping repeat offenders locked up, and we want to know how much it costs to keep them locked up. The crime rate depends on the number of offenders on the street, and the added cost depends principally on the number of offenders incarcerated. Thus, we have constructed a mathematical model (diagrammed schematically in Figure 3.3) that predicts the number of offenders on the street and in prison. The number of offenders on the street depends on four factors:

- The rate at which people who have not yet committed a felony begin a criminal career.
- The rate at which offenders desist from crime.
- The rate at which offenders are removed from the street through incarceration.
- The rate at which incarcerated offenders are released.

The prison population is usefully divided into those who would commit felonies again if released from prison and those who would not.[6] This is an important distinction because if the objective is to keep felons locked up to ensure they do not commit more crimes, keeping ex-felons locked up costs money with no gain.[7] As sentences wear on, some offenders may reach a point at which they give up on a life of crime. Thus, the number of dangerous criminals in prison depends on three rates: the rate at which offenders on the street are incarcerated,

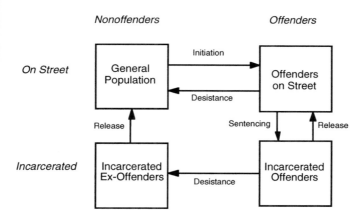

Figure 3.3. Criminal Dynamics

the rate at which still-dangerous criminals are released from prison, and the rate at which incarcerated felons stop being dangerous.

Of the rates (arrows) shown in Figure 3.3, the two release rates are derived from sentence lengths associated with the various policies described previously. Sentencing rates are derived from data on arrests per crime and convictions per arrest and, again, from the sentencing provisions in whichever alternative law is under consideration. We infer annual desistance rates from what is known about the length of criminal careers (they are on the order of 10 years long on average; see Blumstein, Cohen, Roth, & Visher, 1986). We assume that initiation into the criminal population is proportional to the state's population.[8]

Projecting Offense Rates

As mentioned, we use the number of offenders on the street to derive the crime rate, and we use the number of incarcerated offenders (among other things) to derive costs. How is the crime rate related to the number of offenders on the street?

A common way to model mathematically criminals' offending patterns was pioneered by Shinnar and Shinnar (1975). The rates at which active criminals commit crimes, at which crimes lead to arrests, and at which criminals desist or "retire" are assumed to be represented by independent Poisson processes. A Poisson process is one in which the average frequency of occurrence of events (e.g., crimes) is constant, but events occur at random intervals. In fact, Poisson processes are completely random in the sense that knowing how long it has been since the last event does not help in predicting how long it will be until the next one. Thus, active offenders commit crimes at a constant average rate, but any two consecutive crimes might be a day apart or a month apart. Also, the probability that any given offense will lead to an arrest is constant. The independence of the Poisson processes refers to the lack of influence of one on the other. For example, the probability that an active offender will desist at any given time is unrelated to how many crimes he or she has committed.

This simple model, like all models, ignores much of the complexity of real-world offending patterns. For example, offenders go on crime sprees; it is unlikely that a crime would be committed (or an offender rearrested) shortly following an arrest, when the offender would still be in custody, and it is more likely that a very old offender will desist from crime in the next month than that a young one will. Despite such imprecisions, the Poisson-based model has proven useful in modeling criminal behavior at the aggregate level.

Differences in Offense Rates

Not all criminals are equally active. Indeed, both arrest records and self-report surveys suggest that there are enormous differences in individual offense rates. These differences can be modeled by defining different values for rates of offense, arrest, and desistance, that is, by defining different classes of criminals. Pragmatically, keeping track of many different classes of criminals is cumbersome. More important, there are precious few data available for estimating the rates, and the more classes, the more parameters one must estimate.

Hence, we model just two classes of offenders. We divide the population of incarcerated offenders in 1993 in half on the basis of the rate at which they committed crimes, and we call the more frequent half high-rate offenders and the other half low-rate offenders. This even split of the incarcerated population is only for the reference year.

Projections of the future under different criminal justice laws allow the split to vary over time. Because high-rate offenders make up a larger fraction of prisoners than of the population on the street, the recidivism rate of persons released from prison exceeds the arrest rate of persons on the street. We used this fact to estimate the ratio of the offense rate of high-rate offenders to that of low-rate offenders.

There are limitations to this modeling framework. Notably, it ignores the chronological age of offenders. A closely related limitation is that we assume criminals' offense rates and their probability of desisting are constant over time (until their criminal careers end completely). One consequence of this is that the model may overestimate the benefits to be gained from the various alternative laws we evaluate. The reason is as follows. High-rate offenders are more likely to be arrested and thus more likely to be sentenced to prison, and, of course, the objective of the three-strikes laws is to lock up such offenders. Some high-rate offenders, however, would have become low-rate offenders at some point if they had not been arrested (just as some would have desisted entirely), but our model does not allow for that. The gain from locking up high-rate offenders will thus not be as great as the model predicts.[9] (Of course, some offenders imprisoned while committing crimes at a low rate might have become high-rate offenders. In these cases, the laws deliver a "bonus." Does that make up for the overestimates? No, because the low-rate offenders are not being removed from the street population as fast by the repeat offender laws.) This bias will, however, affect all sentencing policies analyzed with this model and, thus, is unlikely to greatly affect inferences drawn about the relative efficacy of different sentencing policies, which is the focus of this analysis.

Other Factors Tracked by the Model

Of course, criminals commit different kinds of crime, and penalties are different for different crimes as well. Thus, we keep track of the offense and arrest rates of high- and low-rate offenders by type of crime—violent felonies, felonies that are serious but not violent, and minor felonies.

For some of the minor offenses, it is difficult to define the exact number of offenses and, hence, an offending rate. For example, a drug dealer may be almost continually in possession of contraband, and it is impossible to say that the individual committed any particular number of possession-with-intent-to-distribute offenses. Because of this and the fact that people are generally more concerned about serious crimes, we specify offense rates only for serious (including violent) crimes, whereas arrest rates are specified for minor crimes. Also, we express crime prevention benefits in terms of serious crimes averted, not the reduction in all felonies. However, when we discuss index crime offense rates and serious crimes avoided, we do mean all such crime, not just reported crime. (We rely on victimization surveys of the general population to obtain data on the total crime rate.)

Once we fully specified the Poisson models, we could construct a simulation that tracks the flows of offenders through different "states" (e.g., boxes in the model). As Figure 3.3 shows, the most important distinctions are whether the individual is free or incarcerated, active or retired. These states alone, however, are not sufficient because sentences sometimes depend on prior records. To preserve the memoryless property of our model, we expanded the number of states tracked to specify the number of previous "strikes" offenders have acquired: zero, one, or two or more.

We ran the simulation model over a 25-year time frame. We chose 1 year as the time step because it is the most common reporting interval for the data used in the model and provides a convenient metric for reporting results.

Estimating Costs

As mentioned, costs are largely influenced by the number of offenders incarcerated; however, the numbers of arrests and trials also affect costs. Each of these factors is an output of the model, and costs are calculated by multiplying those outputs by the factors shown in Table 3.2.

The cost factors are approximations only—gross approximations in the case of the first four lines of the table. The trial costs, for example, are a very rough estimate that does not include losses to government and other employers of citizens who serve on juries. It is important to note, though, that it would take very large errors in the first several

TABLE 3.2 Criminal Justice System Cost Factors	
Cost Item	*1993 $*
Police cost per arrest[a]	624
Adjudication cost per arrest[b]	1,300
Cost per trial[c]	4,000
Jail operating cost per prisoner-year[d]	10,000
Prison operating cost per prisoner-year[e]	20,800
Prison capital cost per prisoner[e]	97,000

a. In 1990, the United States at all levels of government spent $31.8 billion on police protection and made 14.2 million arrests (U.S. Department of Justice, 1992, pp. 2, 432). This is $2,240 per arrest, or $2,500 in 1993 dollars. Assuming that one fourth of police protection funds are spent on making arrests, we get the estimate of $624 in this table.
b. In 1990, the United States at all levels of government spent $16.5 billion on "judicial and legal services." This is $1,160 per arrest, or $1,300 in 1993 dollars (U.S. Department of Justice, 1992, pp. 2, 432).
c. Testimony by Carolyn McIntyre, Legislative Representative, California State Association of Counties, California Senate Appropriations Committee hearing on AB 971 (Jones), March 28, 1994.
d. Jail operating cost is judged to be approximately half prison operating cost.
e. Memorandum by Richard S. Welch, Chief, Offender Information Services Branch, California, March 14, 1994, p. 9.

cost factors to change the overall thrust of the results, as overall costs turn out to be dominated by prison costs, and prison operating costs in particular.

Our cost analysis does not include an attempt to convert crime reduction benefits into monetary equivalents. These benefits include savings to society from reduced property losses, medical attention, and pain and suffering to victims. The property loss and medical costs associated with the average robbery or assault (the most common types of violent crime) are estimated to be less than $1,000. Depending on how they are estimated, the pain and suffering costs could be much larger. However, the basis for calculating them is not well established.[10]

General Limitations

Aside from the simplifications we have already addressed in regard to constructing the model, our analysis is limited in several ways. Some of the more important ones are as follows.

- We consider only adult, not juvenile, crimes and sanctions. Although juveniles currently account for at least 16% of all violent felony arrests, they are not affected by any of the three-strikes laws, and are therefore not included in our analysis.[11]

- The model does not account for the effects of the three-strikes laws on plea bargaining. Some have predicted that many more cases will go to trial under the new law, even accounting for the fact that longer sentences for repeat offenders would cut down on their offenses, arrests, and trials. However, the latter fact is the only one we consider in the model. (Again, though, because we find that prison costs dominate, even a large error in trial costs is not likely to strongly influence our conclusions about total costs.)

- Because we assume that the initiation rate will be proportional to the general population size, we assume that the fraction of citizens who become active criminals will remain roughly constant over the next 25 years. (Our findings about the differential effects of alternative criminal justice laws do not depend on this growth assumption being more than roughly correct.)

- We assume no deterrent effect. That is, we assume that the various alternatives reduce crime by removing criminals from the streets, not by deterring criminals on the street from committing further crimes. This assumption is consistent with recent research (Blumstein, Cohen, & Nagin, 1978; Cook, 1980; MacCoun, 1993). Nonetheless, we analyzed the sensitivity of our results to the no-deterrence assumption.

- Our specific estimates are for the state of California. Although we hope that our qualitative conclusions and analytical framework are relevant elsewhere, caution should be exercised in generalizing our results to other states, where the characteristics of offenders and sentencing laws may be different.

- We assume that the new three-strikes law will be implemented as written, and we make the same assumption when considering the various alternatives. That is, we assume that sentences will be meted out as directed by the law and enough prison space will be added to keep offenders subject to the new extended sentences locked up for the prescribed periods. We address the potential failure of this assumption later in this report.

- Our analysis here considers only what expanded incarceration by itself can do to decrease crime. We omit alternative crime-fighting strategies, such as prevention programs or police force expansion. This limitation is very serious in the opinion of some observers of the criminal justice system. We will return to this topic.

Benefits and Costs of the Sentencing Alternatives

Before proceeding to overall crime reduction and cost results, we present one interesting intermediate output of our analysis—the number of FBI index offenses that typical low-rate and high-rate offenders commit in 12 months on the street (see the top panel in Table 3.3). The differences are large. High-rate offenders commit almost 18 times as many crimes as low-rate offenders. The typical high-rate offender commits seven serious crimes per year, including two violent ones. The typical low-rate offender commits one serious crime every $2\frac{1}{2}$ years.[12] Given such differences between criminals, it is easy to see how enhanced repeat offender penalties can influence the crime rate.

Offense rates, however, are not the same as crime rates. If two persons collaborate in a robbery, each one has committed an offense, but there is only one crime. The bottom two panels of the table show the data that permitted our model to translate reductions in offense rates achieved by locking up criminals into reductions in crime rates.

In presenting our results, we will first compare the Jones three-strikes law with the previous law, because the Jones law is the focus of the current debate. We will then compare the new law with the alternatives defined earlier.

Jones Three-Strikes Compared With Previous Law

We estimate that over the next 25 years, the Jones three-strikes law will reduce the annual number of serious crimes in California 28% on average below the number that would have been committed under the previous law (see Table 3.4).[13] It will also increase the costs of California's criminal justice system by an average of $5.5 billion a year over the same period.[14] That works out to a 122% increase over the $4.5 billion per year estimated for the previous law. (The California Department of Corrections has estimated an annual increase of $5.7 billion.) By dividing the cost increase by the number of crimes reduced, we arrive at an estimated cost per serious crime prevented of $16,300. This may not be easy to conceptualize, given the broad range of crimes covered under the "serious" rubric. Another way to look at it is that

TABLE 3.3   Offenses and Crimes per Offender per Year: Index
Felonies, California

| | Type of Felony | | | |
Type of Offender	Violent	Serious Only[a]	Other Index[b]	Total Index
	Offenses per offender per year			
Low rate	0.12	0.29	0.71	1.11
High rate	2.03	5.03	12.43	19.49
	Offenders per crime			
Low rate	1.54	1.79	1.92	1.84
High rate	1.54	1.79	1.92	1.84
	Crimes per offender per year			
Low rate	0.08	0.16	0.37	0.60
High rate	1.32	2.81	6.47	10.60

NOTE: These are estimates of offenses per offender per year and offenders per crime by index crime, prorated to violent, serious, and other index crimes. The bottom panel in this table is computed from the first two panels.
a. Serious only means serious but not violent.
b. Other index crimes include those felonies on the FBI index list (e.g., auto theft) that are not serious. Some felonies (e.g., drug offenses) are not on the index.

each million dollars extra spent under the new three-strikes law will prevent 4 rapes, 11 robberies, 24 aggravated assaults, 22 burglaries of a serious nature, and 1 arson. Every $5 million extra will prevent five times the number of crimes just listed—plus 1 murder.[15]

We thus see that effects on the number of serious crimes will be dominated by decreases in assaults and burglaries (not the murders, rapes, and robberies that many people may believe to be the law's principal targets). How do the costs break down? As shown by Figure 3.4, prison operating and construction costs clearly dominate the cost difference between the new three-strikes law and the previous law. The new law will result in small savings in the costs of arresting and convicting felons and in the cost of jail operation. However, these savings will be overwhelmed by a large difference in prison operating cost and a 12-fold increase in the annual cost of prison construction.

TABLE 3.4	Changes in Cost and Serious Crime: Jones Three-Strikes Law			
Item	*Previous Law*	*New Law*	*Change*	*% Change*
Annual cost ($ million)	4,520	10,040	5,520	122
Annual serious crimes (000)	1,219	881	–338	–28
Cost/serious crime prevented ($)		16,300		

NOTE: All figures are discounted at an annual rate of 4%.

The extra prison costs result, of course, from the need to build and operate enough additional prison space to accommodate the flow of new prisoners as those subject to the three-strikes law are kept in prison longer. (As explained, our trial cost estimates are very limited in scope. However, as is obvious from the graph, even if our trial cost estimates were off by a factor of 5 or 10, the effect on the total cost difference between current and previous laws would not be large.)

Sensitivity of the Results to Changes in Assumptions

Our estimates are, of course, subject to uncertainty. They are uncertain because some of the model inputs cannot be estimated with much accuracy, and because some of the model assumptions are too simple. (Some of these issues were discussed earlier.) Although all inputs are consistent with published data, some were estimated in a relatively indirect manner, for example, offense rates for high-rate and low-rate offenders. We have already mentioned that we do not allow offenders to switch back and forth between high and low rate. Also, we did not account for any deterrent effect, that is, that longer sentences would deter offenders on the street from committing crimes. Researchers have found little or no evidence that such deterrence occurs (Blumstein et al., 1978; Cook, 1980; MacCoun, 1993), but such an effect is alleged by proponents of the new law.[16]

Without assembling a more detailed database and building a more complex model than the resources available for this analysis permitted, we cannot say exactly by how much we may have over- or underesti-

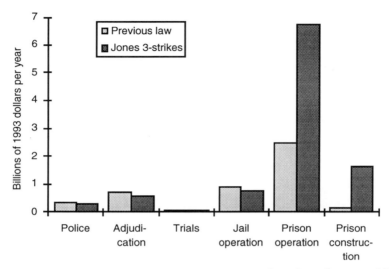

Figure 3.4. Changes in Cost by Component: Previous Law Compared With Jones Three-Strikes Law

mated crime reduction and cost increases. In lieu of such an effort, we have examined the sensitivity of two of our major conclusions to changes in input parameters. In particular, we have examined the effect of changing two critical assumed values:

1. The ratio of the arrest rate of high-rate offenders to that of low-rate offenders (as a proxy or the ratio of offense rates).
2. The desistance rate of persons with one or more strikes under the Jones law. Increasing this rate is equivalent to changing our assumption of no deterrence. We reason that if the Jones law were to have a positive deterrent effect, that should show up particularly among persons with strikes.

We increased and decreased the ratio of the arrest rate (number of arrests per year out of prison) of high-rate offenders to low-rate offenders by 25%, and we increased and decreased the desistance rate of offenders with one or more strikes under the Jones law by 25%. The first of these has the effect of changing the ease with which a repeat offender law can single out high-rate offenders and thus affect the crime rate. The second (in the positive direction) is equivalent to an assumption that the Jones law will each year cause 1 of every 40 felons with strikes to desist.

In each case, we calculated the relative reduction in crime rate brought about by the Jones law under the given assumptions, and the relative increase in the average prison population, the main driver for costs. We then compared these changes with those under our standard assumptions, as reflected in the results shown in Table 3.4. Table 3.5 displays the differences between the two sets of results.

As Table 3.5 shows, none of our sensitivity cases affected our estimate of the decrease in crime rate or increase in prison population by more than 10% in absolute value. At one extreme, if high- and low-rate offenders are "25% more different" than we assumed, and if the Jones law increases desistance by 25%, the decrease in crime rate will be larger by about 6% and the increase in prison population will be about 7% smaller. This means, for example, that the crime rate reduction will be the standard 28% times 106%, or 30% (not 28% plus 6%). At the other extreme, the decrease in crime rate will be smaller by about 8%, and the increase in the prison population will be larger by about 10%.

There may be other sources of error. It is possible that varying other assumptions might show somewhat larger effects, and there are minor differences between the model inputs and the laws. Taking all this into account, we believe that the estimates presented here can be viewed as accurate to within one fifth (20%). For example, when Table 3.4 reports that the Jones three-strikes law will reduce crime by 28%, this may be interpreted as a reduction of at least 23% but no more than 34%.

Given that the cost estimates are driven by prison costs, and that the prison cost factors we use should be quite reliable, our costs should not vary more than we expect our projected prison population to vary. Thus, again, these may be regarded as correct to within 20%. That is, the extra cost of the Jones three-strikes law should fall within the range extending from $4.5 billion to $6.5 billion annually.

Trends

Reporting average annual results, as we have done so far, obscures differences in crimes prevented and cost increases over time. We

TABLE 3.5   Sensitivity of Crime Rate and Prison Population to
Assumptions

Assumption (relative to standard)		Relative Difference in	
Arrest Rate of High-Rate Offenders Divided by Arrest Rate of Low-Rate Offenders	Desistance Rate of Offenders with 1 or More Strikes Under the Jones Law	Decrease in Crime Rate	Increase in Prison Population
25% lower	25% lower	−7.5%	+9.6%
25% lower	No change	−2.8%	+2.2%
25% lower	25% higher	+1.4%	−4.0%
No change	25% lower	−4.6%	+6.8%
No change	No change	0.0%	0.0%
No change	25% higher	+4.0%	−5.9%
25% higher	25% lower	−2.3%	+4.7%
25% higher	No change	+2.2%	−1.7%
25% higher	25% higher	+6.1%	−7.3%

NOTE: Negative results in column 3 indicate smaller decreases in crime, that is, higher crime rates; positive results, vice versa. Results in columns 3 and 4 are percentage of change under standard assumptions, not percentage of results under previous law (see the text).

project that the number of serious and violent crimes prevented each year will increase rapidly during the new law's first 10 years, then more slowly thereafter (Figure 3.5).

As mentioned, the major determinant of crime rates is the number of offenders on the street—particularly high-rate offenders. Figure 3.6 shows how much the Jones three-strikes law is expected to reduce the number of high-rate offenders on the street over the 25-year projection period. Again, note the big change early in the period, culminating after several years in a drop of about one third from the previous-law projection. No graph of the effect on low-rate offenders is presented because the projections under the two laws are so close that the lines virtually overlap. Low-rate offenders will be little affected by the new law because their low rate of committing crimes means a low rate of accumulating strikes, and consequently a low probability of receiving the enhanced sanctions under the second- and third-strike provisions.

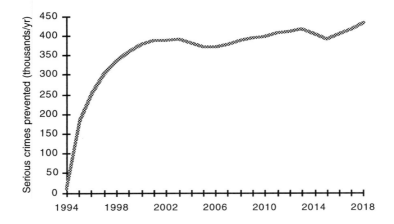

Figure 3.5. Serious Crime Prevented by Year: Jones Three-Strikes Law

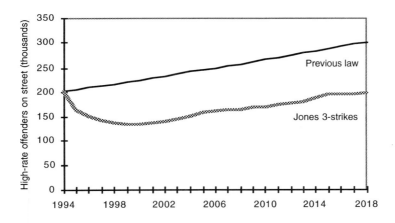

Figure 3.6. High-Rate Offenders on Street by Year: Jones Three-Strikes Law Compared With Previous Law

The additional costs under the new law (Figure 3.7) will fluctuate considerably over time because of the on-again off-again nature of the need to add prison spaces. We estimate, for example, that actual time incarcerated for a serious crime on second strike will go up to

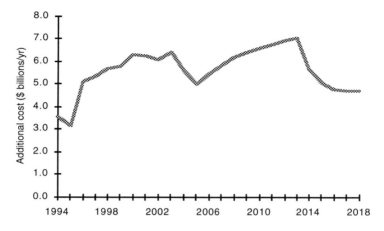

Figure 3.7. Additional Cost per Year: Jones Three-Strikes Law

about 10 years under the new law. It was roughly 3 years under the previous law.[17] Thus, those convicted of their second serious felony in 1992 will be getting out of prison sometime around 1995; those convicted in 1993, around 1996. "Second-strikers" convicted in 1994 will not emerge until about 2004. When coupled with the immediate effects of sending all serious felons to prison, the Jones law's second-strike sentence increases will result in a buildup of prisoners and prison costs, relative to the previous law, until 2004.[18] Then, the first second-strikers convicted under the Jones law will be released and costs will drop for a while on a relative basis. Meanwhile, extra costs associated with third-strikers will be increasing until those prisoners begin coming out in 2014. (The effects of these 10-year and 20-year prisoner releases also show up in a minor way in the crime reduction curve in Figure 3.5.)

Figure 3.8 compares the projected number of prison spaces under the Jones three-strikes law with those expected if the previous law had remained unchanged. Over most of the 25-year projection period, the Jones three-strikes law will more than double the required number of prison spaces. Again, flexes in the curve are apparent around 2004 and 2014.

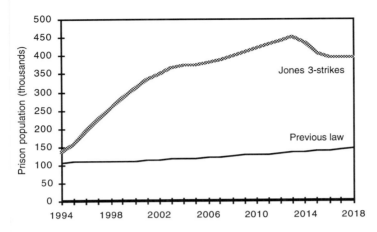

Figure 3.8. Projected Prison Populations by Year: Jones Three-Strikes Law Compared With Previous Law

Comparison With Alternative Laws

We now compare the crime reduction and extra costs anticipated as a result of the Jones three-strikes law with those of several alternatives. These comparisons are in the form of crimes prevented and extra costs incurred relative to the previous law. Results are given in Table 3.6 and discussed through the graphical presentations in the remainder of this section.

First, as might be expected, the less restrictive alternatives would generally reduce crime by a smaller amount than the Jones three-strikes law (see Figure 3.9). However, the second-strike-only alternative would achieve 85% of the Jones law's crime reduction benefit. Because the two options are identical except for the third-strike provisions, this implies that only 15% of the new law's effect will result from those provisions. This is ironic, considering the emphasis on the third-strike penalties in much of the public debate on the law.

The Jones violent-only alternative retains the third-strike provision but invokes second- or third-strike sentencing sanctions only for violent crimes. That alternative would not be as effective as the second-strike-only alternative, but it would still achieve two thirds of the crime reduction benefit of the Jones law.

Item	Previous Law	Alternative	Change	% Change
Jones three-strikes law				
Annual cost (millions)	$4,520	$10,040	$5,520	122
Annual serious crimes (000)	1,219	881	−338	−28
Cost/serious crime prevented		$16,300		
Jones second strike only				
Annual cost (millions)	$4,520	$8,600	$4,080	90
Annual serious crimes (000)	1,219	932	−287	−24
Cost/serious crime prevented		$14,200		
Jones violent only				
Annual cost (millions)	$4,520	$7,100	$2,580	57
Annual serious crimes (000)	1,219	999	−220	−18
Cost/serious crime prevented		$11,800		
Rainey three strikes				
Annual cost (millions)	$4,520	$8,510	$3,990	88
Annual serious crimes (000)	1,219	952	−267	−22
Cost/serious crime prevented		$14,900		
Guaranteed full term				
Annual cost (millions)	$4,520	$8,920	$4,400	97
Annual serious crimes (000)	1,219	877	−342	−28
Cost/serious crime prevented		$12,900		

TABLE 3.6 Summary Cost-Benefit Comparison of Alternative Laws

NOTE: All figures are discounted at an annual rate of 4%.

The Rainey three-strikes bill is also more focused on violent offenders, but is harsher not only to them but also to third-strike serious, nonviolent offenders. It is more lenient than the Jones law on second-strike serious, nonviolent offenders and much more lenient on one- and two-strikers with an additional minor felony conviction. The result of these differences is that the crime reduction benefit would be less and would also be less than that of the Jones law without the third-strike provision.

The guaranteed-full-term alternative matches the Jones three-strikes law in crime reduction. Recall that the full-term alternative contains no second- or third-strike provisions. It simply requires that all offenders convicted of a serious felony serve in prison the full sentence given to them. It would achieve the full effect of the Jones law even though it would cut in half the fraction of offenders convicted of a minor felony who go to prison from 21% to 11%. The Jones law will increase this

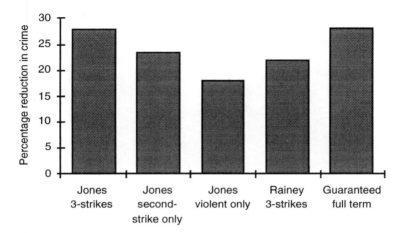

Figure 3.9. Percentage Reduction in Serious Crime From Jones Three-Strikes Law Compared With Alternatives

proportion for those who have at least one strike to 100%. This latter point provides a clue as to how the crime reduction power of a three-strikes law, supposedly targeted to keep violent repeat offenders incarcerated, could be matched by a no-strikes alternative. In fact, the Jones law is not targeted toward violent repeat offenders. Forty percent of the crimes that would cause a strike to accumulate are burglaries, and the chance that the third strike that sends someone to prison for life will be a minor felony is better than even.

The costs of most of the alternatives follow the benefits (Figure 3.10). However, the savings relative to the Jones three-strikes cost would be greater for all other alternatives on a percentage basis than the reduction in benefits. This is shown more directly in Figure 3.11, which displays cost per serious crime prevented. By this criterion, the Jones violent-only alternative would be best; it would deliver two thirds the benefit of the Jones three-strikes at only half the cost, for a cost per serious crime averted of about $12,000, compared with roughly $16,000 for the new law. This alternative is more cost-effective than the Jones law for two reasons. First, it spends less money locking up late-career offenders who might soon give up on crime anyway. Second, it spends less money locking up late-career low-rate offenders, who are

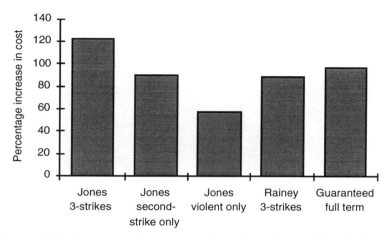

Figure 3.10. Percentage Increase in Costs From Jones Three-Strikes Law Compared With Alternatives

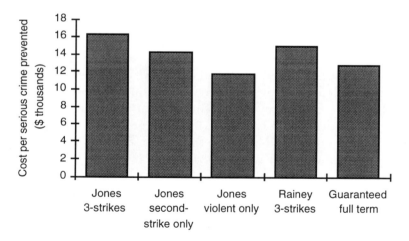

Figure 3.11. Cost per Serious Crime Prevented From Jones Three-Strikes Law Compared With Alternatives

disproportionately affected by the Jones law's counting a minor felony as a third strike.

Because the Jones second-strike alternative falls between the Jones law and the violent-only alternative in number of late-career criminals affected, it also falls between the two in cost-effectiveness. Again, this alternative permits a separate evaluation of the new law's third strike. The bill for the law's other provisions is the same as that for the second-strike-only alternative: about $14,000 for each serious crime prevented. The cost of the third strike is twice as much per serious crime prevented, again reflecting the inefficiency of late-career lock-ups and charging a third strike for a minor felony.

The guaranteed-full-term alternative puts more emphasis on incapacitating offenders early in their criminal careers. It gives short prison sentences to many who are given none by Jones instead of giving long sentences to a few. It requires that even first-time serious felons serve full terms in prison and saves some of the money that the new law spends locking up those convicted of minor felonies. By doing so, the full-term alternative would achieve a cost-effectiveness ratio second only to that of the violent-only alternative.

We do not wish, however, to establish cost per serious crime prevented as a touchstone criterion. The point, after all, is to reduce crime (some would say as much as possible), and the various alternatives are limited in how much they can achieve. Although it is true that the violent-only alternative can achieve two thirds the benefit of the Jones three-strikes law at half the expense, one cannot achieve the entire benefit by putting more money into that approach.

The guaranteed-full-term alternative thus stands out for its ability to realize the full benefit of the new three-strikes law at somewhat less cost. (This is graphically represented in Figure 3.12.) However, both the new law and all the alternatives, even the Jones violent only, represent major increases in spending over current levels. In the next section, we try to gain some perspective on the implications of such expenditures within California's current and prospective budgetary environment.

Footing the Bill

We have estimated that over the next 25 years, the Jones three-strikes law will prevent on the order of 340,000 serious crimes per year in California at an additional cost of roughly $5.5 billion annually, or about $16,000 per serious crime prevented. Alternatively, the guaranteed-full-term alternative could prevent the same number of serious

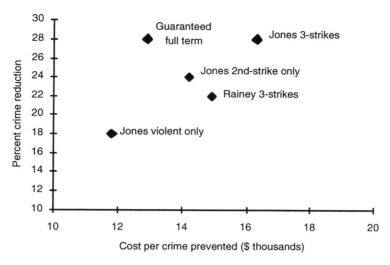

Figure 3.12. Benefits and Cost-Effectiveness From Jones Three-Strikes Law Compared With Alternatives

crimes for an additional expenditure of about $4.4 billion annually, or a cost of about $13,000 per crime prevented.

This analysis cannot determine whether it is "worth it" to increase California's criminal justice budget by such large amounts to achieve a 28% reduction in serious crimes (mostly burglaries and assaults) committed by adults. That determination depends on subjective factors that are difficult to quantify. However, some perspective can be gained on the issue of worth by asking two questions: First, are there other ways in which $5.5 billion per year could be spent that would reduce crime by more than 28%? Second, what must be given up to spend an additional $5.5 billion annually on crime reduction?

How Else Could the Money Be Spent to Reduce Crime?

We restrict ourselves here to two often-mentioned alternatives: increasing police protection and attacking the causes of crime. We cannot assess the value of these alternative expenditures relative to the new three-strikes law, but we can frame the comparison in a way that perhaps allows some perspective.

Governments, ranging from local to federal, have been attempting to increase the size of police forces. In Los Angeles, for example, the mayor hopes to find money for a major expansion of the police department. The financially strapped city may have to settle for a more modest buildup, but even the mayor's plan would increase the police force by less than 50%. The new federal crime law aims to add 100,000 police across the country, a gain of less than 20%. Five and a half billion dollars is on the same order of magnitude as what California spends annually on law enforcement at all levels. By redirecting that amount of money from implementing the Jones three-strikes law to funding police protection, California could thus double the number of police officers in every jurisdiction in the state. Alternatively, a somewhat smaller expansion could be undertaken in exchange for higher police pay, which might result in a force that is not only bigger but one with higher morale and greater aptitude.

In recent years, law enforcement officials have stressed that they can make only so much headway against crime if the root causes are not addressed. The reasons for this are clear: Our analysis suggests that there may be as many as 1 million felons on the street in California. At some point, these individuals will stop committing crimes and will be replaced by another million felons. The typical criminal career lasts roughly a decade. This implies that something on the order of a million California children under the age of 10 will become felons. The new three-strikes law does little or nothing to change that prospect (and neither would the alternatives evaluated earlier). It works by transferring felons from the street to prison; it does not act to shut off the supply.

The root causes of much serious crime are well known. They include broken families, dysfunctional families, poverty, sociopathic inclinations, the drug culture. Can money spent combating these causes be as effective as the three-strikes law? To be so, $5.5 *billion* would have to persuade 28,000 children who would have become felons not to take up criminal careers.[19] At a smaller, program level, the question can thus be rephrased: Can $5.5 *million* be targeted to environments in which children have a high propensity for crime in such a way as to keep 28 children who would otherwise have become criminals from doing so?

What Must Be Given Up to Fund Three Strikes?

Further insight can be gained into whether the Jones law is worth $5.5 billion a year if we ask whether Californians are willing to give up that much in other services. This is a more basic question than the preceding one, as it asks whether Californians want to shift large amounts of current spending to any criminal justice endeavor.

We begin with the assumption that higher taxes are unlikely. In particular, three strikes costs enough that the additional tax required to fund it would not be small—probably at least $300 per year from the average working person. Borrowing would also appear to be out of the question, given recent reactions from the bond-rating services and the electorate, not to mention the impracticality of borrowing as a long-term source of revenue.

But the state will have difficulty deciding what current spending should be reduced to make room for three strikes. Figure 3.13 shows how state spending is currently allocated.[20] By 2002, the new three-strikes law will require an additional 9-percentage-point increase in the fraction of the state budget devoted to corrections, now at 9%.[21] Where will those 9 percentage points come from? They cannot come from K-12 education. Proposition 98, written into the state constitution by California voters, sets minimal levels of funding for K-12 education. Because school enrollment will grow faster than the tax base, the percentage of the budget devoted to K-12 education will have to increase from the current 36 to 47 by 2002.

Health and welfare are also unlikely sources of funds. This portion of the budget has been increasing for 25 years and its share of the general fund is now 7 percentage points higher than it was in 1969. If the state wants federal assistance in funding Aid to Families With Dependent Children and MediCal (California's version of Medicaid), the state must provide its own share of the funds needed to support beneficiaries meeting federal entitlement criteria. Like school enrollment, the number of beneficiaries is expected to grow faster than California's population as a whole, so health and welfare spending will also increase as a percentage of the state's budget.

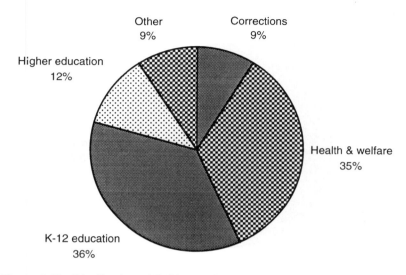

Figure 3.13. Distribution of California General Fund Appropriations, FY 1994

That leaves higher education and other government expenditures. Higher education's share of the budget has already fallen from 17% to 12% in the past 25 years. The result has been sharp increases in out-of-pocket costs for students and substantial cuts in the availability of classes.

Other government expenditures support a broad range of services such as pollution control, park and other natural resource management, workplace safety assurance, and insurance industry regulation. These services have also fallen as a percentage of total state expenditures from 12% in 1980 to 9% now.

Although state funding for higher education and other government services has been falling, these are the only practical sources of funds for the three-strikes law. To support implementation of the law, total spending for higher education and other services would have to fall by more than 40% over the next 8 years. At the same time, these spending categories will face severe pressure from the increasing health, welfare, and K-12 education mandates (for the combined effect of three strikes and K-12, see Figure 3.14). Increases in expenditures on corrections

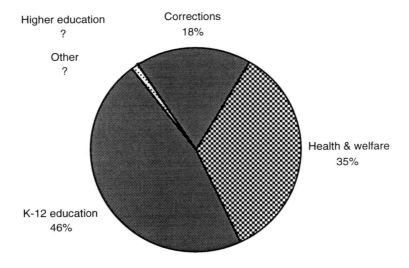

Assumes no increase in health & welfare (unlikely).

Figure 3.14. Budgetary Squeeze on Higher Education and Other Services, FY 2004

have tripled its portion of the state budget since 1980. If the three-strikes law remains in place, by 2002 the state government will be spending more money keeping people in prison than putting people through college. This allocation of funds raises questions of values that cannot be settled through data analysis.

Practical Considerations

Throughout this chapter, we have assumed that the Jones three-strikes law (or an alternative) will be implemented as written. It is clear from the preceding discussion, however, that something's got to give. Even though Californians passed the three-strikes initiative, they are unlikely to accept the state government's abdicating large portions of what they see as its responsibility for higher education, environmental quality, and so on. Legislators who found it politically attractive to vote for the three-strikes law may find it politically unattractive to fully fund its implementation. Voters may balk at the billions of dollars in additional prison bonds that will have to be passed in the coming years.

The results of underfunding the law are difficult to predict. If prison space is insufficient, courts may order the early release of prisoners. If they try to follow the spirit of the Jones law, they may release those with a brief record in favor of retaining older criminals behind bars. This may not be the right choice from the point of view of crime reduction, as younger criminals may have more of a criminal career ahead of them than older ones. On the other hand, prosecutors and judges, who are also politically accountable to the public, may choose to apply the law selectively. In the months since the three-strikes law took effect, the media have reported instances of rebellion against the law within the judicial system. This may continue as judges, prosecutors, witnesses, and juries have to face the possibility that criminals without a history of violence would be given long prison sentences.[22]

Clearly, failure to fully implement the law will decrease both its costs and its crime reduction benefits. Although these reductions should occur in similar proportions, their magnitude is uncertain. Only time and the workings of the criminal justice system will reveal the extent to which the new three-strikes law will realize the benefits Californians expect from it and the costs many of them do not.

Notes

1. Passage of the initiative (it did pass) had the practical effect of making the three-strikes law harder to repeal or to amend in ways that do not further its purpose, as such actions could be taken only by initiative.

2. We emphasize that although we talk about crime and crime rates, the three-strikes law and the analysis of alternatives in this chapter deal with felonies alone—and with *adult* felonies alone.

3. Because of this, when we say *serious crime* in this report, we include violent crime, unless we specify otherwise.

4. The definitions of *serious* and *violent* follow California law and should not be read as reflecting the authors' judgment as to what crimes should be regarded as serious or violent as the terms are used in common parlance. For example, assaults might seem to be inherently violent, but not all assaults are classified as violent under California law.

5. This should conservatively bias estimates of crime reduction and costs.

6. We define an ex-offender pool because it allows us to compute the number of crimes averted by incapacitation. This in no way presupposes the ability to determine which *individuals* have desisted.

7. Of course, there are other reasons to keep ex-felons locked up. A long sentence might deter others from committing similar crimes (although the evidence for this is

weak). Also, many people feel that a crime warrants a punishment of a certain length regardless of whether the criminal's state of mind changes during that period.

8. We use U.S. Bureau of the Census estimates for current and projected state populations.

9. To put it another way, the model makes it seem as if the alternatives can achieve selective incapacitation more easily than they can.

10. A related but more tangible cost is the payments the state makes to victims of crime. These would decrease if crime were reduced. Again, however, these savings would be overwhelmed by the increased prison costs required by the extended-sentence laws.

11. Juvenile convictions count as strikes, but even this is likely to be challenged as unconstitutional.

12. Recall that we define high- and low-rate offenders by halving the states incarcerated population in 1993 on the basis of their offense rates. Naturally, other definitions of high- and low-rate offenders would result in different relative offense rates.

13. Although we have not constrained our model to hold the crime rate constant under the provisions of the previous law, neither have we introduced factors that would make it vary significantly. As a result, the model results for the previous law show a roughly constant crime rate over the next 25 years, so our reported crime reduction benefits can be read as approximate reductions from the current rate.

14. The costs and benefits stated here and elsewhere are annualized values (in constant dollars) computed with a 4% discount rate. Discounting costs and benefits is standard practice in economic analysis of public programs. It accounts for the fact that a dollar today is more valuable than a dollar 20 years from now, because today's dollar can be invested to realize additional earnings or other benefits in the interim. No separate adjustment for inflation is made. Costs may thus be compared directly with costs of other programs in today's dollars. The $5.5 billion difference may be understood as the amount (in constant dollars) that would need to be invested every year to generate, with interest earned, the total discounted 25-year cost difference between the Jones and previous laws. Benefits (crimes prevented) must also be discounted in parallel with discounting of the costs of the alternatives generating those benefits (see Keeler & Cretin, 1983). However, the cost and benefit streams are not strongly skewed over the course of the next 25 years. Thus, most of the annualized discounted costs given in this chapter approximate the undiscounted constant-dollar amounts the state would actually have to pay in an average year. For the same reason, discounted benefits (crimes prevented) also approximate undiscounted benefits.

15. Our analysis may underestimate the cost to prevent a murder. The reason is that murders are often committed by family members or acquaintances who do not fit the profile of a habitual offender and who thus could not be singled out for incarceration.

The law will also prevent 17 minor burglaries, 32 motor vehicle thefts, and 50 other thefts for each $1 million, plus other crimes not on the FBI index. Because we are primarily interested in serious crimes prevented and we apply the full cost of the law to such crimes, the minor crimes prevented may be viewed as requiring no additional expenditure beyond the $16,300 per serious crime.

16. Some evidence suggests the existence of a deterrent effect from increasing the *probability* that a felon will serve time (of whatever length).

17. This applies only to those who were sentenced to prison. Jones provides for a doubling of sentence on second strike, but it also cuts good time from 50% to 20% maximum. The effect is thus to more than triple the current actual time incarcerated for those imprisoned for a second serious offense.

18. We count the full capital cost for adding prison space in the year the space is needed.

19. Over the long run, the Jones law's effectiveness can be equaled if 28% of those who would have become felons are persuaded not to. One year's share of the million felons replaced every 10 years is 100,000. Twenty-eight percent of that is 28,000.

20. We are grateful to RAND colleague Stephen J. Carroll for allowing us to use his analysis of current and future state expenditures; that analysis is part of an ongoing research project.

21. This assumes relatively optimistic growth in money available for the general fund (nearly 50% between FY 1994 and FY 2002, in constant dollars). The growth in the corrections budget is based on growth in the entire pre-Jones budget at a rate equal to that anticipated for prison construction and operation under the previous law (roughly 10% in constant dollars over the 8 years). The extra three-strikes prison costs are then added to that.

22. It is ironic that the sweeping changes required by the three-strikes law, combined with its near-prohibitive cost, may require legislators and criminal justice officials and practitioners to make the very kind of discretionary choices that proponents of the initiative were trying to take away from them.

References

Blumstein, A., Cohen, J., & Nagin, D. (1978). *Deterrence and incapacitation: Estimating the effects of criminal sanctions on crime rates.* Washington, DC: National Academy of Sciences.

Blumstein, A., Cohen, J., Roth, J. A., & Visher, C. (Eds.). (1986). *Criminal careers and "career criminals"* (Vol. 1). Washington, DC: National Research Council, National Academy of Sciences.

California Department of Corrections. (1991). *California prisoners and parolees, 1990.* Sacramento, CA: Youth and Adult Correctional Agency.

California Department of Justice. (1992). *Crime and delinquency in California, 1992.* Sacramento, CA: Division of Law Enforcement, Law Enforcement Information Center.

Cook, P. (1980). Research in criminal deterrence: Laying the groundwork for the second decade. In N. Morris & M. Tonry (Eds.), *Crime and justice: An annual review of research* (Vol. 2, pp. 211-268). Chicago: University of Chicago Press.

Federal Bureau of Investigation. (1993, October). *Uniform Crime Reports for the United States–1992.* Washington, DC: U.S. Department of Justice.

Keeler, E. B., & Cretin, S. (1983). Discounting of life-saving and other nonmonetary effects. *Management Science, 29*(3), 300-306.

MacCoun, D. (1993). Drugs and the law: A psychological analysis of drug prohibition. *Psychological Bulletin, 111*(3), 497-512.

Rohter, L. (1994, May 10). States embracing tougher measures for fighting crime. *New York Times,* p. 1.

Shinnar, S., & Shinnar, R. (1975). The effects of the criminal justice system on the control of crime: A quantitative approach. *Law and Society Review, 9*(4), 581-611.

U.S. Department of Justice. (1992). *Sourcebook of criminal justice statistics–1991.* Washington, DC: Bureau of Justice Statistics.

Chapter Four

Effect on a Local Criminal Justice System

ROBERT C. CUSHMAN

This chapter describes the developing effect of AB 971 (Jones) on justice systems operating within local units of government in California, with the intention of preparing the reader—and officials of local government in other states where similar legislation may be enacted—to anticipate the challenges this law will present.

Local Effects Provide Early Warning System

The effect that "three strikes and you're out" legislation is having on state governments, especially state prisons systems, has received much more press coverage than the effects that three strikes has and will have on city and county governments. This uneven coverage has made it more difficult to accurately estimate the potential effect of the legislation and, as will be seen, has led to some unnecessary and faulty assumptions.

Examining the expected effect at local levels of government first makes sense for a number of reasons. For the most part, it will be city police and county deputy sheriffs who will arrest "strike" defendants.

These defendants will be held in city and county jails awaiting trial. And although they will be adjudicated in state courts, these courts are situated at the county level of government, which, in most states, pays for the bailiffs, court reporters, court clerical staff, the courthouse itself, and perhaps the costs of prosecution and defense, as well. Most of the justice apparatus operates at the local, not the state, level of government. Thus, before strike cases can reach the state prison system, they must be adjudicated within a justice system that is essentially based within city and county governments.

Any crisis that may be created by new legislation can be expected to appear first at the local levels of government. Here is where court delay will emerge, where those accused will stack up in county jails awaiting trials, and where other symptoms of system overload will first appear. Thus, pressure on local institutions will appear long before these pressures appear at the state level of government.

Backlogs that develop within the justice systems operating at the county level of government will actually slow the consequences that will be felt by state governments. Cases have to be adjudicate at the county level before defendants are sent to state prisons. Thus, when backlogs develop at the local level it mutes the development of effects at the state level. This can create a false impression that original state estimates of a large increase in prison admissions were in error, or exaggerated.

Summary of Experience Reported by Local Government

Several California counties have conducted surveys and/or studies to determine the potential and actual effects of the three-strikes legislation. In addition, some statewide survey information is available. This section will summarize the experience reported in the press, in studies conducted by California counties, and the surveys.[1]

Santa Clara County (San Jose) was one of the first California counties to mount a serious attempt to assess the potential effects of the three-strikes legislation. An initial report was issued in August 1994, less than 5 months after the passage of the legislation (Center for Urban Analysis, 1994a). Subsequent reports were also produced (Center for Urban Analysis, 1994b, 1995).

The Santa Clara County effort emerged from the county's prior participation in a multiyear national study of felony sentencing conducted by the National Association of Criminal Justice Planners (NACJP; Langan & Graziadei, 1995). This project, under the leadership of Mark Cunniff, Executive Director of the NACJP, provided Santa Clara County with a scientifically selected sample of persons sentenced on felony matters in Santa Clara County in 1992. The NACJP sample provided a great deal of information that described these cases and how they were actually adjudicated in 1992. Some additional data were added to this database from records provided by the public defender and staff from the municipal and superior courts.

The Santa Clara County strategy was to assign a skilled deputy district attorney to examine each case in the sample and determine which cases would have been three-strikes, two-strikes, or one-strike cases had the three-strikes law been in effect at the time these cases were adjudicated. This provided a reasonable basis for estimating the potential number of strike cases that could be expected in 1994 (Center for Urban Analysis, 1994a, p. 1).

The next step was to compare how these cases were adjudicated in 1992 with how they might have been adjudicated had the three-strikes law then been in effect. This comparison allowed the county to estimate potential effects of the three-strikes legislation.

The analysis was performed in a workshop organized and led by a supervising judge of the Criminal Division of the Superior Court. Seventy-three sample cases, representing 1,395 strike cases, were discussed in a group setting by senior attorneys from the District Attorney's Office, the Public Defender's Office, the Office of Conflicts Administration, the Probation Department, and a representative from the Sheriff's Office concerned with court security. The Honorable John Flaherty and another superior court judge guided the discussion and "presided" as these cases were essentially "readjudicated." Each case was discussed in terms of how it might be adjudicated differently under the three-strikes law. Particular attention was devoted to determining the strike status of the cases; that is, how many strikes would be involved and whether these cases would go to trial. Qualitative and quantitative information was collected as the discussion moved from case to case (Center for Urban Analysis, 1994a, p. 2).

The Most Likely Scenario

An early section of Santa Clara County's report summarizes the most likely scenario. It is titled "The Condition to Be Managed" and provides a useful distillation of the types of changes expected by many California counties. It reads as follows:

> The justice system has a surprising ability to avoid becoming over-whelmed—to adjust, to adapt and absorb challenges and changes. But this time may be different. The "three-strikes, you're out" law is expected to create a crisis in the administration of justice in Santa Clara County and elsewhere in the State.
>
> Where will the system begin to break down first? The strain will appear at many places at once—at the jail, in the municipal and superior courts where felony matters are heard, and by the prosecution and defense, by court security and prisoner transportation and other support services. But the workload impact will most likely be experienced earliest and most directly by the individual attorneys assigned to the cases from the District Attorney's Office, the Public Defender's Office, and Office of Conflicts Administration, an office that also represents indigent defendants.
>
> Strain on the capacity of the District Attorney's Office, the Public Defender's Office, and the Office of Conflicts Administration will most likely exacerbate a growing court process backlog. As the criminal workload increases, periodic "purges" of criminal cases may be required. To do this, the adjudication of criminal matters will displace civil proceedings. This may produce an ongoing reduction in court resources devoted to civil proceedings.
>
> The proportion of the jail system that is devoted to pretrial prisoners will increase dramatically, perhaps to 70%. Because the strike cases are expected to take a long time to adjudicate, large numbers of serious pretrial prisoners will collect in the jail system and the jail population will ramp up until these inmates begin to be sentenced to the state prison system. This will then produce some temporary relief of jail crowding because some of these prison-bound inmates would have been sentenced to County jail terms in the past. This change will further diminish the proportion of the jail population that is made up of sentenced prisoners.
>
> By June 1995, the State Department of Corrections is expected to be full.[2] Imposition of a court-ordered inmate population "cap" on an already crowded state prison system could occur earlier. In either event, felony commitments from the counties will have begun to "back up" in county jails. This will again escalate jail crowding in Santa Clara County.
>
> The characteristics and volume of the felony probation supervision caseload will change. The most serious probation cases will be sent to prison and no longer require supervision at the county level. The number

of felony-level intakes to probation supervision will diminish. This will keep the probation supervision workload from growing; in fact, a small reduction in the caseload is forecast. This could create an opportunity to revitalize the adult probation service.

What are often considered justice support services will also experience considerable strain, and it may be that breakdowns in the less obvious areas will produce important unanticipated and unintended consequences. For example, any crisis in office support staff, investigators in the district attorney and/or public defender offices, laboratory analysis, court security, and/or inmate transportation could temporarily bring the justice system to a standstill.

The juvenile justice system will also experience effects that mirror those of the adult justice system because strikes garnered as a juvenile can be used in adult proceedings.[3] This project did not include an attempt to quantify these effects; however, juvenile strike cases are certain to involve more litigation and require more hearings and more processing time from arrest to final disposition. The additional time to process the juvenile cases and the new seriousness with which they may be regarded will, most likely, lead to a demand for additional juvenile hall bed space for these juvenile cases.

However, unlike the adult system where strike cases are associated with mandatory prison terms, there is no requirement that juvenile strike cases be sent to the California Department of the Youth Authority. Thus, no "savings" in county institution or probation supervision resources can be expected to automatically accrue, because the new three-strikes law will send some juveniles to the state level who were previously managed locally. (Center for Urban Analysis, 1994a, p. 2)

Expected Effects

The reports, surveys, and press accounts that were reviewed converge into recurring themes that serve to summarize the expected and actual effects of the three-strikes law at local levels of government. These are enumerated here.

Thousands of cases are being prosecuted. Santa Clara County determined that 28%, or 2,315, of the approximately 8,400 persons expected to be sentenced on felony matters in Santa Clara County in 1994 would be strike cases. About 2.7% (235 defendants) were expected to be three-strikes cases; another 12% (1,005 defendants) were expected to be two-strikes cases. One-strike cases, 13% (1,075), would include approximately 155 defendants with multiple strike counts (Center for Urban Analysis, 1994a, p. 3).

Three-strikes cases made up 3% of the approximately 68,000 felony filings in Los Angeles County during the year March 1994 through February 1995; two-strikes cases made up about 8% (Legislative Analyst's Office, 1995, p. 3).

A survey of 42 counties conducted by the California District Attorney's Association (CDAA) reported that "at the end of August 1994 (six months after the enactment of the law) there were more than 7,400 'second' and 'third-strike' cases filed" (Legislative Analyst's Office, 1995, p. 3). In Los Angeles County, which represents about half of the state's cases, more than 5,000 second- and third-strike cases had been filed as of the end of November 1994 (Legislative Analyst's Office, 1995, p. 3). In Santa Clara County, public defender, district attorney, and court information all showed in excess of 430 two- and three-strikes cases were open and being processed as of mid-January 1995 (Center for Urban Analysis, 1995).

Many more trials will be required. Estimates provided by three California counties indicate the expected number of trials will increase substantially. Los Angeles County reports an increase in the overall number of felony cases going to trial despite declining felony arrest rates and a declining number of felony filings. The Los Angeles County District Attorney estimated the number of jury trials will increase from about 2,410 in 1994 to 5,875 in 1995, an increase of 144% (Legislative Analyst's Office, 1995, p. 5). Actual experience showed that the number of superior court trials increased from 318 in January through February 1994 to 417 in January through February 1995, or by 31%. Approximately 40% of the trials during the past year were strike cases (Countywide Criminal Justice Coordinating Committee, 1995).

In Santa Clara County, the review of cases performed at the workshop suggested that the expected number of trials per year would increase from 225 to 590, a 160% increase. The number of jury trials was expected to increase from 200 in 1992 to 585, a 193% increase (Center for Urban Analysis, 1994a, p. vi). The San Diego County Public Defender expected the number of jury trials to increase from about 500 in 1993 to 1,500 in 1994, a 300% increase (Legislative Analyst's Office, 1995, p. 5).

According to the California Legislative Analyst, prior to the three-strikes legislation, "about 94% of all felony cases statewide were disposed of through plea bargaining." But according to the report, after the law was passed, about 14% of all second-strike cases and only about 6% of all third-strike cases have been disposed of through pleas (Legislative Analyst's Office, 1995, p. 4). The Legislative Analyst's report also found that counties that relied heavily on plea bargaining in the past were experiencing the most significant increases in the number of cases going to trial after the passage of the new law (Legislative Analyst's Office, 1995, p. 4).

Many more jurors will be needed. The number of jurors needed was expected to increase, not only because there would be more jury trials, but because each side in a life imprisonment case is entitled to 20 peremptory challenges, instead of 10.

Many more hearings will be required to dispose of cases in municipal and superior courts. The 2,315 annual number of strike cases that Santa Clara County expects to process will require an estimated 17,200 appearances in municipal court, or an average of 7.4 per case. This is a 17% increase over the number of appearances that were required by these dockets in 1992. At the superior court level, strike cases that would have been settled by plea in 1992, but are expected to require jury trials now that the three-strikes law is in effect, are expected to produce a demand for 8,740 additional hearings in superior court for 385 additional trial cases; this represents an 85% increase (Center for Urban Analysis, 1994a, p. 24).

The arrest-to-sentencing case processing time will increase. The 2,315 annual number of strike cases that Santa Clara County anticipated were expected to require a total of 143,145 days to move through the municipal court process, an average of 61.8 days. This is a 21% increase over the number of processing days that were required in 1992. At the superior court level, the additional 385 strike cases that were expected to be tried by jury were expected to add an estimated 50,050 days of processing time—an additional 19% of the total number of days it took to process these cases in 1992. Half of the increase was expected to be devoted to the additional 135 cases that were identified as three-strikes cases requiring jury trials (Center for Urban Analysis, 1994a, p. 27).

The number of preliminary hearings will increase. In Santa Clara County in 1992, 56% of the strike dockets had a preliminary hearing. This was expected to increase to 67% of strike cases in 1994. The raw number of strike dockets requiring preliminary hearings was expected to increase from 1,295 to 1,557, or by 20% (Center for Urban Analysis, 1994b, p. 14).

The amount of time spent on preliminary hearings will increase. Because of the increase in the expected number of preliminary hearings, the total number of hours required to conduct preliminary hearings for the strike cases in Santa Clara County was expected to increase by an estimated 20% (Center for Urban Analysis, 1994b, p. 18).

The preliminary hearings will be longer. In addition, preliminary hearings were expected to take longer. In Santa Clara County, the combination of additional preliminary hearings and additional time for conducting each preliminary hearing was expected to increase the total number of additional hours to be devoted to preliminary hearings for the strike cases by 55% (Center for Urban Analysis, 1994b, p. 18).

Fewer felony cases are settling in municipal court. San Diego, Orange, Santa Clara, and Los Angeles Counties all report a substantial reduction in the number of felony cases being settled at the municipal court level. Strike cases are moving to the superior court level for trial.

Costs associated with defense representation by private attorneys on the Conflicts Panel will increase. In Santa Clara County, attorneys handling cases for defendants facing the most serious penalties are paid on an hourly basis; attorneys handling cases for defendants facing less serious sanctions are paid a flat fee. In 1992, 28% of the Santa Clara County strike cases faced severe penalties that merited assignment of counsel paid on an hourly basis instead of a flat fee. After review at the workshop, an estimated 61% will require these more experienced trial attorneys. This is likely to increase defense costs. The current panel of attorneys will have to be expanded in number and experience (Center for Urban Analysis, 1994a, p. 34).

Other backlogs will develop. Strike cases have become a larger and larger proportion of the growing total number of cases set for trial in the superior court in Santa Clara County. At December 31, 1994, it was 30% of 630 cases (Center for Urban Analysis, 1995, p. 8). In Los Angeles County, the percentage of Public Defender's Office open strike cases in the total pending superior court caseload increased from 4% in March 1994 to 57% by December 1994 (Countywide Criminal Justice Coordinating Committee, 1995).

System breakdowns will create delays in processing time. Additional increases in processing times are expected, simply because Santa Clara County will not have the proper resources available at the proper location at the proper time to adjudicate ready cases. For example, a judge, prosecutor, or defender may not be available; a suitable courtroom may not be available; inmate transportation may be unable to deliver a prisoner on time. Simple logistics will become more complex as the capacity of the justice system is strained to keep up with the increased workload (Center for Urban Analysis, 1994a, p. 3).

Legal ambiguity will produce delays. During the next year there will be many motions, court tests, appeals, and other litigation. Eventually, this level of activity will decline but it is likely it will add to the number of hearings and produce delays in processing cases.[4]

The pretrial jail population will increase. The extra 50,050 days it is expected to take to process strike cases requiring jury trials in Santa Clara County translates into 137 additional jail beds, assuming these cases spend all their pretrial time in custody. These beds would be required to be in a security facility suitable for housing such defendants. Strike cases that do not eventually go to trial might also take longer to settle. This would add to the total jail bed requirement (Center for Urban Analysis, 1994a, p. 29). Orange County estimated it would require another 500 beds to absorb the three-strikes load (Orange County Administrative Office, 1994, p. 4). Los Angeles County estimates that more than 1,000 three-strikes cases were in jail awaiting trial as of December 31, 1995 (Legislative Analyst's Office, 1995, p. 5). In San Bernardino County, the jail no longer accepts offenders being booked for misdemeanors because of the growth in its three-strikes presentenced jail population (Legislative Analyst's Office, 1995, p. 7).

The proportion of the jail population that is unsentenced will increase. Prior to the passage of the three-strikes legislation, about 50% of the county jail beds in California were occupied by pretrial prisoners. This percentage has been increasing (Board of Corrections, 1995, p. 1).

In August 1994, Santa Clara County projected that the pretrial jail population might increase from 50% to about 70% as a result of three strikes (Center for Urban Analysis, 1994a, p. 29). Indeed, the number of unsentenced, felony-charged, male jail inmates increased dramatically over March 1994 when the legislation was passed. The increase is almost totally due to increases in the average length of inmate stay, increasing from 81 days in January 1994 to 94 days in July 1994 and 114 days in January 1995 (James, 1995).

The pretrial population in Los Angeles County was about 60% prior to three strikes; it has now surpassed 70% (Walters, 1995).

More high-security inmates will be held in jail. Two-strikes and three-strikes inmates are considered "high security." They need to be identified as strike inmates as soon as they are booked into jail, then classified to secure housing and close supervision. A survey of 15 counties conducted by the California State Board of Corrections found that many counties are modifying their procedures and classification systems to improve management of this potentially more difficult population (Legislative Analyst's Office, 1995, p. 8). In Los Angeles County, for example, the percentage of jail inmates classified as high security increased from 37% in November 1993 to 49% in October 1994 and 53% by February 1995 (Countywide Criminal Justice Coordinating Committee, 1995).

Increased court security will be needed. Three-strikes inmates have nothing to lose. They face 25 years to life in prison. This will make them more dangerous to transport to what is expected to be an additional

number of court hearings. The increased penalties, the increase in
prisoner movement created by the additional hearings, and expectations of court delay and jail crowding all indicate a need to increase
court security. Secure courtrooms will be needed for court proceedings
for strike cases, especially for the prison-bound two-strikes cases and
the three-strikes cases facing sentences of 25 years to life.

There will be sentenced-prisoner jail day savings. If all the 905 Santa
Clara County one-, two-, and three-strikes defendants who were sentenced to jail in 1992 had been sentenced to prison, the jail person-year
savings would have totaled 532 jail person-years, about 20% of the 2,689
jail person-years ordered for all felony sentences in 1992. This is the
maximum effect; it is not likely that all of the strike cases will be
sentenced to prison (Center for Urban Analysis, 1994a, p. 16).

There will be county probation supervision day savings. If all the Santa
Clara County strike defendants received prison sentences, the probation savings would total 2,095 person-years, 14% of the total probation
ordered in 1992. This, too, is the maximum effect; not all the sentenced
strike defendants will be sent to prison. Some will receive jail terms as
a condition of probation and will therefore spend time in jail and later,
on probation (Center for Urban Analysis, 1994a, p. 18).

Civil matters may be forced out by the criminal court workload. Because
criminal work is accorded priority, the very large increase in criminal
trials may force out civil litigation. This could create long delays for
civil matters and make the court virtually unavailable to civil litigants.
This could produce an environment in which consumer fraud and
other illegal business practices cannot be restrained, and where
criminal matters emanate from frustration over an inability to reach
civil remedies, especially in domestic relations matters.

Clearly, more courts are shifting resources to address the challenges
presented by the three-strikes legislation. In Los Angeles, for example,

> more than half of the 50 courtrooms in the central court district that are
> normally used for civil cases were being diverted to criminal trials . . . by
> early 1995, approximately 60 of the 120 judges currently handling civil
> cases are expected to be redirected to criminal cases. Two-thirds to

three-fourths of all courtrooms that hear civil cases will be devoted to criminal trials. (Legislative Analyst's Office, 1995, p. 8)

Developing backlogs are pushing less serious cases out. There are reports that the growing backlog of more serious strike cases is forcing less attention to other matters. For example, some district attorneys are prosecuting fewer misdemeanor cases (Legislative Analyst's Office, 1995, p. 6). Similarly, some counties are releasing inmates to make room for the more serious strike cases. In Los Angeles County, for example,

> prior to enactment of "three-strikes," sentenced offenders generally served about two-thirds of their sentence before being released. Recently, however, offenders are serving only about 45 percent of their sentence, in order to make room for more "three-strikes" offenders awaiting trial. (Legislative Analyst's Office, 1995, p. 7)

Several counties reported a reduction in the number of misdemeanants in jail. As noted earlier, misdemeanor offenders are no longer being booked into the San Bernardino County jail because jail space is being occupied by more serious three-strikes pretrial inmates (Legislative Analyst's Office, 1995, p. 7).

Justice expenditures will increase substantially. In October 1994, the Santa Clara County Board of Supervisors authorized a onetime expenditure of $1.3 million to help justice agencies cope with three strikes through the end of the fiscal year.[5] At about the same time, Los Angeles County provided an emergency appropriation of $10.2 million to its justice agencies (Legislative Analyst's Office, 1995, p. 8). Other counties have augmented justice budgets throughout the fiscal year. As county budgets for FY 1995/1996 are being prepared, very large increases are being reported to help justice agencies cope with the ongoing effects of three strikes.

Lessons Learned

Three-strikes legislation is not a rational response. Table 4.1 shows the number of punishment years produced by the Santa Clara County

justice system in 1992 for what would have been strike and nonstrike
cases, if the legislation had been in effect at that time (Center for Urban
Analysis, 1994a, p. 19). It shows a total of 8,395 defendants were
sentenced to a total of 28,901 person-years of punishment. Although
it is not displayed in the table, the total cost of carrying out these
sanctions (in 1992 dollars) will be $300 million.

This author suspects that in most jurisdictions, these calculations
have simply never been put together before. The analysis done in Santa
Clara County showed that voters, justice officials, and officials of
general government had no idea of the number of punishment years
being produced by local justice systems *prior* to the passage of three
strikes. Undertaking such a profound change in the private sector
without a thorough analysis of the effect would be considered foolish
and unheard of. Yet at the ballot box, California voters, without
knowing the effect of their action, clearly expressed the view that
current levels of punishment were not enough. For example, in Santa
Clara County, the November 1994 three-strikes initiative passed by a
71.9% margin.[6]

Empirical evidence will not necessarily make a difference. We cannot
count on rational argument or "fact sheets" to inform and change
opinion. Empirical, factual information about the consequences of the
legislation does not seem to matter. This puzzles practitioners, and it
is heretical to academics and researchers. A very strong form of
cognitive dissonance drives both thinking and action on this issue;
"people cling to their beliefs with such utter conviction that incompatible evidence is denied or reinterpreted with as much inventiveness
as is necessary to preserve the original beliefs" (author unknown).

*Historical analysis of criminal history records will overstate the number of
strike cases that can be expected to enter the justice system.* The Santa Clara
County research revealed that simply relying on an inspection of a
defendant's criminal history record to determine the number of strikes
will seriously overestimate the number of strike cases and the seriousness of these cases, once they are adjudicated (Center for Urban
Analysis, 1994a, p. 3). Similarly, review of defendant "rap sheets" led
the state Department of Corrections to initially overestimate the num-

TABLE 4.1   Total Person-Years of Punishment Imposed: Persons
Sentenced on Felony Matters, 1992, Santa Clara County,
California

Number of Strikes	Number of Defendants Sentenced	Total Years of Sanctions	Total Years of Incarceration	Prison Years	Jail Years	Probation Years
No strikes	6,080	17,811	4,515	2,358	2,157	13,296
One strike	920	3,961	2,436	2,143	293	1,525
One+[a]	155	1,660	1,630	1,622	8	30
Two strikes	1,005	2,958	2,478	2,267	211	480
Three strikes	235	2,512	2,452	2,432	20	60
Total	8,395	28,901	13,511	10,822	2,689	15,390

SOURCE: Center for Urban Analysis (1994a, p. 19).
a. Indicates one-strike cases with multiple strike counts.

ber of strike cases that could be expected to come into the state prison
system (Tristan, 1994).

There are several reasons for these two sources of error. First, from
the Santa Clara County research, it became clear that once prosecutors,
defense attorneys, and judges sat down to review individual cases,
other important factors became apparent. For example, the prosecution may have had a weak case—a victim who would not testify, difficulty
with witnesses, and so forth. The time between strikes may have been
lengthy, or the offense may have been committed when the defendant
was very young. These factors might make it more difficult to get a
conviction from a jury. In some cases, it was clear the prosecutor might
trade a strike, that is, accept a two-strikes plea agreement to a longer
than usual prison term, rather than pursue a shaky three-strikes prosecution. Thus, when the results of the criminal records research were
compared to the results following discussion of the individual cases in
the workshop, some three-strikes cases became two-strikes cases, some
two-strikes cases became one-strike cases, and so on.

Second, the process of researching, obtaining transcripts, and proving old priors turned out to be very labor intensive, time-consuming,
and sometimes simply impossible.

Third, rap sheets are very incomplete, especially in recording dispositions. The situation is getting worse because the workload has been growing and state funds to keep criminal history records current have been shrinking (Legislative Analyst's Office, 1995, p. 11). Research conducted by the National Association of Criminal Justice Planners found sizable numbers of offenders known to have been convicted of serious offenses in Santa Clara County and Sacramento County, California, whose rap sheets contained no information about their conviction and sentencing.[7] This information is essential to establish a prior strike. The public assumes that the records are much better than they actually are. It is conceivable that litigation could ensue if a future crime victim believes officials should have known about alleged prior serious and/or violent felony convictions during some prior criminal proceeding, especially if proving the earlier priors would have resulted in a life sentence.

Many three-strikes and two-strikes cases are being downgraded. It seems apparent that this "downgrading" of the number of strikes from three to two to one to no strikes has also been driven by other factors that remain to be discovered and articulated, because the original estimates of the number of convictions at each level were much higher than actual experience has shown, not only in Santa Clara County but in many other counties as well. Although the data are still sketchy, there are signs that both the number of strike cases and the *ratio* of two-strikes to three-strikes cases change dramatically as these cases make their passage through the justice process. This suggests that many three-strikes cases are making the transition to two-strikes status.

For example, at the Santa Clara County jail, as of January 1, 1995, there were 174 two-strikes and 138 three-strikes inmates, a ratio of 1.26 "two-strikers" for every three-strikes inmate (Board of Corrections, 1995, Appendix C). Comparing this to state prison admissions from Santa Clara County as of May 31, 1995, there were only 9 three-strikes commitments as of May 31, 1995 versus 275 second-strike commitments, a ratio of 30.5 two-strikes commitments to every three-strikes commitment (Data Analysis Unit, 1995). The change in ratio might be explained if jail inmates are being "overclassified" into the three-strikes category, or it could be a consequence of longer processing times of the three-strikes cases demanding trials. (There were 114 three-strikes cases—about 34% of the cases—awaiting trial in Santa Clara County as of May 31, 1995.) These explanations, however, do not seem sufficient to explain the shift in the two- to three-strikes ratios.

Statewide data show similar patterns. The combined jail populations from 18 counties showed a ratio of 2,870 two-strikes inmates to 1,724 three-strikes inmates, or 1.66 two-strikers to every three-striker (Board of Corrections, 1995, Appendix C). However, the statewide prison commitment total as of May 31, 1995 was 7,795 two-strikes commitments and 424 three-strikes commitments, for a ratio of 18.38 two-strikes to every three-strikes commitment (Data Analysis Unit, 1995).

It is now clear that fewer three-strikes cases survive the entire passage from charging to sentencing. The data available suggest that these ratios are developing differently for each county and that the general transitioning of cases from three-strikes to two-strikes, and perhaps to one-strike and no-strike, status is taking place in its own fashion in each of California's 58 counties. This is a little understood phenomenon, and worthy of further study.

Strike legislation should be viewed as part of a larger movement. This legislation is a lightning rod—symbolic of a much larger trend toward ratcheting up penalties. In California, for example, 315 bills to increase penalties were signed into law in the same year that the three-strikes legislation passed. Three strikes represents a new approach to dealing with the career criminal. Unfortunately, the term *career criminal* has become murky. It is now a montage of three essentially overlapping types of offenders: violent offenders, serious offenders, and repeat offenders. These three categories of offenders can be represented on a piece of paper as three circles, with some overlap. Certainly, all violent offenders are also serious offenders, but burglary, which is considered "serious" in California, is not considered a violent crime, nor are many other of the crimes that carry the label *serious*. They are "serious," but not "violent." And, of course, repeat offenders can be convicted on any one of some 500 felonies in California without being labeled serious or violent. To which target population should a three-strikes law be applied?

Most three-strikes offenders are being charged and convicted of nonviolent, nonserious offenses. Data obtained from California counties by the

Legislative Analyst's Office showed that the trigger offense for about 70% of all defendants charged as second- and third-strikers was nonviolent and nonserious. Similarly, most convictions were for nonviolent, nonserious offenses (Legislative Analyst's Office, 1995, p. 9). Counties vary markedly in terms of their practice and policy concerning the trigger offense in strike cases. Some require it to be a violent or serious offense, others do not. The number of strike cases and the extent to which they are nonserious or nonviolent varies markedly by county. This reflects the ambivalent, inconsistent application of the law to violent, serious, repeat offenders.

The law is not being applied uniformly in California's 58 counties. According to the *San Jose Mercury News,*

> Alameda County . . . has 4 percent of the state's population and accounts for 3.3 percent of the state's prison inmates. When it comes to three-strikes implementation, however, Alameda falls below the curve, accounting for just 1.3 percent of the 6,157 inmates imprisoned under the law, the Department of Corrections says. In contrast, San Joaquin County, with about one third of Alameda's population, sent twice as many inmates to prison under the three-strikes law during its first year.
>
> And, when combined, Los Angeles and San Diego Counties accounted for 58% of strike commitments to the state but only 45% of the overall state prison population. Thus, there is clear evidence that differing prosecution policies are operating in different counties. The Alameda County District Attorney's Office, for example, has decided "to prosecute 'three-strikes' cases only when the crimes involved are violent or serious, even though any felony can constitute a third strike under the law." (Walters, 1995, p. 10)

Even more troubling to many is the disproportionate number of minorities among the two- and three-strikes prison commitments. California Department of Corrections data reveal that 70% were either African American or Hispanic (" 'Three-Strikes' Data Point," 1994; Walters, 1995).

The law is being resisted. Numerous newspaper accounts and a good deal of anecdotal evidence reveal "that some judges, juries, and victims are responding in ways that reduce its effects" (Legislative Analyst's Office, 1995, p. 8). Examples cited in the report by the Legislative

Analyst include "judges reducing minor felony criminal charges to misdemeanors when a felony conviction under the 'three-strikes' law would require a lengthy prison sentence" and some resistance "by superior court judges to consider the qualifying prior convictions when sentencing offenders for new offenses, a practice which is inconsistent with the intent of the measure" (Legislative Analyst's Office, 1995, p. 8).

Focusing only on strike data is difficult and might be a mistake. It should be clear from the discussion of the previous items in this list of lessons learned that narrowly focused efforts to "study the effect of three strikes" may be too limited. It will be difficult to separate out the effect of the three-strikes "iceberg" from the many other icebergs being swept along on this punitive tide. Suffice it to say that the emerging problems of jail crowding, court delay, and justice system overload are only partly due to three strikes. Encouraging officials to blame it all on three strikes obfuscates the issue. This just is not constructive.

Jail crowding will become the new "crisis." Jail population projections forecast additional jail population increases well beyond the capacity of the system to absorb them. In Santa Clara County, nearly all of this growth has been because of increases in the length of stay of persons charged with felonies, not because more offenders are being booked into the jail. The Santa Clara County Director of Corrections says: "We don't have more inmates. The inmates we have are staying longer!" (personal communication, 1994). As noted earlier, the average length of stay of the pretrial felony-charged unsentenced jail population increased from approximately 81 days in January 1994 (about the same length of stay as in January 1993) to 94 days in July 1994, and to 114 days in January 1995. The dramatic increase in the length of stay begins in March 1994, when the strike legislation became effective (James, 1995). Increases in county jail populations are being reported throughout the state, although, here again, there is much county by county variation.

And there are related effects. For example, according to a survey conducted by the California State Board of Corrections, the number of inmate assaults on staff has increased 27% since the enactment of the three-strikes legislation (Board of Corrections, 1995, p. 2). Furthermore, the jails are destined to become filled with a much higher proportion of pretrial inmates. In 1989, the pretrial population was 51% of the statewide average daily jail population. By January 1, 1995, the pretrial population made up 61% of the statewide jail population (Board of Corrections, 1995, p. 1).

The expected effects are developing more slowly than projected. In February 1995, Santa Clara County released a report that confirmed that the full aftereffect of the two- and three-strikes cases that had been filed had been much slower in developing than expected (Center for Urban Analysis, 1995). Few had gone to trial. An increasing inventory of cases awaiting trial was developing, and as of December 1, 1994, two- and three-strikes cases made up about 30% of this inventory. This same phenomenon is being reported by other counties.

As this has occurred, the California State Department of Corrections (CDC) estimates of the number of two- and three-strikes cases that will enter the California prison system have been continuously revised downward. The CDC has simply underestimated how long it is taking to adjudicate cases in which the defendants are being housed in county jails and processed in county courthouses. No "early warning" system has yet been put in place to help state corrections more accurately anticipate this prison system intake. To work, such a system must gather the following data from the counties: the number of strike filings by county prosecutors and the percentage of total filings they represent; the number of strike cases being settled by plea or by trial in each county and their percentage of total dispositions; the time it is taking to adjudicate these cases in each county and whether this is changing; the number of strike cases the courts estimate they will dispose of each month; and the number of strike cases in the jails and their proportion of the total jail population.

The fact that both positive and negative effects are developing more slowly than anticipated has special significance. Stretching out the length of time between the passage of the law and its effects will make it more difficult for the public to discern cause and effect. It is also making it easier for lawmakers to distance themselves from personal responsibility for any negative consequences of the legislation, thus reducing accountability. For example, the law will eventually require vast expenditures (Greenwood et al., 1994). The full weight of these will fall on subsequent administrations. Positive outcomes may be masked by other factors and, because of the lag time, never be associated with the legislation or the initiative. For example, localities may eventually avoid costs, suffering, and other negative consequences associated with crime by having three-time felons removed from their communities.

Furthermore, officials, particularly some officials at the county level of government, are being lulled into a false sense of complacency. The law affects a small number of cases and although the amount of work and the length of processing time for these cases is increasing dramatically, this may not be easy to detect, at first. The law will not increase the number of filings. As noted, the actual number of trials has not increased noticeably. By most measures, the justice system is always overloaded anyway, so claims of additional work may not seem unusual. And, even under pressure, the justice system has always proved to be highly adaptable. There are other incentives for minimizing or choosing to ignore the potential consequences of the legislation. For example, every California county is having budget problems. Why allocate funds to justice until the situation compels this response? These are some of the forces that support complacency.

However, more sensitive measures will find these cases stacking up, awaiting trials. They will find investigators in the District Attorney's Offices and the Public Defender's Offices overwhelmed with work. They will find the court's clerical resources being consumed with trying to find and produce data concerning prior convictions, and they will find attorneys swamped with strike cases. The weight of this surge of two- and three-strikes-related work will eventually become a crisis, but it will build slowly, diminishing the sense of urgency that may be required to plan and adapt to the challenges the legislation will eventually present to state and local governments.

The Santa Clara County study shocked officials (Center for Urban Analysis, 1994a). About $1.3 million in onetime monies was allocated to support a systemwide response. In other counties, realization of the need for action may be taking place much more slowly. They will simply attempt to "cope." In these counties, incremental adjustments may take place, but more fundamental, structural changes will not be as likely to occur, or be adopted early.

Unexpected adaptations are taking place. Some of the most interesting effects are the ones no one anticipated. In Santa Clara County, for example, the district attorney has decided to present many three-strikes cases directly to the grand jury, thus bypassing most or all municipal court processing. Defense attorneys are reporting that persons charged with one-strike offenses are fighting their cases much more aggressively, and demanding trials. They understand that once they have one strike, any subsequent felony arrest will possibly expose them to a much longer prison term. Similar stories come from defense attorneys handling cases in juvenile court.

There are reports that some overworked county prosecutors are referring parole violators being charged with additional crimes to parole officials instead of prosecuting them on a new offense. This practice sends them back to prison to finish their terms and avoids the time and cost of prosecution. The evidentiary standard of proof for a parole violation is much less than that needed for conviction of a new offense. But this practice can also allow the offender to avoid a strike conviction and, perhaps, a long prison term. This procedure would make sense in the occasional case where a return to prison as a parole violator will lead to more prison time for a parolee, or where the case involving the new offense is a weak one that the prosecutor believes will be difficult to prove; however, according to news reports, this practice is now common in some counties (Spiegel, 1994). These and many other surprises will emerge. And, of course, as has been discussed throughout this chapter, there will be great variations from county to county.

Conclusions

It is difficult to write a conclusion to this chapter or to this book. The effects of the three-strikes initiative are still unfolding, not fully experienced, not fully understood. Will local justice systems be able to adapt to the challenges presented by this new legislation? Will the money that will be required materialize? Or will the new law unintentionally produce the very conditions it seeks to remedy, a degradation in public safety caused by a deterioration of the justice apparatus? Court backlog, release of offenders because speedy trial requirements cannot be met, early release of offenders from crowded jails too full to contain them, and disparity in the administration of justice are all threats to the very integrity of the law. The justice systems operating within some counties will do better than others. They will find ways to manage the tension between what appears to be an insatiable demand for punishment and an endless supply of perpetrators.

Notes

1. The *Los Angeles Times* reviewed all 98 third-strike cases that were resolved between March 1994, when the law took effect, and August 31, 1994 (Colvin, 1994; Colvin & Rollich, 1994). In addition, the Countywide Criminal Justice Coordinating Committee (1995) of Los Angeles County conducted an assessment of the effects of the three-strikes legislation 1 year after enactment. The San Diego Municipal Court analyzed a sample of prestrike legislation cases to establish case-processing baseline information that could be compared to cases that were adjudicated under the three-strikes law (Angene, 1994; Miller, 1994). The Orange County Administrative Office (1994) prepared a report outlining the effects they expected. The California District Attorney's Association (1994) conducted a survey in August 1994. The California Legislative Analyst's Office (1995) produced a statewide preliminary assessment report in January 1995. Under sponsorship of the state Board of Corrections (1995), the California Sheriff's Association completed an 18-county jail survey. And, finally, the California Department of Corrections has completed a number of studies (see Tristan, 1994, for an example of an early study).

2. The Tristan (1994) memo indicates that "by June 1995, the overcrowding will be at 188 percent . . . all available beds will be occupied" (Attachment B, p. 1). This date has been moved out into the future several times, mainly because strike cases have not come into the state system as quickly as forecast. They are backing up in the courts at the county level of government.

3. Although the initiative intended that serious and/or violent juvenile crimes be counted as priors, this has been subject to serious legal challenges. In Santa Clara County, and most everywhere else, juvenile strike priors are not being presented to the court when adults are adjudicated.

4. A number of the provisions of the initiative and the original three-strikes law are being challenged. Because of drafting errors, the Jones law inadvertently excluded felony convictions for crimes committed outside of California. It also accidentally precluded the death penalty for anyone who had already been convicted of a violent or serious felony. The law provides the prosecutor with the discretion to dismiss priors due to the interest of justice. Litigation may emerge to force definition of just what this means. The law says a juvenile offense can be counted as a strike but is not clear about what qualifies as a juvenile offense. Furthermore, prosecutors fear the section may be struck down as unconstitutional because juveniles do not have the same kind of due process rights as adults. Some advocates predict that long sentences for a minor third-strike offense might be deemed cruel and unusual punishment. The issue of whether the court may dismiss a prior has yet to be decided.

5. On October 18, 1994, the Santa Clara County Board of Supervisors approved a $1.3 million emergency interim augmentation to four Law and Justice Departments: Office of the District Attorney, 9 positions and $423,261; Office of the Public Defender,

13 positions and $489,644; superior court, 12 positions and $399,295; and Office of the Sheriff, 0 positions, $25,000.

6. This figure was obtained by phone from Sandra Gonzales, *San Jose Mercury News* reporter.

7. This research was discussed with Mark Cunniff by phone.

References

Angene, L. (1994, July 1). *Sampling of "strike" cases prior to AB971: November 1 through November 15, 1993.* San Diego, CA: San Diego Municipal Court, Special Projects Unit.

Board of Corrections. (1995, March). *Three strikes jail population report.* Sacramento: State Sheriff's Association Detention and Corrections Subcommittee and California State Board of Corrections.

California District Attorney's Association. (1994, September). *Two- and three-strike survey results: Report of the California District Attorney's Association.* Sacramento: Author.

Center for Urban Analysis. (1994a, August 10). *Assessing the impact of AB971 "three-strikes, you're out" on the justice system in Santa Clara County, California: Report prepared for the Santa Clara County Board of Supervisors, Bench/Board Committee.* San Jose, CA: Office of the County Executive, Santa Clara County,

Center for Urban Analysis. (1994b, December). *Assessing the impact of AB971 "three-strikes, you're out" on the municipal court system in Santa Clara County, California: Report prepared for the Santa Clara County Board of Supervisors, Bench/Board Committee.* San Jose, CA: Office of the County Executive, Santa Clara County.

Center for Urban Analysis. (1995, February). *Up-date to three-strikes, you're out. Workload in process within the justice system in Santa Clara County, California: Report prepared for the Santa Clara County Three-Strikes Committee.* San Jose, CA: Office of the County Executive, Santa Clara County.

Countywide Criminal Justice Coordinating Committee. (1995, March 15). *Preliminary report on the impact of the "three-strikes" law on the Los Angeles County justice system.* Los Angeles: Countywide Criminal Justice Coordinating Committee, Los Angeles County.

Colvin, R. L. (1994, October 23). Tough judge assails "three strikes." *Los Angeles Times,* p. 1.

Colvin, R. L., & Rollich, T. (1994, October 23). Courts toss curve balls to "three-strikes." *Los Angeles Times,* p. 1.

Data Analysis Unit. (1995, June). *Second and third strike data–June 1995.* Sacramento: California Department of Corrections, Estimates and Statistical Analysis Branch, Offender Information Services Branch, Data Analysis Unit.

Greenwood, P. W., Rydell, C. P., Abrahamse, A. F., Caulkins, J. P., Chiesa, J., Model, K. E., & Klein, S. P. (1994). *Three strikes and you're out: Estimated benefits and costs of California's new mandatory-sentencing law* (Report No. MR-509-RC). Santa Monica, CA: RAND.

James, W. G. (1995, January 5). *Jail population report, 1993-1995.* San Jose, CA: Department of Corrections, Santa Clara County.

Langan, P., & Graziadei, H. (1995, January). *Felony sentences in state courts, 1992: Bulletin.* Washington, DC: U.S. Department of Justice, Bureau of Justice Statistics, Office of Justice Programs.

Legislative Analyst's Office. (1995, January 6). *Status: The three strikes and you're out law–A preliminary assessment.* Sacramento, CA: Author.

Miller, E. L. (1994, September 1). *"Three strikes and you're out" public and press information.* San Diego, CA: Office of the District Attorney, County of San Diego.

Orange County Administrative Office. (1994, April). *Impacts of three strikes and you're out (AB971).* Santa Ana, CA: County Administrative Office, Orange County.

Spiegel, C. (1994, October 24). Three strikes loophole can give offenders a break. *Los Angeles Times,* p. 1.

Three-strikes data point to racial disparities. (1994, October 12). *The Daily Breeze,* p. 5.

Tristan, D. (1994, March 7). *Estimates of the three strikes initiative: Memo to wardens.* Sacramento: California Department of Corrections.

Walters, D. (1995, June 19). Three strikes law is a sledge—Or a scalpel. *San Jose Mercury News,* p. 10.

PART

System Effects

Chapter Five

"Three Strikes and You're Out"
Rethinking the Police and Crime Control Mandate

MICHAEL D. WIATROWSKI

||| The development of "three strikes and you're out" legislation promises to have significant implications for the debate over the control of crime in the United States. From a deterrence and incapacitation perspective, it is felt that if there are certain consequences to crime, that individuals, when confronted with the third crime, will choose not to offend. In the past, the police have been at the forefront of crime control strategies. On evaluation, those strategies have not been effective in having the police achieve the objective of controlling crime. Although the police will not be directly involved in three-strikes policies, this legislation has significant implications for policing. This chapter will investigate the relationship of this legislation to the police role in crime control.

The idea of the police and how they operate reflects the core of values of the society in which they are embedded (Bittner, 1973). The literature on policing frequently discusses the history, development, organization, and functions of the police in American society, but rarely discusses the philosophy, theory, or concept of the police. In totalitarian societies, the police are brutal and repressive, reflecting the values of those holding wealth and power. In socialist societies, the police may, in theory (probably not in reality), espouse principles of social justice representing collective interests as well as individual justice.

In democratic societies, the police, at least in theory, reflect the values associated with due process and the protections found in the documents of the country that creates the police. When the police become unbound by these democratic values, the potential exists for actions that erode the legitimacy of the core institutions of society. The death squads of Chile and Argentina, the "plumbers" of Nixon's Watergate era, and the secret police of Russia and Cuba are legacies that illuminate that thesis.

The perspective that will be developed in this chapter is that the nature of policing reflects the broad pattern of political, social, and ideological change in the United States (Gordon, 1974; Miller, 1974; Walker, 1977) and this in turn affects how the police interact with both society and the criminal justice system. Embedded in this are internal debates about what are appropriate missions and mandates for the police and how policing will be conducted. The question addressed is, should the police attempt to control crime and criminals through very aggressive and proactive measures in the community or should they promote the development of functioning institutions in the community that have the net effect of reducing the amount of crime in the community? The three-strikes policies to control crime through incapacitating offenders do not develop in a vacuum. Instead, they result from the inability of the criminal justice system to control the seemingly intractable crime problem. In the previous quarter century, various types of crime control strategies have emerged that have placed different emphases on different parts of the criminal justice system. Programs that are now viewed as ineffective have emphasized the proactive role of the police in apprehending and deterring crime through preventive patrol. Court reforms that have removed judicial discretion in sentencing have increased prison capacity but not reduced crime. Rehabilitation has been repudiated in most states as a primary goal of prisons.

It is therefore understandable that a "lock 'em up and throw away the key" approach would by default emerge as a proposal to control crime. As new ideas do not seem to be forthcoming, old ideas are dusted off. Prior to the American Revolution, the United States and Australia were used as penal colonies (Hughes, 1987). Science fiction writers have promoted the use of the moons of Jupiter as penal colonies, although it is not presently economically feasible. Short of mass public executions, there appear to be few alternatives that promise to have an effect on the crime problem.

In the United States, the nature of policing has changed dramatically in the past 30 years. This reflects not only the development of policing as an organization but also what the police should be doing and how the police interface with the criminal justice system (Kelling & Moore, 1988). As the goals of the criminal justice system change, the possibility exists that the nature of policing and the manner in which it is conducted will also change.

The implementation of three-strikes laws is significant because they frame the arena in which the police operate. These laws are premised on assumptions about how the crime problem can be controlled in the United States (Bayley, 1994). The distinct possibility exists that these laws will in turn affect how the police operate to support that mandate, particularly if they feel they can be viewed as in the forefront of the crime control issue. The possibility also exists that these laws will alter the manner in which the public views the police. This chapter is, in part, speculative. Clearly, a crime control strategy that emphasizes the incapacitation of offenders who have committed serious and multiple offenses is based on the idea that the criminal justice system can neither deter nor rehabilitate these offenders (Zimring & Hawkins, 1995). Societies therefore have the right to punish and, if need be, incapacitate these individuals by taking away their liberty for the remainder of their lives (Van Den Haag, 1975). With rehabilitation repudiated as a primary goal of criminal justice, the system has been in search of a replacement for the theoretical equilibrium between justice and punishment that had existed for a century (Allen, 1981). The frustration with previous crime control models that stressed the police and then sentencing by default has left the public with the use of prisons to incapacitate those offenders who have not responded to other measures. The question to be addressed, then, is how the police will fit in with the newly emerging strategy of incapacitation.

Order and Society

There are two dominant theories on how order is maintained in society (Tyler, 1990). In one view, described as the instrumental perspective advanced by social control theorists, the threat of sanctions is the primary mechanism through which criminal, deviant, and other undesired types of behaviors are controlled. People decide whether the advantages of a course of action meet or exceed the costs of that action. A crime or delinquent act potentially has significant costs, including arrest, incarceration, physical punishment, social humiliation, and the loss of financial status. In addition to the potential rewards, the sanctions should be sufficiently certain and severe to prevent the vast majority of the population from considering those acts. If criminals and delinquents choose to commit a crime and come before the criminal justice system, then they suffer the consequences of that choice.

The other view, the normative perspective, emphasizes the role of legitimacy of the social structure in whether laws are obeyed. This view states that social order is based on the premise that individuals will not risk the social, economic, and psychological investments that they have made in their jobs, education, and community by committing crimes. Correspondingly, those who have not made or had the opportunity to make such investments have few incentives to obey the law. Many street corner drug dealers, gang members, and petty criminals in inner-city areas in which economic and social disinvestment has occurred are symbolic of this perspective (Wilson, 1987). This perspective looks critically at the stratification system and the notion of social contract and would argue that in many inner cities, the state demands socially responsible behavior from individuals, but that the relationship of society to the individual has not been reciprocated (Tyler, 1990). It is understandable that individuals would have low levels of commitment to the norms of a society that demonstrates low levels of commitment to them.

Police resources are directed—consistent with the instrumental perspective—into inner-city areas where the social contract has been broken down. It is not uncoincidental that police managers concentrate "jump out squads" here, which leap out from vans to chase drug dealers, generating large numbers of arrests that have had little effect on crime in those communities with drug problems. In recent years, there have been programs described as "weed and seed," which have targeted the criminal elements in high-crime areas. The police are good at weeding but have done little to sow the seeds that create the sense of community that does not exist in high-crime areas. Traditionally, the police have blamed the court and correctional system for letting out the criminals to roam the streets "before the ink is dry on the paperwork." This would indicate that the police believe that they are upholding their part of the crime control strategy, consistent with the social control and incapacitation theorists, and that the problem resides in other parts of the criminal justice system.

From a policy perspective, then, it makes sense to increase the opportunities for investments in conformity in the same manner that corporations are given incentives to invest in businesses that create jobs. This means that when societies invest in the education of young people, promote economic investments in communities and their revitalization, treat drug users, and so forth, there is a reasonable expectation that potential offenders in high-crime areas will choose conformity over crime. The disinvestment or the shifting of resources out of depressed communities is well documented but receives little attention from crime control strategists. Not uncoincidently, in both Florida and California, the cost of new prison construction is viewed as coming out of funds that had been reserved for education. In an era in which individuals are held to high standards of personal legal accountability for their actions, it is ironic that society is not held to the same high standards to care for its children and adolescents and their successful integration into adult society (Curtis, 1993).

Evolutions and Revolutions in Policing

In the United States, there have been dramatic changes in the nature of policing over the past century. Early in this century, the police were heavily involved in corruption and partisan politics. To confront this, civil service reforms removed the police from the direct influence of the political system (Walker, 1977). In the 1960s, the examination of the criminal justice system by the President's Commission on Law Enforcement and Administration of Justice (1967) confronted policing in three important areas. First, the police were moved from their

position as a branch of municipal government to become a component
of the criminal justice system (Kelling & Moore, 1988).

The second element of this movement was perception that the
status of policing would be improved through "professionalization"
(Wilson, 1977). This was supported through the passage of legislation that created the Law Enforcement Assistance Administration
(LEAA). Through this federal agency, sums of money that were very
large ($7 billion during the life of LEAA) but relatively small in relation
to the total expenditures on policing at the local and state level were
allocated to the states (Duffee, 1980). These funds were used for a
variety of programs in the areas of police, courts, and corrections. For
the police, the ideal of police professionalism was promoted through
enhanced and advanced educational opportunities for officers. The
developing knowledge in the social and behavioral sciences would be
used to improve the effectiveness of the police along with the development and application of computers and advanced scientific technologies. The police also established state criminal justice planning coun-
cils, which in theory attempted to coordinate and integrate the
activities of the collection of agencies, now called the criminal justice
system (Hudzik & Cordoner, 1983).

The third major issue was the police assuming a major responsibility
for the control and suppression of crime in the community as the
organizational mandate for their portion of the criminal justice system.
It is ironic that prior to the creation of the modern criminal justice
system, the police were responsible for maintaining order in the
community; the judicial system was responsible for the adjudication of
guilt and innocence; and the correctional system, with the rehabilitation of offenders and their reintegration into society.

The crime control theorists sought the creation of the vision of an
integrated criminal justice system in which offenders flowed through
the system like the components of a car on an assembly line. This would
result in a convicted offender at the end of the process who would then
be either rehabilitated, punished, or incapacitated. The charge of
crime control became the mission for this newly conceived system, with
the police in the forefront. Historically, the police had been concerned
with the idea of order in the community. Their actions were directed
at resolving problems in the community using legal and sometimes
extralegal sanctions, including illegal use of force, as remedies to keep

the community a desirable place to live (Kelling & Moore, 1988). They were effective in apprehending criminals based on their knowledge of the community. Also, the smaller, less urbanized communities of the period between the world wars had lower crime rates (Felson, 1994).

In the period following World War II, the urbanization and suburbanization of the United States created massive shifts in the demography of the country as the population shifted from a "Gemeinshaft to a Gessellshaft" society (Bell, 1973). The prosperity of the nation in the post-World War II era allowed for larger families. This cohort, combined with the urbanization of the country, resulted in a massive increase in the amount of crime in American society in the 1960s.

During this same period, the social fabric of the country, which had been bound together with the force of laws segregating the races, was ripped apart in a devastating series of riots in major cities. The legislation of the newly enacted civil rights, fair housing, equal employment, and school desegregation laws created a set of expectations in which a newly desegregated society lagged far behind the changes in the statutes (National Advisory Commission on Civil Disorders, 1968). In the aftermath of these social catastrophes, it was repeatedly noted that racial discrimination and the unjustified use of force by the police were responsible for the precipitation of these urban riots. In practically every major urban area in the United States, over a 10-year period, destruction occurred at a level comparable to the recent riots that devastated Los Angeles (Christopher Commission, 1991).

The police responded to these challenges through the refinement of the unarticulated tenets of the emerging professional model. The field of police-community relations emerged as the police response to their poor relations with the public and minority communities (Radelet, 1986). Although the police know that crime is disproportionately concentrated in communities that are being destroyed by economic and social forces beyond their control, the police continued to use crime control strategies and allusions to "wars on crime" derived from the American military involvement in Vietnam.

The Preeminence of Crime Control and the Police

The post-Vietnam War era saw the emerging criminal justice analysts apply the concepts derived from general systems theory to both policing and the control of crime. It was hypothesized that the police could respond quickly to reports of crime, then conduct scientific investigations and present the evidence in court that would result in the conviction of the offender. After their rehabilitation, the offenders would lead productive lives in the community.

The ideas of preventive and random patrol developed by O. W. Wilson (1977) evolved into a police strategy in which the language of utilitarianism and deterrence theory were shaped and adapted to the requirements of the police (Wiatrowski & Vardalis, 1994). The numbers of police in urban areas increased as cities became larger and chiefs of police demanded more resources. Through rapid response of police patrol cars, centrally dispatched from police headquarters, the certainty of apprehension and conviction would result in an arrest rate that would be high enough to deter the general population from committing a crime. In achieving a high enough level of general deterrence, the crime rate would be significantly lowered through the perception that the commission of a crime would result in apprehension, conviction, and incarceration of the offender.

The theory of policing advanced under the professional model came under challenge almost as quickly as it was articulated. In a critical experiment, the Kansas City Police Department attempted to determine the effects of police patrol on crime (Kelling, Pate, Dieckman, & Brown, 1974). During the previous decade, police managers demanded more resources to carry out the war on crime. It was hypothesized that if the density of the police became high enough, the criminals would view the likelihood of apprehension as being so high that crimes would not be committed. In an extensive evaluation conducted by the Police Foundation, it was found that neither fear of crime, levels of criminal victimization, nor reports of crime were affected by the density of police patrol operations (Kelling et al., 1974).

Bayley (1994) reviews the literature on the relationship between levels of policing and crime and concludes that the police will behave as a bureaucracy and demand more resources, although the evidence shows that these are unrelated to the levels of crime in the community. As the linchpin of their argument about the relationship of levels of police to crime control was shattered, the police adapted a number of tactics at specific types of crime and achieved some modest successes

(Sherman, 1992) but have not achieved the theorized massive suppression of crime.

In related research activities, the relationship between the celerity of the police response time to crime and the level of crime was also closely examined (Spelman & Brown, 1981). The study determined that unless the police could arrive within 2 minutes of the actual commission of the crime, the clearance rate declined to less than 5%. When people are criminally victimized, they first call their spouses or friend rather than call the police, allowing offenders to escape. Similarly, retrospective investigations by police detectives were called into question (Eck, 1982; Greenwood, Petersilia, & Chaiken, 1977). It was determined that with the exception of certain types of serious crimes, the police detectives added little to the case beyond that developed by the police officer in the initial investigation.

The issue of fear of crime began to emerge. Theoretical linkages between fear and actual victimization were being formulated, as was the link between fear and the creation of conditions in the community that were conducive to crime (Reiss, 1986; Skogan, 1990). The result of the disappointing research findings on the principles of the professional model and fear of crime was that some police departments began developing alternatives. Many of these alternatives took the form of community policing, in which police worked with the community to define and deliver police services that were demanded by residents.

The Shift From Offenses to Offenders

The recurring debates over "criminal justice policy" in recent years have foreshadowed massive shifts in the public response to the U.S. crime problem that in only some instances have helped to shape police responses to crime. In *Delinquency in a Birth Cohort,* Wolfgang and his associates (Wolfgang, Figlio, & Sellin, 1972) marked a fundamental reconceptualization in terms of how researchers looked at crime. Prior to their research, the dominant sources of information about crime were obtained from official statistics, with little research on the careers of delinquents and criminals. Wolfgang and his colleagues (Wolfgang, Thornberry, & Figlio, 1987) studied a cohort of youths born in Philadelphia in 1945 and a subsequent cohort study conducted of those born in 1958 and arrived at three important conclusions.

1. A small number of youths (about 6%) committed a majority of the offenses (about 50%).
2. The vast majority of youths who offend at least once desist in their pattern of offending before committing five offenses.
3. Those who become serious or chronic offenders have significant social correlates of their behavior, including poor school performance, low intelligence, serious family problems, and so forth, and what starts in early childhood will probably persist into adulthood with the creation of the chronic habitual offender. These youths were also unaffected by the intervention of the juvenile justice system.

These works prompted an immense amount of research into the nature of criminal careers and the process through which adolescent offenders became career adult offenders (Blumstein, Cohen, & Nagin, 1978; Blumstein, Cohen, & Visher, 1986; Petersilia, 1980). It was noted that chronic delinquents frequently continued their pattern of offending as they matured and accounted for the vast majority of offenses committed as adults.

The findings were viewed by prosecutors and state attorneys general as offering the "magic bullet" with which to achieve significant reductions in the amount of crime in the community. Repeatedly, before the media, they displayed lengthy arrest records. They argued that if they had the ability to incapacitate these offenders, the effect of crime could be ameliorated. Their response was to go before state and federal legislatures and demand mandatory and enhanced sentencing practices for career criminals and serious habitual offenders.[1]

Programs such as the Serious Habitual Offender Criminal Apprehension Programs (SHOCAP) and the Integrated Criminal Apprehension Programs (ICAP) were established to track both juvenile and adult offenders. The result of these programs was the burgeoning prison population of the United States with California, Texas, and Florida at the forefront. The failure of these programs was also manifested by the perception of the public that crime had not decreased. A critical and not often noted element of Wolfgang's and subsequent research is that these studies are retrospective. The difficulties of predicting who should be incapacitated to reduce crime should not be minimized (Greenwood & Turner, 1987).

Three-strikes type arguments are based on uninformed under- standings of incapacitation and deterrence arguments. The literature on these subjects has been most recently reviewed in *Incapacitation,* by Frank Zimring and Gordon Hawkins (1995). This work reveals that the intuitive idea behind locking up career criminals and hoping that it will reduce the amount of crime in society has far exceeded the research that has gone into that proposition. The authors note statements by a former U.S. president and U.S. attorney general in which it is noted that high officials in the Department of Justice support three-strikes arguments on what appear to be pragmatic if theoretically uninformed grounds.

Zimring and Hawkins (1995) provide a cogent and comprehensive review of the various research models and the assumptions that have dominated this research over the past 20 years. These include works by Shinnar and Shinnar (1975), Greenwood and Abrahamse (1982), Greenberg (1975, 1991), and Blumstein (1983). As assumptions or parameters are changed, then estimates of potential decreases in crime in relation to increases in the amount of incarceration expand and contract like a balloon. If there is one summary statement that can be made with mathematical precision, it is that the current prison con- struction programs will provide more prison spaces and that those prisons spaces will be filled in response to three strikes. The research does not document that these incarcerations will be associated with a reduction in the amount of crime in the community.

Police, Civility, and Society

At some point, it should be noted that there are some parallels between these types of crime control strategies and those implemented by Great Britain during the 18th and 19th centuries. During that period, England had a large portion of its population displaced from small, rural communities into the cities. This excess population found little legitimate employment, and crime expanded to where large cities were not safe at night. The crime control strategy consisted of increas- ing the number of crimes punishable by death. Although there is debate about the extent to which these laws were implemented and wholesale executions conducted (Radzinowicz, 1948), this did reflect their crime control strategy. Many condemned and imprisoned criminals were sent to the United States as indentured servants, where these former offenders became farmers and craftsmen and productive members of American society.

During this period, England was involved with wars with France and Spain and with the rebellion of the American colonies. After the defeat of Napoleon at Waterloo, England experienced massive unemployment of the former soldiers and sailors who had defended Great Britain. There were periodic riots for bread, culminating with the British Yeomanry firing into crowds (Critchley, 1967).

This appalled the English, who did not believe that the military should be used to maintain civil order.

The British historically distrusted the idea of a "police force" in part due to the effectiveness of the French police force used by Louis XIV to suppress political dissent. Nonetheless, the problem of maintaining civil order led to the creation of the first English police force by Sir Robert Peel. The principles that were articulated by Peel reflect the theory that an orderly society was maintained by the idea of informal social control and that the police did full time what was the responsibility of all citizens. The idea that an orderly society was the product of a civil society led to gradual reforms including education, the establishment of a social welfare system, and the expansion of the industrial revolution to incorporate unemployed workers. Although England has historically had a society that is more stratified than that of the United States, it nonetheless reduced its reliance on draconian punishments to maintain social order and incrementally implemented measures of social security that reduced class tensions (Alderson, 1995; Trojanowicz & Dixon, 1974).

The Emergence of Community Policing

In the United States, there has been a fundamental reconceptualization of the police mission. The police have repudiated the idea that they are responsible for controlling the crime problem in the community and that it was brought about by conditions over which they had relatively little control (Trojanowicz & Bucqueroux, 1993). The police do not determine the location of businesses that provide jobs and make communities viable or the policies of schools that fail to prepare high-risk teenagers for work and participation as adults in society. In community policing, the police work with the community in solving the problems that contribute to crime in the community. This view is based on the thesis that crime is a symptom of the breakdown of the structure of the community and that the police, in conjunction with the community, can work to improve schools, housing, employment and economic opportunities, and health and human services. It is ironic that the police have adopted a theoretical framework that repudiates the deterrence- and utilitarian-based arguments of conservative ideologues of the 1980s and 1990s for those associated with the positivist arguments of the 1960s and 1970s that there are root causes of crime in the community and that those problems can be solved.

To summarize the arguments to this point, it is established that the police have not been effective in controlling the amount of crime in the community through the resources commonly thought to be at their disposal, including high rates of arrests, intensive patrolling, retrospective investigation, and speedy responses. I have also discussed that crime control strategies that related increased levels of incarceration to decreased levels of crime are ill formed and that, at best, we will end up with more prisons filled up with more people.

Three Strikes and Related Effects on the Police

Other speculative elements related to three-strikes type arguments are that they will affect the criminal justice system by increasing the number of trials and potentially overloading the capacity of the judicial system to hold trials. As the incentive for plea bargaining is removed, more defendants will demand trials. In the area of policing, it is possible that the increase in the possibility of incarceration may increase the number of assaults on and murders of police officers. A criminal faced with the prospect of arrest and incarceration for the rest of his or her life may decide to attempt to escape rather than surrender. A similar situation occurred several years ago when people advocated life imprisonment for rapists. It was noted that this could affect the likelihood that an assailant would murder a rape victim if he could be identified to eliminate the possibility of life imprisonment.[2]

Crime, Arrests, and Race

In a similar manner, it is necessary to assess whether the criminal justice system is filling up the prisons with the types of offenders predicted by the increased use of incarceration. In *Malign Neglect: Race, Crime and Punishment in America* (1995), Michael Tonry specifically addresses the issue of race and crime. He notes that the incarceration rate for blacks is 1,895 per 100,000 population compared with 294 per 100,000 for whites. Tonry notes the massive increase in drug arrests and demands an explanation for why a policy would be adopted that falls so disproportionately on one segment of the population. He describes the reductions in federal funding for policies to reduce the historical effect of racism on minority populations. He argues that the policies of the conservatives accelerated the disinvestment in inner-city areas, in effect making the drug economy in some cases the most viable alternative. He notes that between 1986 and 1991, the number of blacks in prison for the sale of drugs increased more than $3\frac{1}{2}$ times to account for 25% of those in prison.

As part of the "get tough" approach, mandatory minimum sentences were enacted for those crimes most likely to be committed by minorities. The possession and sale of crack cocaine was punished more severely than the sale of cocaine in its powdered form. Because of the ability to turn small amounts of cocaine into even smaller amounts of crack cocaine, which would be used by lower-class, black, street corner drug addicts who could only afford a $5 or $10 rock, the police focused on those more visible crimes in minority communities. The cocaine use by middle- and upper-class whites correspondingly received less attention and less severe penalties. A staple of the television show "Cops" is the purchase of drugs, filmed by an undercover camera; the attendant chase through the neighborhood; and arrest, using snarling dogs and guns aimed at the heads of black, street corner drug dealers. Never are such scenes filmed at white, upper-class cocktail parties, where cocaine is laid out on mirrors in the bathrooms along with the finger towels and little bitty pieces of decorative soap.

As a final piece of informed speculation, a question that might be asked is whether the organization and structure of the police would be significantly changed in response to the implementation of three-strikes type legislation. It has been argued that police departments developed their present bureaucratic structure in response to the crime control mandate of the professional mandate (Kelling & Moore, 1988). It might also be argued that with crime control once again a mandate, the movement toward community policing would be removed. The result would be more of a movement away from what has been described as the "due process model" in which the rights of the defendant are protected and the needs of the community considered, and movement toward the "crime control model." In this later model, the emphasis is on aggressive law enforcement at the expense of individual rights (Goldstein, 1977).

The purpose of this section has been to lay out the scenario for what may happen if police are tantalized with another prospect similar to that presented with the war on drugs. The potential does exist that police may target those who have had two strikes and who have fouled off a number of inside fast balls, which are nicking the corners. These three-strikes laws may once again give the police a sense of "mission" under the old and failed mandate that they are having an effect on crime by concentrating on those offenders who have had two strikes. As the police and prosecutors developed programs for serious habitual offenders, the police became increasingly innovative at developing strategies for arresting offenders, which increased the likelihood of an enhanced arrest. For example, the police would maneuver offenders to within 1,000 feet of a school to come under the sanctions associated with selling drugs near schools.[3]

The allusion to baseball may be the policy equivalent of a malapropism. If the United States had not developed an affinity for baseball, then would we be kicking offenders through the goalpost after the fourth quarter or would there be a real sudden death component to settling the crime problem as they do to resolving ties in basketball or soccer? Sports are probably not suitable analogues for criminal justice policy.

The ideological component of criminal justice policy has not been adequately explicated. As stated by Miller (1974) and Greenberg (1975), crime policy is based on assumptions about the nature of society and the different frameworks in which we place individuals. John Rawls in *A Theory of Justice* (1971) notes that we do not pick our individual social circumstances and that a major component of social policy is for one class to transmit its social advantages to its children.

Incapacitation is not the logical consequence of a third choice to commit a crime but is the choice of those with inequitable social choice. As we abandon our inner cities and minority children, as we fail to invest in our children and communities, then we can expect that crime will be the logical consequence of our ideologically based decisions.

Notes

1. The early discussions with Florida state attorneys of the potential for incapacitating large numbers of habitual offenders always showed that none had read Wolfgang's original research or understood that each year there were factors that generated another cohort in which high-rate offenders were created (personal conversations by author with state attorneys).

2. In the mid-1970s, the mandatory-sentencing laws for drug offenders in the state of New York created a situation in which juveniles rather than adults were recruited to carry and sell drugs because of the lesser sentences that they received. It was also noted that the mandatory sentencing increased the likelihood of an offender killing a police officer to escape a mandatory sanction.

3. These observations were recorded in personal conversations with police officers enforcing the laws regulating drug sales near schools.

References

Alderson, J. W. (1995, November). *Community policing in Great Britain.* Paper presented to the Academy of Criminal Justice Sciences, Boston.
Allen, F. A. (1981). *The decline of the rehabilitative ideal: Penal policy and social purpose.* New Haven, CT: Yale University Press.
Bayley, D. H. (1994). *Police for the future.* Oxford: Oxford University Press.
Bell, D. (1973). *The coming of post-industrial society.* New York: Basic Books.
Bittner, E. (1973). *The functions of the police in modern society.* Washington, DC: National Institute of Mental Health.
Blumstein, A. (1983). Incapacitation. In S. H. Kadish (Ed.), *Encyclopedia of crime and justice* (Vol 3., pp. 873-880). New York: Free Press.
Blumstein, A., Cohen, J., & Nagin, D. (Eds.). (1978). *Deterrence and incapacitation: Estimating the effects of criminal sanctions on crime rates.* Washington, DC: National Academy of Sciences.
Blumstein, A., Cohen, J., & Visher, C. A. (Eds.). (1986). *Criminal careers and "career criminals"* (Vol. 1). Washington, DC: National Research Council, National Academy Press.
Christopher Commission. (1991). *Independent commission report on the Los Angeles police.* Los Angeles: Author.
Critchley, T. A. (1967). *A history of the police in England and Wales, 1000-1966.* London: Constable.
Curtis, L. (1993). *Investing in children and youth, reconstructing our cities.* Washington, DC: Milton S. Eisenhower Foundation.

Duffee, D. (1980). *Explaining criminal justice: Community theory and criminal justice reform.* Cambridge, MA: Oelgeschlager, Gunn & Haine.

Eck, J. E. (1982). *Solving crimes: The investigation of burglary and robbery.* Washington, DC: Police Executive Research Forum.

Felson, M. (1994). *Crime in everyday life.* Thousand Oaks, CA: Sage.

Goldstein, H. (1977). *Policing a free society.* Cambridge, MA: Ballinger.

Gordon, D. (1974). Capitalism, class and crime in America. In C. E. Reasons (Ed.), *The criminologist.* Pacific Palisades, CA: Goodyear.

Greenberg, D. F. (1975). The incapacitive effects of imprisonment: Some estimates. *Law and Society Review, 9,* 541-586.

Greenberg, D. F. (1991). Modeling criminal careers. *Criminology, 29*(1), 17-46.

Greenwood, P., & Turner, S. (1987). *Selective incapacitation revisited: Why high rate offenders are hard to predict.* Santa Monica, CA: RAND.

Greenwood, P. W., with Abrahamse, A. (1982). *Selective incapacitation* (Report prepared for the National Institute of Justice). Santa Monica, CA: RAND.

Greenwood, P. W., Petersilia, J., & Chaiken, J. (1977). *The criminal investigation process.* Lexington, MA: D. C. Heath.

Hudzik, J. K., & Cordoner, G. (1983). *Planning in criminal justice organizations and systems.* New York: Macmillan.

Hughes, R. (1987). *The fatal shore.* New York: Knopf.

Kelling, G., & Moore, M. (1988). *The evolving strategy of policing.* Washington, DC: National Institute of Justice.

Kelling, G., Pate, T., Dieckman, D., & Brown, C. E. (1974). *The Kansas City preventive patrol experiment: A summary.* Washington, DC: Police Foundation.

Miller, W. C. (1974). Ideology and criminal justice policy: Some current issues. In C. E. Reasons (Ed.), *The criminologist.* Pacific Palisades, CA: Goodyear.

National Advisory Commission on Civil Disorders. (1968). *Report of the National Advisory Commission on Civil Disorders.* Washington, DC: Government Printing Office.

Petersilia, J. (1980). Criminal career research: A review of recent research. In N. Morris & M. Tonry (Eds.), *Crime and justice: An annual review of research.* Chicago: University of Chicago Press.

President's Commission on Law Enforcement and Administration of Justice. (1967). *The challenge of crime in a free society.* Washington, DC: Government Printing Office.

Radelet, L. A. (1986). *The police and the community.* New York: Macmillan.

Radzinowicz, L. (1948). *A history of English criminal law and its administration.* London: Stevens.

Rawls, J. (1971). *A theory of justice.* Cambridge, MA: Harvard University Press.

Reiss, A. J. (1986). Why communities are important in the study of crime. In A. J. Reiss & M. Tonry (Eds.), *Communities and crime.* Chicago: University of Chicago Press.

Sherman, L. W. (1992). Attacking crime: Police and crime control. In M. Tonry & N. Morris (Eds.), *Modern policing.* Chicago: University of Chicago Press.

Shinnar, S., & Shinnar, R. (1975). The effects of the criminal justice system on the control of crime. *Law and Society Review, 9,* 581-611.

Skogan, W. G. (1990). *Disorder and decline.* New York: Free Press.

Spelman, W., & Brown, D. K. (1981). *"Calling the police": Citizen reporting of serious crime.* Washington, DC: Police Executive Research Forum.

Tonry, M. (1995). *Malign neglect: Race, crime and punishment in America.* Oxford: Oxford University Press.

Trojanowicz, R., & Bucqueroux, B. (1993). *Community policing.* Cincinnati, OH: Anderson.

Trojanowicz, R., & Dixon, S. C. (1974). *Criminal justice and the community.* Englewood Cliffs, NJ: Prentice Hall.

Tyler, T. C. (1990). *Why people obey the law.* New Haven, CT: Yale University Press.

Van Den Haag, E. (1975). *Punishing criminals: Concerning a very old and painful question.* New York: Basic Books.

Walker, S. (1977). *A critical history of police reform: The emergence of professionalism.* Lexington, MA: Lexington Books.

Wiatrowski, M. D., & Vardalis, J. (1994). Community policing and a model of crime prevention in the community. *Journal of Police and Criminal Psychology, 10*(2).

Wilson, O. W. (1977). *Police administration.* New York: McGraw-Hill.

Wilson, W. J. (1987). *The truly disadvantaged.* Chicago: University of Chicago Press.

Wolfgang, M. E., Figlio, R., & Sellin, T. (1972). *Delinquency in a birth cohort.* Chicago: University of Chicago Press.

Wolfgang, M. E., Thornberry, T., & Figlio, R. (1987). *From boy to man, from delinquency to crime.* Chicago: University of Chicago Press.

Zimring, F. E., & Hawkins, G. (1995). *Incapacitation.* Oxford: Oxford University Press.

Chapter Six

The Effect of "Three Strikes and You're Out" on the Courts

Looking Back to See the Future

MALCOLM M. FEELEY
SAM KAMIN

To judge from the public and professional reaction to the recent spate of "three strikes and you're out" laws enacted between 1992 and 1994,[1] one would have to conclude that these acts are sui generis—unlike anything that had come before. We have been inundated over the past few years with predictions of massive and unprecedented effect on the courts, jails, and prisons of those states that have enacted these laws. Judges, prosecutors, and defense attorneys have all argued that their resources will be stretched to the breaking point by the enforcement of these laws; corrections officials have maintained that current jail and prison space will be insufficient to support the number of expected inmates.

No doubt these three-strikes laws are best understood in Durkheimian terms, as moral panics or symbolic crusades with only marginal instrumental value in terms of improving the effectiveness and efficiency of crime control.[2] As such, however, they are hardly unique.

The recent history of criminal justice policy has seen a number of spasmodic attempts by the public and politicians to respond in an extreme manner to what they perceive as skyrocketing crime rates and a permissive criminal justice system.

This chapter assesses recent three-strikes laws in light of our experience with other panics.[3] In particular, it explores the consequences of the Rockefeller drug law of 1972, state and federal mandatory minimum laws, federal sentencing guidelines, and California's recent Victim's Bill of Rights. We identify a standard pattern of response to law embraced in the midst of moral panic: First, even if judges, prosecutors, and other court personnel vigorously oppose such laws, they nonetheless find it useful to embrace the exaggerated claims of the laws' proponents to secure more resources for themselves. Second, the laws' passage usually produces an initial period of hyper-concern and confusion, which produces a fair amount of injustice. Third, after the salience of the issues has subsided, officials employ a host of discretionary devices to adapt to the law in ways that reinstitute long-standing operating procedures. Finally, once lower salience of the issue has been maintained for a period, court officials quietly but publicly press to amend the harshest provisions of these laws to reinstitutionalize traditional procedures and to rectify disparities and inequities caused by the law.

We do not mean this analysis to suggest that "nothing works," or that all effects of mandatory-sentencing laws are nullified through adaptive behavior. Most certainly they are not. Indeed, on the whole, they clearly "ratchet" up sentence severity (Casper & Brereton, 1984). But we do want to suggest that all of these moral panics produced outbursts of draconian policies followed by adaptive behavior and recision that appreciably reduced the laws' effect. Outbursts and adaption, we believe, may be the norm rather than the exception, not only for criminal justice policy but for public policy in general. Jeffrey Pressman and Aaron Wildavsky (1973, p. 109) make the same point, although for somewhat different reasons. They suggest that we turn our standard concern on its head, and ask not why so many new policies are not implemented but why it is that some occasionally are.[4]

We thus begin our analysis of current three-strikes laws by looking backward, by investigating the adaptive behavior that has arisen in response to earlier moral panics and attempts to limit discretion. We complete our analysis by looking at the most well known of the recent three-strikes laws, California's. By analyzing the California law in light of several recent moral panics, we hope to be able to make some reasoned predictions about the future of three-strikes enforcement, rather than simply adding another warning cry to the debate. In doing so, we hope to cast a self-critical eye on the role of criminal justice scholars in responding to moral panics. The overwhelming majority of criminal justice scholars oppose harsh mandatory minimum sentencing laws. Despite this opposition—some might say because of it—these scholars find themselves caught up in the moral crusade, and their language often becomes the mirror image of the crusaders, responding to hyperbole with hyperbole. We hope this chapter will contribute not to furthering the language of crisis and panic but to the calm and reasoned analysis of the future of criminal justice policy.

The Recent Panics

The Rockefeller Drug Law

Our first example is what came to be known as the Rockefeller drug law. In 1972, New York State passed the "nation's toughest drug law." Enacted at the behest of then Governor Nelson Rockefeller, the proposed new law provided for a mandatory life sentence for anyone convicted of the sale or possession of narcotics, prohibited plea bargaining, and eliminated parole. It also proposed mandatory life sentences for those convicted of committing violent acts while under the influence of narcotics and a 100% property tax on drug dealers, so that on conviction, the state could seize all of a person's private property. Although some of the stiffest provisions were ultimately watered down in the face of quiet opposition from defense attorneys, prosecutors, and judges alike, the final version of the law was extremely harsh.

The Rhetoric of Passage

Rushed through from first reading to enactment in less than 4 months, the law created three categories of Class A drug offenses: A-III, A-II, and A-I, which provided for mandatory minimum penalties of 1, 6, and 15 years, respectively. The maximum sentence in all categories was life imprisonment, and all parole releases required lifetime supervision. The final version differed from the initial proposal in one key respect, however: It permitted plea bargaining in A-II and A-I felonies but not in A-III felonies. Thus, the most serious felonies could be downgraded, but the least serious could not and the most serious A-III felonies could be accorded the same response as the least serious. This weakening of the law notwithstanding, by all accounts the provisions of the Rockefeller drug law were draconian. Indeed, at the time he introduced it, Governor Rockefeller promised that the law would be "brutal" and repeatedly emphasized that it was designed to provide "the strongest possible tools to protect our law abiding citizens from drug pushers" (Goldstein, 1973, p. 1).

Although judges, prosecutors, and defense attorneys as well as most other criminal justice professionals opposed the law, they were nevertheless caught up in its dramaturgical enterprise. Robert McKay, dean of the New York University School of Law and president of New York City's Legal Aid Society, warned, "[The law is] completely counter to everything the civilized world has been working for" (Feeley, 1983, p. 119, n. 10). New York's chapter of the American Civil Liberties Union called the bill "a frightening leap towards the imposition of a total police state" (Feeley, p. 119, n. 9). New York City judges warned that if enacted, the bill would cause the courts to stop functioning altogether, and the state would "have to multiply by many, many times the number of judges, nonjudicial personnel, and ancillary personnel" to cope with the increased work load. Still other prosecutors and defense attorneys warned that because the mandatory minimum sentences were so severe, defendants would insist on trial rather than plead guilty, and the courts would come to a grinding halt. Others warned that the courts would have to cease all civil business, as they struggled to cope with the massive increase in criminal trials. One judicial council estimate was that the trial rate would jump from 9% to 85% of all narcotics cases, and this led Mayor Lindsay to estimate that the number of judges in New York City alone would have to be increased from 79 to 370, simply to keep abreast of the anticipated increase in trials. His Criminal Justice Coordinating Council continued this line of reasoning, saying the city would need an additional $400 million for construction of courtrooms and prisons alone, and another $150 million to $200 million annually to staff and operate them (Feeley, 1983, p. 121, n. 12). Still others warned that the draconian sentences would probably lead New York police officers to change their policing practices and forgo the arrest of drug users, in an effort to avoid tying up so many police resources in the courts.

Despite these warnings, however, the law was adopted with only minor modifications. Rockefeller got his tough drug law, and he was off and running for an unprecedented fourth term as governor with an eye cast toward the presidency.[5] But he was not the only winner in the battle over the drug law. New York City politicians and criminal justice officials also received something they had long wanted: additional judges, prosecutors, auxiliary personnel, and courtroom space. Local political leaders received a patronage bonanza, and criminal court officials received a substantial infusion of new resources. New York City criminal justice agencies obtained $55 million in appropriations for new "drug" judges, a substantial increase of support, but well below the hundreds of millions of dollars that some had claimed was necessary if the courts were not to grind to a halt. Nonetheless, given the city's and the state's budgetary woes at the time, this constituted a substantial and welcome increase of support for the city's strapped criminal justice system.[6]

Early Implementation: Confusion and Unfairness

The effects of the Rockefeller drug law were closely watched at the time. Indeed, it was perhaps the most carefully studied new sentencing law in the United States before the adoption of the Minnesota sentencing guidelines and the federal sentencing guidelines over a decade later (see, e.g., Japha, 1976a, 1976b, 1976c). What did all of this work reveal? In short, it showed that neither the bold promises nor the predicted dire consequences materialized.

First, contrary to some predictions, New York City police did not change their priorities and flood the courts with easily arrested petty user-dealers, who were now subject to substantially harsher penalties. Instead, they continued to concentrate on the harder-to-locate large-scale drug dealers. By the best available estimates, drug prices did not increase, thereby suggesting that the new law had a negligible effect on availability (Japha, 1976a; see also Feeley, 1983, p. 124).

Furthermore, despite the important new "weapon" in the hands of criminal justice officials, there were both fewer drug convictions and fewer offenders sent to prison in the 3 years following passage of the act than in the 3 years preceding its adoption. Part of the explanation seems to be that because of the high stakes involved, judges began dismissing charges at a higher rate than they previously had.[7] Dismissal rates jumped from 6.8% in 1972 before the law was passed to 21.3% in 1975, the second full year after the law was enacted (a figure that markedly decreased the following year after repeal of the harshest provisions in the law; Japha, 1976b, p. 2).

Plea bargaining also played a role in limiting the law's effects. As predicted, the trial rate for drug cases jumped (from 6.5% in 1973 to 15% in 1975) and the rate for A-I drug cases, the most serious, jumped even more dramatically despite the continued availability of plea bargaining. Although the increases were lower than many had predicted, especially when considered as a proportion of all offenses and not just drug cases, they constitute a substantial jump that helped account for the increased backlog of all cases. The law continued to allow limited plea bargaining, however, and plea bargaining was widely used in the same ways that it had been prior to adoption of the new law. For example, it was routinely used, both before and after the passage of the law, to reduce legal sanctions in proportion to prior record and the "real" seriousness of the offense in the eyes of criminal justice officials.

Although prior to adoption of the new law court administrators had predicted that it would take 5 years to adjust to the new law (*New York Times*, January 26, 1973, p. 18, cited in Feeley, 1983, p. 125) and that the system might collapse under the weight of increased motions and trials, the court system adjusted much more quickly. Initially, both the proportion of defendants charged under the new law choosing to be tried by a jury and backlogs rose dramatically, but within 2 years, both returned to earlier levels. This occurred in part because an increase in the number of available judges took some of the pressure off, in part because defense attorneys quickly learned to "work with" the new law, and in part because the court system adapted in a number of other ways. The result was that a new equilibrium was established and the new law was normalized. Although the new law clearly put a strain on the courts, they found a variety of ways to adapt.

This is not to say that the law had no effect. Clearly, it did. It ratcheted up sentence severity for some types of drug violations, established new ways of doing business in the courts, and above all, it created grossly inequitable sentences for a handful of criminal offenders who were hit by the full force of the law. Some of these offenders had been prosecuted and sentenced shortly after adoption of the law before the courts had learned to adapt to the new law. Others were unlucky enough to have their cases handled by prosecutors and judges who were unwilling to bend the new law's provisions as most of their colleagues eventually chose to. Overall, however, the Rockefeller drug law had a very limited effect both on drug availability on the streets and on the operations of the criminal court system.

From Adaption to Amendment

The glaring inequities that enforcement of the law yielded and the problems of prosecuting A-III felonies led officials to seek ways to further thwart its effects. In 1976, 3 years after the law's adoption, New York City's chief drug prosecutor quietly announced that his office would no longer enforce the law's prohibition against plea bargaining A-III-level felonies. This nonenforcement policy permitted prosecutors to better distinguish serious from not so serious cases, something that the prosecutor thought necessary for fair sentencing and expedited adjudication.

There was virtually no public reaction to his announcement. Despite the public popularity of the law, the moral crusade had passed. By that time, Nelson Rockefeller had moved from the governor's mansion in Albany to Blair House in Washington, having been appointed vice president by Gerald Ford. Three years later, significant steps were taken to dismantle the law. In 1979, after hearing testimony from judges, prosecutors, and defense attorneys, the New York legislature quietly took the first of several steps that systematically dismantled the Rockefeller drug law, restoring prosecutorial discretion to negotiate pleas and flexibility in sentencing. Some of these amendments permitted resentencing for those sentenced under the harsh conditions of the original law. This process was far from an instantaneous adjustment, however. The last provision modifying some of the draconian provisions was enacted by the state legislature and signed into law by

Governor George Pataki in 1995, more than 20 years after the law's initial adoption. Nonetheless, although some of the law's effects lingered on for years, most of the adjustments had taken place by 1979, when New York City's courts had resumed their prelaw standard operating procedures.

Ultimately, the Rockefeller drug law failed to have much of a lasting effect on the state's criminal justice system because the courts were already imposing stiff sentences on serious drug pushers prior to the adoption of the new law. The law was, simply put, premised on a false assumption, one that prosecutors, judges, and public defenders—and perhaps Rockefeller himself—knew to be false, namely, that the state was treating drug offenders permissively. Such is the fate of many mandatory attempts to limit discretion enacted in the midst of moral crusades; because they are based not on operational realities but on public perceptions of those realities, they are often ineffectual because they push the system in the direction it is already headed.

Other Moral Panics

Studies of other mandatory minimum sentencing laws tell a story that looks very much like what happened in New York after the passage of the Rockefeller gun law. After an initial period of upheaval, these mandatory minimum laws have a limited-to-no long-term effect, due in large part to the efforts of criminal justice professionals to thwart the laws' harshness and reestablish discretionary practices.

Other Mandatory Minimum Laws

Studies of the mandatory minimum sentences for gun possession in both Massachusetts and Michigan—at various times both promoted as "the Nation's toughest gun law"—reveal pervasive adaptation that effectively nullified the new laws. In Michigan, the passage of a mandatory 1-year minimum sentence for gun possession, left the rate of imprisonment for most major crimes essentially unchanged. Many gun possession charges were dropped when prosecutors believed full enforcement would result in injustice. And when prosecutors refused to drop these charges, as some occasionally did, judges became more deeply immersed in plea bargaining, often dismissing these charges outright. Ironically, the single most important consequence of the mandatory minimum sentencing laws in Michigan may have been not the diminution of discretion, but rather an expansion in the scope and nature of the judge's role in plea bargaining (Feeley, 1983, pp. 128-138).

Similarly in Massachusetts, the much-heralded Bartley-Fox gun law had little effect because of adaptive behavior by criminal court officials. The law's effect was not nearly so dire as had been predicted, in part because prosecutors brought fewer charges carrying the mandatory sentence, judges and juries were reluctant to convict in the shadow of the mandatory sentences, and the law was in many ways redundant on existing sentencing enhancements, such as the one for armed robbery (Feeley, 1983, p. 130). In fact, one of the reasons that the gun law sailed through the state legislature with such little opposition from criminal justice officials is that they knew that the law would have little effect on how they actually did their jobs.

Thus, in both Massachusetts and Michigan, the reasons for adaptive behavior were the same. Court officials already thought they were handling gun-related cases in an adequate manner, and they resented a law that restricted their discretion to discriminate between serious and not-so-serious situations. As a result, they bent the laws to fit existing policies or ignored them to the degree they were incompatible with accepted practices.

Sentencing Guidelines

Similar to mandatory minimum laws, systems by which defendants are sentenced according to legislative guidelines are another attempt to constrain the power of the prosecutor and judge. One of the most well-publicized sentencing reforms in recent years has been the establishment of the U.S. Sentencing Commission and the creation of mandatory sentencing guidelines for federal offenses. Some have criticized these guidelines because they are not sufficiently subtle to permit prosecutors and judges to tailor sentence recommendations and sentences to particular offenses and offenders. Others argue that the guidelines, rather than eliminating sentence disparity, simply serve to mask increases in penalties' severity (Alschuler, 1991; for a somewhat different view, see Marvell & Moody, 1996).[8] For whatever reason, it appears that the guidelines are also being weakened by adaptive behavior on the part of prosecutors and judges.

Former U.S. Sentencing Commissioner Ilene Nagel and University of Chicago Law Professor Steve Schulhofer estimate that in more than 30% of all cases, prosecutors manipulate case records to downgrade the seriousness of offenses and to bring sentencing exposure into line with what prosecutors and judges think are the appropriate levels (see, e.g., Nagel & Schulhofer, 1992). The federal system was once regarded as a model criminal justice system, in part because of the virtual absence of plea bargaining; this regard has weakened in recent years, in part because prosecutors now routinely plea bargain cases as a way to avoid unreasonable mandatory sentences.[9]

One of the more important consequences of the implementation of sentencing guidelines is the imposition of uniformity on a set of cases where officials may see differences. Where this occurs, we generally see adaptive behavior and in turn reinforced and increased discretion of criminal justice officials. The federal sentencing guidelines have expanded the scope of plea bargaining, shifted still more responsibility for sentencing away from judges to prosecutors, expanded reliance on plea bargaining, and at times driven this discretion underground.

Victim's Rights Initiative: A Plea Bargaining Ban

In 1982, the voters of the State of California approved the "Victim's Bill of Rights" initiative, which, inter alia, forbade the plea bargaining of any "serious" felony. Similar bills, when introduced before the state legislature, had been criticized by both public defender and district attorney organizations (presumably because both groups felt they were properly handling the disposition of serious felonies), but there was very little public opposition to the initiative (McCoy, 1990, pp. 30-31). Notwithstanding its voter-friendly title and the lack of any real opposition, however, the Victim's Bill of Rights managed to pass with just 56.4% of the votes.

The law's effect was, not surprisingly, far from an end to plea bargaining. An early study showed that in the first few years of implementation, the trial rate in California went down rather than up, indicating that more, not fewer, pleas were being negotiated (McCoy, 1990, pp. 90-92). What the investigation revealed was that the initiative had the effect not of removing plea bargains from the prosecution's repertoire, but of changing the way in which they are negotiated—shifting them further forward in the adjudicative process to comply with the letter, if not the spirit, of the law.[10]

In light of the attempts to limit discretion discussed above, the result in California should not be surprising. It seems clear that court officials' norms are not easily changed by edict. A ban on plea bargains has the effect not of removing plea bargains from the realm of acceptable procedures but of shifting, perhaps subtly, the way in which pleas are understood and effected.

Back to the Future: Three-Strikes Laws in Perspective

This detour into the history of attempts to minimize discretion should sensitize us to the possible long-term consequences of three-strikes laws. In particular, it suggests that get-tough laws (a) generate exaggerated language that is used by criminal justice officials, even if they oppose the proposals, to obtain additional resources, and (b) create short-term disequilibria and confusion that increase backlogs and rates of trials but that (c) are followed by a variety of adaptive behaviors that restore equilibrium among the courthouse work group. These are fairly obvious "lessons." But given the hype that surrounds moral panics—generated by both proponents and opponents—it is useful to be reminded of the obvious. They help us to locate three-strikes laws within a realm of comprehensibility.

These lessons also suggest that researchers should guard against being caught up in the rhetoric of the symbolic crusade lest they contribute to it. By characterizing three-strikes laws as unique or taking at face value the claims of many of their proponents or opponents, researchers themselves become participants in the dramaturgy. Three-strikes laws should be assessed as the latest of a long line of laws associated with episodic moral panics and wars on crime, another in a series of attempts to limit the discretion of criminal justice actors perceived to be too lenient by a fearful public or cynical legislature.

Although the past is not a perfect predictor of the future, there is no reason to think that three-strikes laws will be appreciably different than previous attempts to limit discretion. If this is true, we can expect bold claims about the laws' potential effects to be coupled with opportunities for continued discretion, adaptation, and flexibility, allowing the laws' seemingly brutal harshness to be mitigated to some extent and in the long run permitting something akin to long-standing standard operational norms to reemerge. This is not to say that "nothing works" or that policy makes no difference on implementation. These laws will certainly have considerable effect on outcomes and in the direction their proponents wish them to have. Clearly, they can and will ratchet up sentencing severity (Casper & Brereton, 1984). But perhaps more than most public policies, their promise is likely to be far greater than their actual effect. All this suggests, once again, that three-strikes laws must be understood in Durkheimian terms (see note 2). Kai Erikson's *Wayward Puritans* (1966) and Joseph Gusfield's *Symbolic Crusade* (1963) may yield more insight into the nature and function of support for three-strikes laws than any instrumental concerns about a more effective and a more efficient criminal justice system.

California–The Shape of Things to Come

California has implemented both the most severe and most closely studied three-strikes law to date. In effect for little more than a year as of this writing, we can use the new law as a test case for our theory that three-strikes laws may behave very much like other attempts to curtail the discretion of criminal justice professionals.

Rhetoric

During the debates over three strikes before the legislature and the public,[11] both the supporters and the skeptics of three strikes often mounted equal and opposing claims and counterclaims about the consequences of three strikes. In so doing, both sides dramatically exaggerated the significance of the law. Even as the law's proponents made outrageous claims about the benefits it would bestow on the state, opponents generated their own exaggerated claims. Philip J. Romero (1994), chief economist in the Governor's Office of Planning and Research, issued a position paper purporting to show that "the social benefits of the crime reductions from a 'three strikes' approach vastly exceed the costs of implementation—from the first year of implementation" and that by the year 2027, the law would provide the state net social benefits of $48 billion per year (p. 5). A skeptical RAND Corporation report offered an assessment that was as bleak as the governor's assessment was optimistic. RAND estimated that if fully implemented, California's three-strikes initiative would cost the state's taxpayers a net increase in tax burden of $5.5 billion annually (Greenwood et al., 1994). Other observers made similar dramatic calculations. Mike Reynolds (Reynolds, Scully, & Huffington, 1994), the law's chief backer, argued during the initiative campaign that three strikes will mean that taxpayers will no longer have to pay "the outrageous costs of running career criminals through the judicial system's revolving door over and over again" (p. 36). A state Legislative Analyst's Office (1995) report estimated that the cost of California's three-strikes law would "increase state prison operating costs by hundreds of millions of dollars annually, reaching about $3 billion in 2003 and about $6 billion in 2026, and increase the state's prison construction cost by about $20 billion."

This rhetoric was not limited to politicians: Criminal justice officials also contributed their voices to the cacophony.[12] The Los Angeles County District Attorney's Office estimated that the number of felony jury trials would increase from a little more than 2,400 in 1994 to nearly 5,600 in 1995 (Weinstein, 1994, p. A24). Robert M. Mallano, an administrator for the Los Angeles courts, warned that the number of judges hearing civil cases in Los Angeles courts would be halved, from 120 to 60, by mid-December and that in short order it would be virtually impossible for anyone to get a jury trial on a civil matter in Los Angeles. Estimates from the Public Defender's Office estimated that there would be a tripling of the number of jury trials—from around 500 in 1993 to 1,500 in 1994, and officials in Santa Clara County (San Jose) announced that they expected a doubling of the trial rate during the same period (Legislative Analyst's Office, 1995, p. 5).

It is not hard to see why both proponents and opponents of the law saw it in their interest to make dire predictions about the law. Corrections officials, judges, district attorneys, and public defender offices all used them to mount well-timed campaigns for increased funding. Just as official figures on prison population capacities are malleable enough to be easily manipulated for budgetary purposes, "estimates" of the consequences of three-strikes laws are contingent enough to serve the same functions.

These campaigns have met with some success. The budgets of criminal justice agencies increased at a significantly higher rate than they otherwise would have. It remains to be seen, however, whether the warnings and the initial projections of the effects of the three-strikes law will materialize. If California's three-strikes law is like so many other mandatory minimum sentences, we can expect to see officials adapt to it through a variety of discretionary practices that remain well within their purview to embrace.

Implementation and Adaption

Although as of this writing it is too early to provide any definitive reading of the longer-term consequences of three strikes on the courts, there is increasing evidence that the process of adaptation has already begun to set in, at least in some counties. In the more conservative southern part of the state (and in particular, Los Angeles and San Diego Counties), prosecutors continue to press for something close to full enforcement of the law. In the urban northern areas (San Francisco and Alameda County [Oakland]), however, the courts have found ways to adapt. In San Francisco, Supervising Public Defender Daro Inouye told us that the county's prosecutors were "cautious" in interpreting the law. Rather than overtly flouting the law, Inouye told us, prosecutors get around the law with a wink and a nod. "A district attorney will tell us something like, 'We might have difficulty proving some of the prior convictions,' but that 'if the defendant insists on going to trial [rather than pleading to something less than a three-strikes conviction], we'll do everything we can to prove them.' " By caging the offer of a plea in terms of insufficiency of the evidence rather than the "interests of justice," which the law no longer permits, district attorneys can maintain that they are following the letter of the law even as they avoid it.

The Alameda County prosecutor's office is even more direct in its adaptive response to the law it did not want. According to Chief Deputy Richard Igelhart, a case will not be brought as a third strike unless the current felony is either serious or violent, despite the fact that the language of the statute mandates the charging of any felony as a third strike. Furthermore, Igelhart maintained, once a determination has been made to charge a case as a third strike, the allegations of prior convictions are not bargained with. Unlike some other counties that may plea bargain when they feel a three-strikes cases is weak, Alameda County prosecutorial policy is to dismiss a weak case rather than bargain it down. The threat of life imprisonment, Igelhart told us, is not something to be trifled with—it is a threat too great to be held over a defendant's head.

In describing his office's policy, Igelhart emphasized that he was not claiming that the three-strikes law had no effect. Obviously, he said, it has contributed to harsher sentences in some cases. His larger point was that even before three strikes, his office had vigorously prosecuted the "really bad repeat offenders." What his office wanted to continue to do was to make distinctions between the truly bad repeat offender and the less bad repeat offenders who either because of a lengthy time between offenses or the nature of the current offense did not warrant the same severe sanctions. The three-strikes legislation, he continued, fails to make important distinctions where common sense dictates that they be made. This was the identical point made by the drug prosecutor in New York City when he announced, after Governor Rockefeller's departure from Albany, that he would no longer insist on the Rockefeller drug law's mandatory minimum provisions. It is the same point made by judges and prosecutors in other jurisdictions when they confronted the prospects of a law they thought eradicated distinctions that their experience and professionalism led them to believe were important.

It remains to be seen whether other counties will follow the adaptive behavior we see in northern California's more liberal counties. But whenever other mandatory minimum sentencing schemes have been put into effect, their effect has been significantly eroded over time as prosecutors and judges have sought to reassert the power to make distinctions they deem important. One analysis by the staff of the California Judicial Council anticipates precisely this. It observed, "Typically, after any major change affecting criminal cases, caseloads adjust to available resources, and to new sentencing expectations." It then went on to note that "the trend toward stiffer penalties [often accompanied by prohibitions against plea bargaining] over the past decade has actually been accompanied by a fall in the relative number of contested felony cases. . . . The reason for this may be that more and more criminal defendants have been induced to enter guilty pleas

rather than risking the heavier penalties which the law has permitted"
(California Judicial Council, 1994, p. 3).

How might this adaption occur? The law provides that *all* felonies,
not merely violent and serious felonies, are to be charged as third
strikes and purports to close loopholes and ban plea bargaining so that
its tough effects cannot be thwarted. However, the law has no self-
enforcing mechanism. If prosecutors decide not to charge all strikes of
which they are aware, there is no one to complain. The decision not to
charge an individual defendant is a very low visibility, highly discretionary event—usually the only individual aware of the decision not to
charge is the defendant, who is unlikely to complain. If a judge attempts
to circumvent the statute and show leniency for a defendant, however,
the prosecutor is entitled to appeal. Just as we have become aware of
prosecutors refusing to charge second and third strikes where they
could, there are also a handful of reported instances of prosecutors
appealing judges' decisions to *dismiss* a prior conviction to avoid the
full force of the three-strikes law.[13] Thus, ironically, this law, like so
many other laws designed to restrict discretion, has the effect of
enlarging the discretionary powers—and hence sentencing powers—of
the prosecutor at the expense of the judges.

Scale Back

There are still other indications that California's three-strikes law is
being blunted. In October 1995, Assemblyman Richard Rainey, formerly the sheriff of Contra Costa County and the author of a much
more limited (and eventually unsuccessful) three-strikes bill, succeeded
in shepherding the Community-Based Punishment Act through the
legislature. Signed into law by Governor Wilson, the law provides for
some nonviolent offenders to be directed away from terms in state
prisons and placed in county-based community service, restitution, and
electronic-monitoring programs. As written, the law can apply to some
second- and third-strike offenders currently serving double term or life
terms under the three-strikes law. Another bill (SB 760) under consideration in winter 1995 would move up to 20% of prisoners currently in
state prisons back to the county level, to serve time in local jails and in
various noncustodial intermediate-sanction programs. This bill would

also cover some types of second- and third-strike offenders currently serving lengthy prison terms.

Conclusion

Although as of this writing it may be premature to argue that the California criminal justice system is adapting to and nullifying the three-strikes law, nevertheless, the early stages of its implementation resemble the adaptive and corrective moves seen in New York after passage of the Rockefeller law. In light of this, it is not unreasonable to expect, once moral panic subsides or takes another form, that the state's three-strikes law will eventually be robbed of much of its draconian strength. Of course, this is much easier to do with a law enacted by a legislature than through initiative,[14] but it would not be the first set of provisions imposed on criminal justice officials that has been adopted through the initiative process and widely ignored by local prosecutors.[15]

If California does follow New York, we can expect the application of the law to be uneven, with some prosecutors' offices vigorously pressing for three strikes whenever they can and others routinely undermining the law in instances where they do not believe it is warranted. The process is likely to occur in differing ways and to differing degrees across the state, meaning that disparities and inequalities will continue. Furthermore, we can expect the process to be a slow one: In 1994, almost precisely 20 years after enactment of the Rockefeller drug law, New York's new conservative governor, George Pataki, signed a law repealing the last of the provisions of the law and setting in motion a process of sentence rehearings for a handful of offenders who had been caught up in its full enforcement.

Notes

1. See the other discussions of the history and provisions of three strikes, including California's three-strikes initiative and statute, in this volume. See also Turner, Sundt, Applegate, and Cullen (1995).

2. In a study based on interviews of a random sample of residents of the San Francisco Bay Area, University of California at Berkeley Professor Tom Tyler reports that support for three strikes in California is best accounted for in terms of a belief that the state faces a problem due to ethnic and racial diversity and the breakdown of the traditional family,

rather than crime-specific concerns or some specific concerns that the courts are not doing a good job convicting and punishing criminals, or even that increased sanctions will increase deterrence ("Bases for Supporting the Three Strikes Initiative," Talk at the Center for the Study of Law and Society, UC Berkeley, November 19, 1995).

3. The recent spate of three-strikes laws is closely akin to various habitual offender laws that have been embraced with great enthusiasm from time to time since the mid-19th century. Indeed, many opponents of three-strikes laws argue that they are unnecessary because habitual offender laws are already on the books. Although three-strikes laws are probably closest to habitual offender laws, this chapter contrasts them to recent mandatory minimum laws because these laws not only have sought to impose harsh sentences, but also they have been notable for their efforts at limiting judicial discretion at sentencing and their effects have been closely assessed.

4. There is, of course, no question that sentences have become harsher since 1980. But one of the interesting features of this increased harshness is that it is difficult to account for it in terms of any specific "big" pieces of legislation. Although some jurisdictions that now have harsher sentencing practices have adopted harsher penalties for selected offenses or offenders and the like, other states have not enacted such new policies, and they too have experienced the same upward trend in penal severity. It is not that things do not change; rather, they may change for a host of reasons. In this sense, laws like three strikes may be more effect than cause of such shifts in policy.

5. Actually, the governor did not even run for reelection in November 1974. Sometime earlier, he had been named vice president by Gerald Ford after the collapse of the Nixon presidency.

6. Although the law applied generally throughout the state, by all accounts the overwhelming share of the drug problem and effects on the courts was in New York City. Roughly 70% of all new drug law sentences were in New York City, and city agencies received roughly this proportion of all new resources earmarked by the state legislature to implement the new law.

7. This appears to have been due to two quite different factors: Some dismissals were a form of nullification of the law, an effort to avoid the law's harshness for a sympathetic defendant. Others were because judges began scrutinizing claims of procedural irregularities more carefully and when they did this began excluding evidence more frequently.

8. No doubt there is some truth in both these claims, but defenders of the guidelines point out that these effects are due at least in part to congressionally imposed mandatory minimum sentences rather than the guidelines. Furthermore, they argue that mandatory minimum sentences are themselves inconsistent with the idea of guidelines; they point out that when it adopts mandatory minimum sentences Congress bypasses the Sentencing Commission altogether and attaches its own penalties to selected politically salient offenses in ways that wreak havoc with the guidelines' ideal. It is Congress's political expediency and not the commission's efforts, they argue, that have led to the most egregious sentence increases in the federal system, and which in turn have led to the most blatant efforts by courts to thwart the law's intent.

9. U.S. attorneys' offices have long used plea bargaining as an investigative tool to trade information for leniency and the like. But most observers say that until recently these offices did not routinely exchange pleas of guilty for leniency to facilitate rapid handling of cases.

10. The new law forbade plea bargaining in any case "in which the indictment or information charges any serious felony" (McCoy, 1990). If a case pursued without an

information or indictment is pleaded, therefore, the law has not been violated. Thus, if cases were pleaded in municipal court and then certified for sentencing in superior court, the law would be followed. McCoy (1990) found that this was precisely what occurred.

11. In reality, California has two identical three-strikes laws—one enacted by the legislature and one through the initiative process.

12. The media contributed its own apocalyptic observations, as well. With story headings like "The Law That Brought the Criminal Justice System to Its Knees" and "3 Strikes-Spawned Flood of Cases Crowds Out Civil Suits," newspapers reported on the reaction of the courts immediately following the adoption of three strikes. These accounts chronicled the law's early, dramatic effects: lower guilty plea rates and higher trial rates, the shift of civil court judges to criminal duty, and the like.

13. In summer 1995, Lawrence Antolini, a Sonoma County Superior Court judge, dismissed a prior felony ("strike") for a defendant facing sentencing as a "second-striker" and hence liable to be sentenced to twice the normal term. The defendant, Jeffrey Dean Missamore, was apprehended with 8 grams of marijuana while serving a 3-month misdemeanor sentence for shoplifting food and cigarettes from a local supermarket. Possession of marijuana in jail is a "serious" felony under the law, and thus counts as a second strike. Missamore's first strike was a 1986 conviction for burglary. Incensed at the prospects that Missamore would have to serve 10 or more years in prison, Judge Antolini *dismissed* his prior conviction over the strenuous objections of the prosecutor. Judge Antolini's decision was overturned by a state appeals court panel by a vote of 2 to 1.

14. The California three-strikes initiative, for example, can be overturned only by a two-thirds vote of the legislature or public.

15. See the section in this chapter: Voter's Rights Initiative: A Plea Bargaining Ban.

References

Alschuler, A. (1991). The failure of sentencing guidelines: A plea for less aggregation. *University of Chicago Law Review, 58,* 901-951.

California Judicial Council. (1994, April 19). *Three strikes document* [for the Town Hall Meeting on "three strikes and you're out"]. San Francisco: Bar Association of San Francisco.

Casper, J. D., & Brereton, D. (1984). Evaluating criminal justice reforms. *Law and Society Review, 18,* 121-144.

Erikson, K. (1966). *Wayward Puritans: A study in social deviance.* New York: John Wiley.

Feeley, M. M. (1983). *Court reform on trial.* New York: Basic Books.

Goldstein, T. (1973, May 9). [Article]. *New York Times,* sec. 1, p. 1.

Greenwood, P. W., Rydell, C. P., Abrahamse, A. F., Caulkins, J. P., Chiesa, J., Model, K. E., & Klein, S. P. (1994). *Three strikes and you're out: Estimated benefits and costs of California's new mandatory-sentencing law* (Report No. MR-509-RC). Santa Monica, CA: RAND.

Gusfield, J. (1963). *Symbolic crusade: Status politics and the American temperance movement.* Urbana: University of Illinois Press.

Japha, A. (1976a, August). *Crime committed by narcotics users in Manhattan* (Drug Law Evaluation Project report) [staff memorandum]. New York: Association of the Bar of the City of New York.

Japha, A. (1976b, August). *The effects of the 1973 drug laws on the New York State courts* (Drug Law Evaluation Project report) [staff memorandum]. New York: Association of the Bar of the City of New York.

Japha, A. (1976c, August). *Sentencing patterns under the 1973 New York State drug laws* (Drug Law Evaluation Project report) [staff memorandum]. New York: Association of the Bar of the City of New York.

Legislative Analyst's Office. (1995, January 6). *Status: The three strikes and you're out law–A preliminary assessment.* Sacramento, CA: Author.

Marvell, T. B., & Moody, C. E. (1996). Determinate sentencing and abolishing parole: The long-term impacts on prisons and crime. *Criminology, 34,* 107-128.

McCoy, C. (1990). *Politics and plea bargaining: Victims' rights in California.* Philadelphia: University of Pennsylvania Press.

Nagel, I. H., & Schulhofer, S. J. (1992). A tale of two cities: An empirical study of charging and bargaining practices under the federal sentencing guidelines (Symposium on federal sentencing). *Southern California Law Review, 66,* 501-554.

Pressman, J. L., & Wildavsky, A. B. (1973). *Implementation.* Berkeley: University of California Press.

Reynolds, M., Scully, J., & Huffington, M. (1994, August 16). Argument in favor of Proposition 184 [the three-strikes initiative]. California ballot pamphlet for the general election on November 8, 1994.

Romero, P. J. (1994, March 31). *How incarcerating more felons will benefit California's economy.* Sacramento, CA: Governor's Office of Planning and Research.

Turner, M. G., Sundt, J. L., Applegate, B. K., & Cullen, F. (1995, September). Three strikes and you're out legislation: A national assessment. *Federal Probation, 59,* 16-35.

Weinstein, H. (1994, November 30). 3 strikes-spawned flood of cases crowds out civil suits. *Los Angeles Times,* p. A24.

Chapter Seven

The Effect of "Three Strikes and You're Out" on Corrections

JAMES AUSTIN

The past few years have witnessed a popularization of the "three strikes and you're out" sentencing reform movement. First adopted by Washington State in 1993 and later by California and the federal government in 1994, a number of other states have either adopted such legislation or proposed to do so. As these bills have gained popularity, there has been a growing debate on what effect these reforms will have on the correctional system.

These initiatives pose enormous potential challenges to prisons and jails on a number of levels. Just how much effect will be felt by each state will depend on how laws are worded and implemented by the courts. If the list of "strikeable" offenses is quite broad and the law is faithfully applied to the vast majority of eligible offenders, the effect on jails and prisons could be immediate and substantial. Conversely, if the law is narrowly worded and/or its provisions not applied to most offenders who meet the criteria for a three-strikes sentence, the effect could be minimal.

For state prisons that house convicted felons, the expectation has been that these laws are expected to greatly increase both the number of offenders sentenced to state prison and their lengths of stay, which in turn will significantly increase the prison population and its costs (both operational and capital). For jails that house pretrial defendants, their populations may rise as increasing numbers of defendants who previously had relatively short periods of pretrial detention now decline to accept what must be viewed as meaningless "deals" from the prosecutors and plea bargains and opt for prolonged jury trials. In so doing, the time to dispose of a case will increase as will the period of pretrial detention, also increasing the court's backlog of cases.

Related to both jails and prisons, correctional officials have also been concerned about the effect of these long-term offenders on the management of their facilities. Prison officials face a dual problem. Some feel that "three-strikers" represent a higher management risk population because these inmates, who face either very long sentences or no possibility of release, will have no incentive to conform to the prison's disciplinary regime. Consequently, there will be a need in the short term for very expensive maximum-security facilities to house these maximum-security inmates. However, over time the need for such beds will subside as these inmates age and become less of a security problem. What will then emerge is the need for low-security facilities with increased medical services to house a low-risk and elderly inmate population that must die in prison.

For jails, the problem is largely limited to the additional need for high-security pretrial beds. Jail administrators are concerned that pretrial defendants who face life without the possibility of parole sentences if convicted will pose a higher risk for escape. Consequently, many jail administrators like Sheriff Sherman Block in Los Angeles have adopted a policy that all pretrial defendants must be housed in the maximum-security units of their jail. It is also likely that few of these inmates will be considered for pretrial release, further increasing the pretrial population.

This chapter reviews the merits of these scenarios based on the early experiences of states that have adopted three-strikes laws over the past few years, with a focus on state prison systems. The concerns raised above, in many states, appear to be largely false and overstated, and in others, limited to a small number of jurisdictions. But to understand why there will be such extreme variation among the states and why the effect of three-strikes legislation on corrections may be less than anticipated, one must have a historical perspective on recent sentencing reforms that have been adopted by many states over the past two decades and how they have already affected prison populations.

Recent Trends in Prison Admissions, Length of Stay, and Population Growth

During the 1980s, dramatic increases in the number of offenders sentenced to prison for drug offenses were largely responsible for the doubling of the prison population. Between 1970 and 1986, inmates committed solely for drug crimes comprised about 10% of state prison admissions. By 1992, however, these admissions represented approximately 30% of prison sentences (Bureau of Justice Statistics [BJS], 1994). However, by 1993 drug arrests had dropped to 1 million from a peak of 1.4 million in 1989 (see Figure 7.1), which in turn began to slow down prison admissions. However, there has been a slight upturn in drug offense arrests, which may once again begin to fuel prison admissions.

In August 1995, the Department of Justice announced that the nation's prison population reached 1 million on June 30, 1994 (BJS, 1995b). During 1994, the prison population jumped by 83,294—the second largest annual increase in history. What has been fueling these massive increases in prison population growth? Most people assume that the major reason has been prison admissions. As more offenders are convicted and sentenced to prison, the population must increase. And this factor has been true to a certain extent. But an equally important trend—increases in the length of stay fueled by more stringent sentencing reforms—is now the more significant factor.

The National Council on Crime and Delinquency (NCCD) routinely issues a national prison population forecast based on the experiences of a selected number of states. In the 16 states for which NCCD developed projections in 1990, the number of drug offenders admitted to prison had grown by a staggering 96% between 1988 and 1990, whereas the total number of admissions to prison in those states increased by 38%. However, due in large part to changes in law

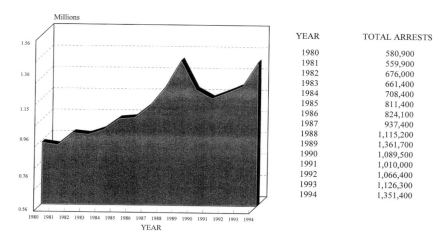

YEAR	TOTAL ARRESTS
1980	580,900
1981	559,900
1982	676,000
1983	661,400
1984	708,400
1985	811,400
1986	824,100
1987	937,400
1988	1,115,200
1989	1,361,700
1990	1,089,500
1991	1,010,000
1992	1,066,400
1993	1,126,300
1994	1,351,400

Figure 7.1. National Estimates of Drug Arrests—1980-1994
SOURCE: Federal Bureau of Investigation, *Crime in the United States* (1980-1993). Washington, DC: Government Printing Office.

enforcement practices, prison and jail crowding, the aging of the baby boom population, and the fiscal constraints of state and local governments, growth in admissions began to slow by 1991. Drug admissions as a percentage of prison intake leveled off or declined in many states just as drug arrests declined. In 1991, total prison admissions in the 16 states grew by less than 3% and drug admissions actually declined by an average of 10% (Austin, Jones, & McVey, 1991). Table 7.1 shows the trend in the number of new court commitments to prison in 18 states for which NCCD did projections between 1990 and 1994.[1] The total number of court commitments declined for these 18 states, although there was considerable variation among the states. The largest declines were recorded in Florida (40% decline), Michigan (18%), and Kansas (12%), and substantial increases occurred in Rhode Island (60%), Massachusetts (42%), Illinois (41%), and Kentucky (35%).

In marked contrast to overall prison admission trends, the prison populations grew by 38% during the same period (Table 7.2). In 12 of 18 states, growth in prison populations greatly exceeds changes in prison admissions. In states with indeterminate-sentencing structures, daily populations are increasing at a rate far greater than new court commitments. This is a direct consequence of changes in sentencing

TABLE 7.1   New Court Commitments to Prison, 1990-1994

	1990	1991	1992	1993	1994	% Change
Arkansas	3,267	3,358	3,551	3,491	3,520	+7.7
California	39,272	41,282	41,282	41,282	42,987	+9.5
Colorado	3,642	3,799	4,494	4,303	3,567	−2.1
Florida	44,701	37,184	34,524	30,530	26,623	−40.4
Illinois	12,397	14,052	15,120	16,062	17,496	+41.1
Kansas	2,840	2,678	2,811	2,802	2,509	−11.7
Kentucky	3,339	3,483	4,117	4,473	4,520	+35.4
Massachusetts	2,765	3,147	3,710	4,277	3,914	+41.6
Michigan	9,333	9,154	9,068	7,654	7,614	−18.4
Mississippi	3,563	3,729	3,729	3,729	3,700	+3.8
Nevada	2,691	2,690	3,211	3,705	3,300	+22.6
Ohio	17,409	19,646	20,594	19,837	18,892	+8.5
Oklahoma	5,866	5,720	6,512	6,285	6,677	+13.8
Oregon	2,950	3,034	3,034	3,034	3,500	+18.6
Rhode Island	2,109	2,240	2,240	2,240	3,364	+64.2
Tennessee	6,536	6,438	6,565	6,842	6,300	−3.6
Texas	46,290	39,646	35,720	33,044	48,338	+4.4
Virginia	6,839	7,040	7,616	7,804	7,642	+11.7
Total	215,809	208,320	207,898	201,391	214,563	−0.1

SOURCE: Department of Corrections personnel, National Council on Crime and Delinquency records, and published reports (*The Impact of Truth in Sentencing: The NCCD Prison Population Forecast*).
NOTE: Figures may represent fiscal or calendar years.

and parole board policies that result in longer lengths of stay and increased numbers of parole revocations.

This so-called stacking effect has been noted by NCCD for a number of years. Although prison admissions have increased significantly due to more arrests, convictions, and higher proportions of convictions resulting in prison sentences, the long-range consequences of previous sentencing reforms and more conservative parole board policies are now beginning to be felt as the length of stay increases.

The effects of previous sentencing reforms can be seen by comparing national data on the length of stay expected for new court commitments with those now being released. The mean and median length of stay for inmates released in 1992 was 22 and 13 months, respectively (BJS, 1995a). The projected minimum length of stay for 1992 new court

TABLE 7.2	Sentenced Prisoner Populations by Selected States, 1990-1994					
	1990	*1991*	*1992*	*1993*	*1994*[a]	*% Change*
Arkansas	6,718	7,667	8,129	8,567	8,916	+32.7
California	94,122	98,515	105,467	115,573	124,813	+32.6
Colorado	7,108	8,347	8,997	9,462	9,954	+41.8
Florida	44,387	46,531	48,302	53,041	56,052	+26.3
Illinois	27,516	29,115	31,640	34,495	35,614	+29.4
Kansas	5,777	5,903	6,028	5,727	6,090	+5.4
Kentucky	9,023	9,799	10,364	10,440	10,724	+18.9
Massachusetts	7,899	8,998	9,382	9,315	10,072	+27.5
Michigan	34,267	36,423	39,019	39,529	40,220	+17.4
Mississippi	8,179	8,848	8,877	9,798	10,631	+30.0
Nevada	5,322	5,879	6,049	6,198	6,745	+26.7
Ohio	31,855	35,750	38,378	40,641	41,156	+29.2
Oklahoma	12,322	13,376	14,821	16,409	16,306	+32.3
Oregon	6,436	6,760	5,216	5,118	6,723	+4.5
Rhode Island	2,394	2,717	2,923	2,675	3,049	+92.4
Tennessee	10,388	11,502	11,849	12,827	14,397	+38.6
Texas	49,197	49,608	51,592	64,313	91,875	+86.7
Virginia	17,124	18,755	20,989	22,635	24,822	+45.0
Federal institutions	58,021	64,131	70,656	79,779	85,850	+48.0
Total	438,055	468,654	498,678	546,542	604,009	+37.9

SOURCE: Bureau of Justice Statistics, *Sourcebook of Criminal Justice Statistics–1993*. Washington, DC: U.S. Department of Justice, Bureau of Justice Statistics.
NOTE: Counts of prisoners with sentences of more than 1 year were taken immediately after the end of each calendar year.
a. Data are based on the BJS midyear report dated October 27, 1994, and reflect jurisdictional populations.

commitments was much higher: 37 (mean) and 24 (median) months. Although these data may be somewhat suspect because they may not take into account good-time credits and early-release programs, they demonstrate that inmates will be serving far longer periods of imprisonment than in the past.

The most dramatic example of the stacking effect is Florida. Since 1990, prison admissions *declined* from 44,701 to 26,623 while the prison population *increased* from 44,387 to 56,052. These results were produced by sentencing reforms that diverted drug offenders from prison but increased to 80% the portion of mandatory sentences that inmates must serve if convicted of violent offenses.

Current Sentencing Initiatives

Despite the past flurry of conservative sentencing reforms, many legislatures are still considering policy changes such as abolishing parole, enhancing mandatory minimum sentences, and implementing various truth-in-sentencing measures—all changes intended to increase lengths of stay for selected inmates. In many instances, these legislatures lack a clear understanding of the effects of the changes. The broad, long-range outcome will be the continuing escalation in the size of prison populations—this despite moderations in prison admissions trends.

Mandatory Minimum Sentences

A recent NCCD study funded by the Bureau of Justice Assistance (BJA) found that all states have some form of mandatory minimum sentences or habitual offender statutes that allow the courts to sentence repeat and violent offenders to long prison terms (Austin, Jones, Kramer, & Renninger, 1996). Many of these laws are discretionary and allow considerable leeway on the part of prosecutors and judges in applying the statutes. However, states are enhancing existing statutes to limit judicial and prosecutorial discretion and mandate extremely long prison sentences, including life without parole.

Truth-in-Sentencing Statutes

Also receiving serious consideration in legislatures around the country are various truth-in-sentencing proposals. The recently passed 1994 federal Omnibus Crime Bill rewards states that want to play the "85% rule game" for inmates sentenced for violent crimes by providing nearly $8 billion in prison construction funds. Amendments to the 1994 act now being proposed by Congress increase the prison construction pot to $10 billion.

Generally, these proposals are designed to require offenders sentenced to prison for violent crimes to serve 85% of the imposed sentences. Because most truth-in-sentencing proposals are calculated to increase serving times regardless of the number of prior convictions and many more offenders would fall under the scope of these laws, these proposals will have implications that are more serious than the implications of three-strikes legislation. This is because the number of inmates convicted of violent crimes is large, and these inmates now serve less than 50% of their sentences.

On a national level, one can make some broad estimates of the consequences of such legislation if adopted by all the states. According to the U.S. Department of Justice's BJS, offenders admitted to prison in 1992 for violent crimes were estimated to serve a minimum of 52% of their sentences (approximately 5 years) before being eligible for parole or other forms of release (BJS, 1994, p. 29). Should they be required to serve 85% of their terms, the additional increase in the prison population for offenders convicted of violent crimes would be a 63% increase (BJS, 1994).

An estimated 400,000 inmates of the 1 million in prison are now serving terms for violent crimes. If they were required to serve 85% of their sentences, this population would increase by more than half, to 652,000.

The state of Texas recently completed a formal impact assessment of a recent truth-in-sentencing or no-parole proposal (Texas Criminal Justice Policy Council, 1995). The proposal would require all offenders convicted for the following aggravated violent offenses to serve 85% of their sentences: capital murder, murder, aggravated sexual assault, aggravated robbery, aggravated kidnapping, indecency with a child, and any felony where a deadly weapon was used or exhibited.

The report concluded that implementation of the truth-in-sentencing proposal only for *aggravated* felonies would result in the need to construct an additional 30,600 prison beds at a total cost of $980 million in construction funds and $510 million in annual operation costs. If the bill were amended to include nonaggravated and aggravated violent offenders, 60,000 additional beds would be needed by the year 2046, a 50% increase over current inmate population figures. The cost to taxpayers for additional prison construction alone was estimated to be $1.9 billion.

An even broader statute was proposed in Illinois in which all inmates would serve 85% of their sentences. This legislation would double the current prison population and increase projected bed needs by more than 42,000 over the next 10 years. The total additional cost to taxpayers was estimated to be $4.6 billion in operating costs and $1.5 billion in construction (Illinois Department of Corrections, 1995).

A Closer Look at the Three-Strikes Movement

In 1995, the NCCD and the Pretrial Services Resource Center (PSRC) conducted a National Institute of Justice (NIJ) funded national survey of states that had adopted three-strikes laws. The objectives of this survey were to better identify those 15 states that had implemented such laws and to learn what the likely effects would be on the courts, local jails, and state prison systems. The results of this survey are shown in Table 7.3.

The first state to enact a three-strikes law was Washington in December of 1993. According to the National Conference of State Legislatures, 10 state legislatures by May 1, 1994, had passed similar legislation and another 12 had similar bills pending (Hunzeker, 1994).[2] Although all these initiatives purport to play the same sentencing game, they have very different rules on how the game will be played.

The Two Extremes of Three Strikes–Washington State and California

California's recently enacted three-strikes law represents the most expansive version of three-strikes legislation. It has broadly defined strikeable offenses, which include frequently occurring crimes such as burglary and assault with attempt to commit a robbery. It also limits the ability of repeat offenders to earn good-time credits while incarcerated and includes as strikes crimes committed by a minor who is at least 16 years of age (Austin, 1994).

The California Department of Corrections (CDC) initially estimated that the measure would increase the prison population from 125,000 in 1994 to 210,000 by the year 2000. By the year 2027, the prison population could reach a staggering 400,000 inmates. However, the CDC has now reduced these early estimates based on the application of the law in several key counties. In particular, there is some evidence that due to plea bargaining maneuvers designed to circumvent the effect of the law or demands by strikeable defendants for jury trials,

TABLE 7.3 Summary of Three-Strikes States

Category/State	Strikeable Offenses	Start Date	Effect on Court and Jail	No. of Prison Admissions to Date	Prison Projections
Two-strike provisions					
Georgia	Life without parole for 2nd violent felony (murder, armed robbery, kidnapping, rape, child molestation, aggravated sexual offenses); maximum sentence must be served for any 4th felony conviction	January 1, 1995	No effect yet in Fulton County (Atlanta)	20-80 two strikes No four-strikes cases yet	4,218 increase by 2008
Tennessee	Life without parole for 2nd conviction for designated violent felonies; same for 3rd conviction for other violent felonies	July 1, 1994, amended July 1, 1995	No effect in Shelby County (Memphis)	0	Unknown
California	Doubled prison sentence for any felony if 1 prior conviction for serious or violent felony; mandatory life for any 3rd felony if 2 prior convictions for serious or violent felony	March 7, 1994	Documented increases in case processing and jail populations	9,574 two strikes 594 three strikes	61,000 increase by 1999
Mandatory life without parole for 3rd serious or violent felony					
Indiana	Most violent offenses, drug dealing	1994	No effect in Allen County (Fort Wayne)	Unknown	Unknown
North Carolina	Violent offenses	May 1, 1994	No effect in Mecklenberg County (Charlotte)	Unknown	Unknown
Virginia	Most violent offenses	1994	No effect statewide	Unknown	Unknown
Washington	Many violent offenses, Class B felonies with sexual motivation	December 1993	23 three-strikes cases filed to date in King County (Seattle)	24 three strikes	250 increase by 2003

State	Offense	Effective date	Cases		
Wisconsin	"Serious felonies" including murder, rape, robbery, aggravated assault, abduction, sexual crimes against children	April 28, 1994	None. Only 1 case filed to date statewide	0	Unknown
New Jersey	Certain 1st-degree crimes	July 1, 1995	Unknown	0	1,400 increase within 40 years
Mandatory life with parole possible					
Colorado	Eligible for parole after 40 years for 3rd violent conviction	1994	Unknown	Unknown	Unknown
New Mexico	Eligible for parole after 30 years for 3rd violent conviction	1994	No cases filed yet in Bernalillo County (Albuquerque)	Unknown	Unknown
Discretion allowed in sentencing					
Connecticut	Range of 25 years to life for 3rd conviction for many violent offenses	1994	None	Unknown	Unknown
Kansas	Allows judge to double sentencing guidelines for 2nd and 3rd conviction for many "person felonies"	1994	Unknown	Unknown	Unknown
Adding charges to already existing habitual offender laws					
Louisiana	Mandatory life without parole for 3rd conviction for many violent offenses, some drug offenses, any offenses punishable by more than 12 years in prison	1994	None	Unknown	Unknown
Maryland	Life without parole for 4th violent felony conviction for which separate prison terms were served for first three	October 1, 1994	Unknown	Unknown	Unknown

the number of cases being convicted for three or two strikes will not be as great as originally projected. Nevertheless, this legislation could result in half the state's inmate population being composed of three-strikes inmates—many of whom will grow old and eventually die in prison. According to our analysis (Figure 7.2), by the year 2020, approximately 20% of the male and female inmates will be at least 50 years old in contrast to the present 4% (Jones, 1994).

At the other end of the three-strikes spectrum, opposite California, is Washington State, with its much smaller "strike zone." Washington's law is unlikely to have any significant effect on the prison system, because few offenders qualify for a third strike and those who do already receive lengthy prison terms. According to state officials, the prison population would increase by only 250 inmates by the year 2003, and even this assumes full compliance with the law by prosecutors and the court (Austin, 1994).

Other State Versions of Three Strikes

Returning to the state survey data shown in Table 7.3, we have tried to classify the states according to the structure of their three-strikes laws. These groups are as follows:

Two-strikes provisions. Three states (Georgia, Tennessee, and California) have mandatory enhanced-sentencing provisions for persons convicted of two strikeable offenses. Offenders can also receive the more commonly known three-strikes provision with a mandatory life term without parole. All three states already allow for sentences of life with and without the possibility of parole.

Three-strikes provisions with a mandatory life term without parole. Indiana, North Carolina, Virginia, Washington, and Wisconsin fall into this category—as does New Jersey, which enacted its three-strikes law on July 1, 1995. Both California and Tennessee have three-strikes provisions in addition to two strikes.

Three-strikes provisions with a mandatory life term with parole possible. In these states, three-strikes offenders are eligible for parole considera-

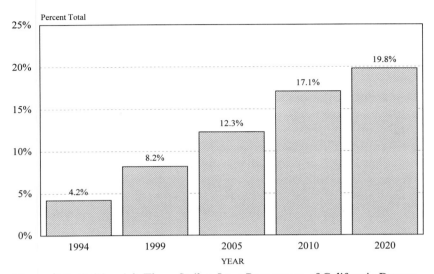

Figure 7.2. California's Three-Strikes Law: Percentage of California Department of Corrections Prison Population Aged 50 Years and Over
SOURCE: M. A. Jones and J. Austin, *The 1995 NCCD National Prison Population Forecast: The Cost of Truth-in-Sentencing Laws. NCCD Focus* (1995, July). San Francisco: NCCD.

tion after having served a portion of their life sentences. In Colorado, parole is possible after serving 40 years and in New Mexico after 30 years. However, given that the average age at admission for these inmates may well be 30 and above, it is unlikely these provisions will have much effect.

Discretion allowed in sentencing three-strikes offenders. Two states (Kansas and Connecticut) allow for the application of the three-strikes provision to be used at the discretion of the court. In other words, it is not a mandatory-sentencing provision. Its effect will depend on the use of the law by prosecutors and the courts. For these reasons, the effect is not expected to be significant.

Adding eligibility criteria to existing habitual offender laws. Louisiana and Maryland, like most states, already have mandatory life terms without parole for repeat offenders. Their laws simply add the type of crimes that makes one eligible for a three-strikes sentence.

The table also reports the expected effect of these laws on prison populations. With the exceptions of Washington and California, very little is known regarding the effect on prison population growth. Only 4 of the 15 states completed impact studies. Of those that did, only Georgia and California (which are both two-strikes states) are anticipating a significant increase. Conversations with correctional officials in these other states suggest that very little effect will be felt for at least 10 years because the offenders targeted by the three-strikes laws are already receiving very long sentences due to previous mandatory-sentencing guideline, parole guideline, and truth-in-sentencing reforms.

Thus, although most states have passed laws or are considering legislation that is more narrowly defined, adopting a California style three-strikes statute for prison populations across the country clearly would further extend already increasing lengths of stay for many inmates. However, playing the Washington version of the same game, which seems to be the dominant model, will have no initial effect and even minimal long-term effect.

Summary

Previous sentencing reforms have already served to increase prison admissions and provide a preliminary analysis of the effects of these laws on correctional populations. More directly, most states have crafted their three-strikes laws so that they only target offenders who by virtue of previously enacted sentencing reforms are already expected to serve long prison terms. Coupled with an anticipated level of manipulation by the courts to avoid the full application of such laws to those who qualify, the likely effect of such laws is greatly exaggerated. In other words, we may finally be exhausting our capacity and willingness to further increase the extent, duration, and costs of imprisonment. The lack of effect of such laws on prison populations also means that for most jurisdictions, the pretrial jail population will not be affected by such reforms.

Future Prison Population Growth

As in the past, NCCD has calculated a national estimate based on data gathered from NCCD's "bellwether" 23 states and the Bureau of Prisons. In making the estimate, two forecasts of the nation's prison population through the year 2000 have been developed. The first scenario assumes that policies affecting prison admissions and lengths of stay in effect at the end of 1994 will continue through the rest of the decade. The second assumes that all states would adopt the 85% rule for offenders sentenced to prison for committing violent crimes and that it would take effect in 1995.

Despite a projected admissions increase of 19% between 1995 and 2000 for 19 states, their prison population will increase by 30% (Table 7.4). Here again we see considerable variation among the states. States anticipating the lowest increases are Kansas (no increase), Arkansas (4%), Rhode Island (7%), Indiana (8%), and Ohio and Connecticut (12% each). States with the largest increases are Oregon (84%), California (64%), and Virginia (47%). These three states have recently adopted three-strikes statutes, truth-in-sentencing laws, and/or have abolished parole.

Applying these forecasts to all states, NCCD projects that under current policies the U.S. prison population will reach 1.4 million inmates by the year 2000—an increase of 40% over the 1994 population of 1 million (see Figure 7.3). However, should all states adopt the 85% rule this year, our national estimate would increase by 190,000 to 1.6 million by the end of year 2000.[3] At an estimated cost of $55,000 to $75,000 per cell, between $10.6 and $15.1 billion would be needed to construct additional bed space. A further $21.9 billion would be required to operate the additional prisons by the end of the decade (based on an annual cost of $25,000 per bed). This combined $32.5 to $37 billion cost does not include additional billions of dollars required to service the debt associated with the public borrowing necessary to pay for additional prison construction. Furthermore, the growth might not end for several decades, as tens of thousands of inmates would have to die in prison from old age or expensive medical complications.

This forecast underscores a number of points. First, despite recent declines in the rate of growth in prison admissions across the country,

TABLE 7.4 Prison Population Projections of Study States, 1995-2000

	1995	1996	1997	1998	1999	2000	% Change
Arkansas	9,024	9,079	9,106	9,185	9,264	9,337	+3.9
California	128,553	142,551	159,992	176,013	192,814	210,422	+63.7
Colorado	11,403	12,261	13,308	14,326	15,455	15,455	+35.5
Connecticut	12,489	12,989	13,301	13,458	13,684	13,999	+12.1
Florida	65,398	72,357	73,999	75,493	76,512	77,896	+19.1
Hawaii	1,961	2,102	2,290	2,415	2,540	2,261	+15.3
Idaho	2,646	2,759	2,836	2,941	2,979	2,989	+13.0
Illinois	38,390	41,726	43,586	46,105	48,561	51,216	+33.4
Indiana	14,900	15,100	15,300	15,500	15,800	16,100	+8.1
Kansas	6,671	7,045	6,997	6,839	6,637	6,637	−0.5
Kentucky	11,551	12,320	13,072	14,518	15,227	15,987	+38.4
Louisiana	25,800	28,000	29,500	31,000	32,500	34,000	+31.8
Massachusetts	10,209	10,632	11,250	11,580	11,911	12,356	+21.0
Michigan	42,291	44,073	45,796	47,580	49,440	51,365	+21.5
Mississippi	11,700	12,194	12,684	13,184	13,664	14,170	+21.1
Nevada	7,385	7,670	8,101	8,530	9,032	9,516	+28.9
Ohio	42,180	43,059	43,915	44,850	46,080	47,215	+11.9
Oklahoma	17,745	18,466	18,918	19,327	19,825	20,112	+13.3
Oregon	7,134	7,472	8,600	9,764	11,440	13,116	+83.9
Rhode Island	3,130	3,181	3,215	3,248	3,293	3,337	+6.6
Tennessee	17,630	18,372	18,758	19,227	19,671	19,886	+12.8
Texas	126,808	140,882	148,866	153,654	151,842	149,444	+46.6
Virginia	27,964	31,700	34,659	38,050	39,005	40,984	46.6
Federal institutions	91,537	97,845	104,605	109,389	113,854	120,169	+31.3
Total	734,499	793,835	842,578	886,176	921,030	958,009	+30.4

NOTE: Figures represent fiscal or calendar years. Not all states report official projections through the year 2000; in some cases reported projections were extrapolated through the year 2000.

prison populations will continue to increase at record levels due to truth-in-sentencing statutes that include three-strikes laws and mandatory sentencing, plus greater restrictions on parole boards and the availability of good-time credits. Such statutes increase the chances of a convicted criminal's being sentenced to prison and that he or she will have a greater length of stay.

Increases in the length of stay are now being driven by the four following trends:

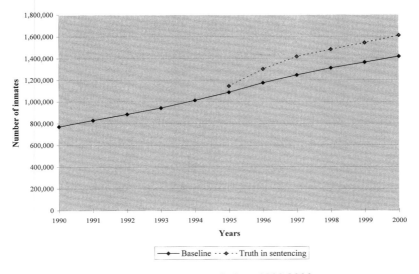

Figure 7.3. Projected U.S. Prison Population, 1990-2000
SOURCE: M. A. Jones and J. Austin, *The 1995 NCCD National Prison Population Forecast: The Cost of Truth-in-Sentencing Laws. NCCD Focus* (1995, July). San Francisco: NCCD.

1. Previous sentencing reforms adopted by the states (including sentencing guidelines) have increased sentence lengths and lengths of stay
2. More conservative criteria adopted by parole boards for granting parole have increased lengths of stay
3. Truth-in-sentencing laws requiring inmates to serve higher proportions of their sentences have increased lengths of stay
4. Three-strikes laws that greatly extend lengths of stay for certain crimes with prior convictions have greatly increased lengths of stay

Of these trends, the more recently touted three-strikes laws will have the least effect on prison and jail systems. In particular, claims by conservatives and liberals are exaggerated for most states. Only California's model is likely to have draconian effects on the criminal justice system. But even in that state, the projected effects may well be overstated.

On the other hand, adoption of a truth-in-sentencing scheme as being debated by the current Congress and many state legislatures would have a far more significant effect on the prison system because it targets a much larger pool of offenders, who would be required to spend a far longer period of imprisonment than presently occurs.

The Offsetting Benefits of Crime Reduction

Few would argue that truth in sentencing and, to a lesser degree, three strikes are inexpensive. But there is considerable debate on whether the prison buildup will have a significant reduction in crime rates.

There are two reasons—maturation and misprediction—that argue against the value of longer prison terms as an effective crime control strategy. If there is one factor that is consistently associated with criminal behavior, it is age. Criminal behavior in most males begins at age 14 and peaks by age 21. National arrest data show that about two thirds of all arrests occur for persons under age 30. The average age of a person admitted to prison is 31 and increasing. This means that a substantial proportion of prisoners are statistically well beyond the peak years of their criminal behavior. Further incarceration of these inmates has little effect on crime rates and can actually represent a substantial waste of incarceration.

To illustrate this point, I compared statewide crime statistics with the crimes committed by inmates released from California prisons for the year of 1991. As shown in Table 7.5, parolees returned to California's prisons with a new sentence for a violent crime represented less than 2% of all violent crimes that resulted in a felony arrest in 1991. Although the number is large (2,520 newly sentenced parolees), it is quite small relative to the total number (143,970) of felony arrests for these same crimes.

Nonetheless, the chief economist of California, Governor Pete Wilson, has promised that taxpayers will receive a $55 billion windfall if another $6 billion is invested in prisons. And there are preliminary data showing that crime is declining in California. However, the same downward trend is occurring for jurisdictions that have not adopted such laws. Others believe truth in sentencing will have no effect on crime or may even worsen the current situation because other areas of life will suffer as money continues to be diverted away from school budgets and other vital services.

As the nation braces itself for its second baby boom and unprecedented numbers of unemployed, poorly educated young people fill the nation's prisons, the debate will continue. During this debate, prison

TABLE 7.5 California Violent Crimes Attributed to California Parolees in 1991

Crime	Total Crimes	Total Felony Arrests	Convicted Parolees	% of Crimes	% of Arrests
Homicide	3,876	3,720	136	3.6	3.7
Robbery	125,105	31,346	1,553	1.2	5.0
Assault	188,993	104,487	751	0.4	0.7
Rape	12,942	4,417	80	0.6	1.8
Total	330,916	143,970	2,520	0.8	1.8

SOURCE: California Department of Justice (1991), California Department of Corrections (1991).

populations will increase by an additional 1,500 to 2,000 persons each week. To date, most would agree that the nation's imprisonment policies have not reduced crime in America or made the public feel any safer. It is unlikely that policies aimed at incarcerating older offenders in prison for longer periods of time will make America safer.

Notes

1. New court commitments are inmates admitted to prison who were not on parole status at the time they were sentenced to prison. According to the U.S. Department of Justice, 60% of all admissions are classified as "new court commitments," with parole revocations representing 30% of all admissions (BJS, 1994, p. 10).

2. The 10 states are California, Connecticut, Georgia, Indiana, Kansas, Maryland, New Mexico, North Carolina, Virginia, and Wisconsin. The 12 states with pending legislation are Alaska, Colorado, Delaware, Illinois, Michigan, New Jersey, New York, Ohio, South Carolina, Vermont, Rhode Island, and Pennsylvania.

3. The truth-in-sentencing scenario was developed using NCCD's Prophet simulation model, data, and projections supplied by states using NCCD's projections methods and data published by BJS. The states of California, Florida, and Virginia as well as the federal system were excluded from this impact assessment because these jurisdictions presently require violent offenders to serve approximately 85% of imposed sentences; furthermore, the effect of this policy is already included in official projections.

Simulation results from sample states were weighted to reflect national prison populations. The scenario is based on the assumption that inmates confined in 1995 and admitted in 1995 or later in the following offense groups will serve 85% of their sentences: homicide, manslaughter, rape, robbery, kidnapping, assault, burglary and "other" violent crimes.

References

Austin, J. (1994). Three strikes and you're out: The likely consequences. *Saint Louis University Public Law Review, 14,* 239-258.

Austin, J., Jones, C., Kramer, J., & Renninger, P. (1996, February). *National assessment of structured sentencing.* Washington, DC: U.S. Department of Justice, Bureau of Justice Assistance.

Austin, J., Jones, M. A., & McVey, A. D. (1991). *The NCCD prison population forecast: The impact of declining drug arrests.* San Francisco: National Council on Crime and Delinquency.

Bureau of Justice Statistics. (1994, October). *National Corrections Reporting Program, 1992.* Washington, DC: U.S. Department of Justice, Bureau of Justice Statistics.

Bureau of Justice Statistics. (1995a, April). *Prison sentences and time served for violence.* Washington, DC: U.S. Department of Justice, Bureau of Justice Statistics.

Bureau of Justice Statistics. (1995b, August 9). *The nation's prison population grew by almost 9 percent last year.* Washington, DC: U.S. Department of Justice, Bureau of Justice Statistics.

Hunzeker, D. (1994, August). *"Three strikes" legislation.* Denver, CO: National Conference of State Legislatures.

Illinois Department of Corrections. (1995, January). *Corrections Impact Note: House Bill 298.* Springfield: Author.

Jones, M. A. (1994). *The aging of California's prison population: An assessment of three strikes legislation.* San Francisco: National Council on Crime and Delinquency.

Texas Criminal Justice Policy Council. (1995, March). *Abolishing parole for offenders sentenced to prison for violent crimes.* Austin: Author.

PART

Special Issues

Chapter Eight

News From Nowhere, Policy to Follow

Media and the Social Construction of
"Three Strikes and You're Out"

RAY SURETTE

However irrational as a crime control measure, Three Strikes and You're Out appears to have mesmerized the public and politicians from one coast to the other and across party lines. It may be the most potent conjoining of crime and politics in the history of the Republic . . . in the post modern world of satellite technology, a crime committed in Petaluma, Ca. frightens viewers in Poughkeepsie, NY. Another contribution to fear of crime may, paradoxically, be the response of politicians. Does a Willy Horton advertisement respond to fear of crime or cause it? It is probably both, consequence and cause—and an opportunity for political exploitation. In any case, a combination of shocking crimes—Polly Klaas's abduction and murder in such a serene place as Petaluma, California, the killing of tourists in south Florida, the roadside murder of basketball star Michael Jordan's father, televised reportage of grisly murders in a variety of workplaces and the killing of commuters on a Long Island railroad train, as well as an outbreak of political advertisements focusing on fear of crime—sent a scary message of social breakdown to the majority of Americans who do not reside in the inner cities. The Message? You are no longer immune from random violence anywhere—not in your suburban home, commuter train, office building, or automobile—and the police and courts cannot or will not protect you.

Skolnick (1995, pp. 5, 7)

The term *news from nowhere* is derived from observations of the news media's ability to assemble and deliver news stories from far-distant localities and subsequently present them in a way that suggests that they have local significance. It reflects the fact that a murder in Maine can be a part of local news in San Diego and that news of distant crime can influence the course of local criminal justice policy. The recent passage of the "three strikes and you're out" law in California presents an opportunity to study this relationship between the media and criminal justice policy. On reflection, however, the question of the relationship between the media and criminal justice policy is found to be complex. The media cannot be simply tagged as manipulating mechanisms that force criminal justice policies down the public's throat. Nor can they be dismissed as objective neutral bystanders in the public policy arena.

Attempting to understand the media-criminal justice policy relationship leads initially to two bodies of research. The first is communication and journalism research. The second is the social construction of reality literature that examines the media's role in the creation and promulgation of social knowledge. Combined, the research provides a foundation to explore criminal justice policy initiatives such as the three-strikes law.

The chain of events that resulted in the three-strikes phenomenon, described as 1994's fastest-spreading anticrime fad, began in Seattle, Washington, in the fall of 1988 (Gest, 1994). A television commentator coined the slogan "three strikes, you're out" to denote a policy where anyone who had been convicted of two serious crimes would subsequently face life without parole if convicted of a third serious offense. The reaction to the initial idea was not enthusiastic. However, the following year a young woman, Diane Ballasiotes, was abducted and stabbed to death by a convicted rapist who had been released from prison. In reaction to this crime, a group, Friends of Diane, formed seeking harsher penalties for sex crimes. This group eventually joined forces with the three-strikes group, but despite the combined efforts, through 1992 there was little legislative or criminal justice professional interest in three strikes in Washington State. The proposed legislation was perceived as similar to a habitual offender law already on the books, and a petition drive to get three strikes on a statewide ballot failed (Gest, 1994).

In 1993, however, the three-strikes group (renamed the Washington Citizens for Justice) allied with the National Rifle Association and succeeded in getting the proposition on the November ballot. Despite some opposition from elements of the criminal justice community, 77% of Washingtonians approved the three-strikes law. As the Washington vote approached, a young girl in California, Polly Klaas, was abducted and murdered, and a three-strikes campaign took off in California. Unlike prior years, this time politicians and citizens across the nation and the political spectrum embraced three strikes. Some estimates indicated that more than 80% of Americans came to favor three-strikes laws (Egan, 1994, p. A1). Political support cumulated with President Clinton endorsing three strikes in his 1994 State of the Union address.

This series of events raises the question of how three strikes rose from an initial lukewarm reception to a national policy with presidential support. Part of the answer lies in the logical appeal of three strikes. Such laws have a commonsense base of support because such offenders are generally perceived by the public as beyond redemption—as "three-time losers." Three strikes, therefore, matches a popular, intuitive response to crime. Most everyone is motivated by the urge to retaliate and the wish for safety (Skolnick, 1995, p. 3). The mainstream American response to crime is composed of a commonsense perspective that focuses on morally deficient criminals and on preventing them from committing crime. The immediate effect is strong support for policies based on punitiveness and individual responsibility (Gans, 1988, p. 80). And although such policies may be ineffective or even countereffective in the long run, they are more palatable to society and are regularly championed in a cycle of short-term politically defined periods demarcated by elections.

In this atmosphere, three strikes emerges as the latest in a string of fast-paced, punitive-oriented, heavily media-covered crime panaceas that periodically sweep the nation. The most notable ones have been the Scared Straight shock incarceration programs of the 1970s and the juvenile delinquent boot camps of the 1980s (Austin, Jones, & Bolyard, 1993; Cavender, 1981; Sechrest, 1994). It is easy to assume that the media are the primary current in such tides, but the actual relationship of the media and criminal justice policy development is not simple. To comprehend the role of the media in the three-strikes legislation, it is necessary to first review the research findings regarding the role of the media in past criminal justice policy initiatives.

Communications and Journalism Research

Arguably, the relationship between the mass media and criminal justice policy is one of the most important factors in contemporary crime and justice policy formation (Duffee, 1980; Elias, 1986; Schein-gold, 1984). Despite much interest, however, the exact nature of the relationship between the media and criminal justice decision making and policy is not well understood, and it has proven difficult to delineate the causal role of the media in criminal justice policy (Cook, Kendzierski, & Thomas, 1983; Cook, Tyler, et al., 1983; Doppelt & Manikas, 1990; Surette, 1992b). There is a long tradition in mass communication research to link the media with public opinion forma-tion, and it is felt that the media are a significant source of public attitudes and perceptions concerning crime and justice (Barber, 1987; Page, Shapiro, & Dempsey, 1987; Stroman & Seltzer, 1985). In addition, agenda-setting research indicates that the media have an influence on the list of issues that are rated as urgent and that therefore receive policy attention. Emphasis on crime has been credited with raising the fear of victimization to disproportionate levels and in giving crime an inappropriate high ranking on the public agenda (Gordon & Heath, 1981, pp. 228-229).

In general, the research has painted the media as having a moderate, widely fluctuating relationship with criminal justice policy. This re-search currently recognizes the media as playing a role in a criminal justice public policy ecology made up of social, political, and media factors (Doppelt & Manikas, 1990). In this perspective, the media's influence nearly never works in isolation of other social variables and is felt to be pervasive enough to reach even isolated individuals (Zucker, 1978, p. 226). In gist, the media's influence is common but not easily predicted.

The general conclusion of the communication research is that three social groups are normally involved in criminal justice policy formation (Doppelt & Manikas, 1990). They are the mass media, the public, and criminal justice professionals and policy decision makers. Initially, researchers assumed the relationship between these three groups to be linear, with the media arousing the public concerning a crime or justice issue, the public responding by pressuring criminal justice officials and legislators for action, and the officials and legislators thereafter creating or altering a policy. However, this linear relationship is actually the exception, not the rule. The direction of influence between the three groups can flow in any direction, and the public is frequently excluded from the process.

Thus, although the media are acknowledged as a source of strong influence in some situations, their effects are difficult to discern and do not operate in direct or simple ways. In addition, media-based echo and anticipatory effects add unique features to the media and criminal justice policy relationship. These media-related effects are found to interweave with criminal justice policy effects and make it especially difficult to clarify the media-criminal justice policy relationship. An echo effect occurs when the news media sensitize a criminal justice system regarding a particular type of crime or offender, such as when the coverage of child abuse within child care facilities during the 1980s resulted in an increased emphasis on the prosecution of child abuse cases (Surette, 1989, 1992b). Rare for other social science research areas, media-related anticipatory effects seem to reverse the causal order of media and criminal justice policy change. In these situations, effects on criminal justice policy occur before any change in media coverage. Policy changes because criminal justice system officials will often respond proactively to anticipated media coverage. For example, Pritchard and his colleagues (Pritchard, 1986; Pritchard, Dilts, & Berkowitz, 1987) found that Illinois state prosecutors' anticipation of news media stances determined their decision to prosecute or not to prosecute pornography cases. Offenders can also display a type of anticipatory reaction due to the media. Invoked in offender populations, this effect occurs when media publicity causes behavior changes in anticipation of a media-publicized criminal justice policy change. This media-induced behavior effect will occur with or without an actual criminal justice policy change. Termed an *announcement* effect, this effect has been well documented in the research literature for driving under the influence, speeding, subway, and street crimes (Surette, 1992a).

These research problems are especially a concern when studying the relationship of the media and public policy because they present the researcher with three competing models of potential effects. The media may actually be the direct cause of a criminal justice policy change with or without a triggering external event as follows:

Media coverage → Criminal justice policy change

An example would be a news program investigative report of ticket fixing by a police department, leading to a new department policy regarding traffic tickets.

Or an external event may be the cause of the policy change and the media cover the event simultaneously:

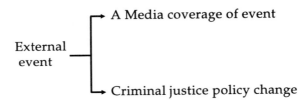

In this case, the media appear to be an influence, but their coverage is simply correlated with the policy change. For example, an external evaluation reveals that low-income defendants are less likely to be offered alternatives to jail sentences. The review and selection process is adjusted as part of a preplanned program refinement cycle at the same time as local media report on the existence of program bias.

Or the media's coverage of an external event and the event may both influence criminal justice policy, a simultaneous influence:

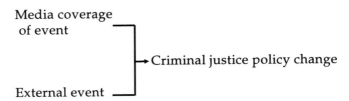

An example would be the case where an offender out of prison on a furlough program commits a violent rape, and as a result, the correctional department reviews and alters furlough programs. Due to media publicity of the rape, the program is also suspended for a number of months and more severe restrictions than otherwise considered are instituted. As the three models reflect, a researcher's task of deciphering the effects of the media, as distinguished from the effects of external events, and from the effects of the coverage of external events, is extremely difficult.

The Social Construction of Crime and Justice Reality

In addition to the communication and journalism research, the social construction of reality perspective assists in understanding the media-criminal justice policy relationship by focusing on the manner in which the dominant view of social reality is created. In this perspective, the media are felt to be crucial in the creation of social reality, especially in the crime and justice realm. To understand their role, it is useful to conceptualize social reality as a changing, socially created phenomenon, not as fixed or universal but as evolving and subjective. In dealing with society, people use world models to understand factual information and to simplify and direct their decisions and social behavior.[1] These models are constructed over time from information gained through social interactions and personal experiences. An individual's direct experiences makes up his or her *experienced reality* (Adoni & Mane, 1984; Cohen, Adoni, & Bantz, 1990; Gergen, 1985; Schneider, 1985). Because its knowledge is firsthand, this reality has the strongest influence on the social reality each individual constructs and subsequently on each person's social behaviors, attitudes, and perceptions.

In addition to experienced reality, humans have access to a second source of knowledge about the world. Termed *symbolic reality*, it is obtained from our extensive capability to manipulate abstract symbols as representations of objects and concepts. This information is gained from interpersonal networks and the mass media. Examples of symbolic reality systems include written and spoken language, art, music, and mathematics. Symbolic reality provides a vast amount of knowledge of the world and allows individuals to incorporate knowledge of experiences that they have not directly experienced into their world models. For modern people, most of our worldly knowledge is, in fact, gained not from experienced reality but from symbolic reality. In the final world model construction step, the experienced and symbolic realities are combined by each individual to create a model *subjective reality*. Thus, reality is subjective in that each individual's final world model will slightly differ from every other individual's model because the knowledge mix will differ slightly from individual to individual. However, people exposed to similar experiences and similar communicated knowledge will naturally construct subjective realities that are more alike than different. One can conceive of "culture" and "cultural heritage" as sets of similar world models created from long-term social reality construction under similar objective and symbolic realities.

In sum, in the social construction of reality, individuals construct their reality based on their interaction with an experienced reality (i.e., the physical world) and information they receive from a culture's symbolic reality (language, art, the media) to create a subjective reality that directs their social behavior. When other sources of knowledge are not available, the media play a greater role in the construction and dissemination of social reality. The mass media have evolved in present-day America to become the dominant player in the symbolic reality realm and by default in the construction of social reality.

Important concepts in the social construction of reality are symbolic campaigns, claims, and claims-makers. Claims-makers are various social groups who advance competing reality constructions containing differing explanations of the nature of reality and the causes of events. In the three-strikes effort, claims-makers include the gubernatorial candidates (especially Pete Wilson) and citizen groups such as the Friends of Diane and Mad About Rising Crime, and ultimately the White House and the California Correctional Peace Officers Association, a powerful union. Claims-makers advance their respective realities through their claims. Claims, in turn, are the assertions that describe and explain a social issue or event. Claims significant to the three-strikes construction included the effect of the law (crime reduction vs. explosive costs and system overcrowding), causes of violent crime (system leniency with predatory criminals vs. social and political inequalities), and the need for the law (out-of-control violence and violent criminals and reduced public safety vs. negligible and counterproductive three-strikes effect).

Competing claims-makers advance their claims through symbolic campaigns, which are periods of intense competition and forceful assertions. Symbolic campaigns involve the media dissemination of selected events by claims-makers that are felt to support their causal explanations and interpretations. The mass media serve as the mechanism of campaign dissemination and exemplify events that are paraded as evidence of the validity of the symbolic campaign's claims. The period prior to the California gubernatorial election was a time of intense symbolic campaigning on behalf of three strikes, and the Polly Klaas kidnapping and murder became the key symbolic crime for the pro-three-strikes campaign. The symbolic campaign for three strikes, however, did not begin with the brutal murder of Polly Klaas. It lies in the media's long historical focus on predatory crimes and predatory criminals. News and entertainment media stand as a long-term symbolic campaign against predator crime and for punitive criminal justice policies.

Predator Criminality and the Symbolic Campaign for Three Strikes

Predator criminals and predator crime, defined as interpersonal, stranger-to-stranger, injury-causing crime in which usually innocent, helpless victims are randomly chosen, are the modern icons of the mass media. Whether in entertainment or news, the crimes that define criminality for the public are acts of predator criminals.[2] The modern mass media have raised the specter of the predator criminal from a rare criminal character to a common, ever-present image, and the public is led to see violence and predation between strangers as a way of life (Scheingold, 1984, p. 63). Predator criminality, as with other icons, represents a largely unquestioned set of beliefs about the world—a constructed reality that as the aphorism "perception is reality" suggests, has the ability to shape the actual world to fit the media image. In their content, the media influence official action by reinforcing the distorted stereotypes of crime and criminals (Cromer, 1978). In its general content, crime in the media emphasizes the uncertainties of modern life that criminals are evil, abnormal people and that victims are vulnerable. Media crime is nearly universally due to individual characteristics rather than social conditions, and the causes of crime are rooted in individual failings rather than social ills. In the end, media predatory crime is a metaphor for a world gone berserk, for life out of control. Forging a partnership between the police, the media, and the audience, this construction of dangerous fugitives loose in a violent and uncertain world encourages ever-broader social controls.[3]

Historical examples of claims-makers employing the media and their predator criminal icon to influence criminal justice policy are common. Becker (1963), for example, recounts how the Federal Bureau of Narcotics in the 1930s successfully launched a symbolic campaign through the news and film media to convince the public that marijuana was a social menace and that its use results in drug-crazed predatory criminals. The criminal justice policy that resulted was the Marijuana Tax Act of 1937, which criminalized marijuana possession. More recently, Cavender (1981) described the role of the media in driving the explosive growth of juvenile shock incarceration programs in the 1970s based on the Scared Straight documentary. Cavender recounts how most of the media coverage presented crime as a problem separate from other social issues and criminals as one-dimensional predators. Juvenile delinquents were portrayed simply as younger versions of irredeemable, adult, predatory criminals.

The most recent example of a media-based predator criminal construction, and the campaign that laid the foundation for the public embrace and political popularity of three strikes, is the social construction of serial homicide in the 1970s and 1980s by both the news and entertainment media. Jenkins (1994) describes the symbolic campaign that constructed a specific, broadly accepted reality of serial homicide and came to significantly influence criminal justice policy. The constructed image was one of serial homicide as the result of roaming, predatory killers who represented a new, rapidly increasing, more vicious type of murderer than previously encountered. Matching the three policy groups of the media, the public, and criminal justice decision makers alluded to in the communication research literature, Jenkins describes three social groups that constructed the serial killer reality. One group is made up of law enforcement organizations. In the case of serial homicide, the FBI played a central, reality construction role and helped to define serial murder as an interjurisdictional crime needing federal intervention and expertise. A second force is the popular culture, precultivated by the long-term entertainment and news media emphasis on predator criminality. The popular culture embraced the claim of serial murders as an exploding problem and portrayed serial murderers as cunning predators needing special law enforcement attention. The novel and movie *The Silence of the Lambs* cemented the reality construction process and its legitimacy in the public's consciousness. The multimedia coverage of serial murderers such as Jeffrey Dahmer and Ted Bundy and the movie *The Silence of the Lambs* link real and fictional cases together, allowing the coverage of actual predator crimes to blend with popular fiction. Third, the news media played a key role in the dissemination and legitimizing of the claims concerning serial homicide. The development of the True Crime genre in books during this same period exemplifies the combined popular culture's and news media's roles. Our cultural and media traditions thus set the tone and prepared a receptive social setting for the interaction between the mass media, public officials, and the public (Jenkins, 1988, p. 67). The resulting criminal justice policy effect was a Behavioral Science Unit within the FBI and increased public concern over predator criminality.[4]

Current criminal justice policy, including the three-strikes law, is linked to these prior reality construction efforts. Recent media coverage provides the reinforcement and linkage necessary for a unified image of violent predatory crime to dominate (Kappeler, Blumberg, & Potter, 1993, p. 245). The media-attuned public comes to evaluate the criminal justice system poorly while paradoxically supporting more crime control-based law enforcement and punitive-oriented policies (Graber, 1980, p. 83). The resulting policy drives, including three strikes, result from the convergence of the goals of politicians seeking an issue, the punitive predispositions of the public, the historical focus of the news and entertainment media, and the professional proclivities of the crime control establishment (Scheingold, 1984, p. 81). In the final analysis regarding crime and justice, the media project the horrendous crime as the norm; the rare as common; the reactive, symbolic policy as significant. Into this receptive cultural bed the three-strikes law needed only a symbolic crime to flourish.

Three Strikes as a Social Construction of Reality Case Study

The three-strikes law emerges as the most recent in a series of criminal justice policies based on the socially constructed, media-centered image of predator crime. To more closely examine its construction, an exploratory review of the news reporting of three strikes in the *Los Angeles Times* newspaper was conducted concerning the amount, tone, and nature of the coverage. An assumption of this research is that coverage in the *Los Angeles Times* is an acceptable proxy measure of the total news coverage and inferences can be extrapolated from its content to the general news media. Using the *Los Angeles Times* index to identify stories, a 13-month content analysis of the *Los Angeles Times* from November 4, 1993 (the date the first story was noted) to September 22, 1994 (the date of the final included story) was undertaken. A total of 86 stories (75 news reports and 11 editorials) related to three-strikes legislation were found. Thirty-four stories dealt with the U.S. crime bill, which included a three-strikes provision; 52 reported on the California three-strikes bill. For the most part, the stories were extensive and prominent. They had a median length of 22 inches, and two out of five began on the front page. Twenty percent of them were run with accompanying pictures; relatively few had graphs or tables.

The stories were classified by their tone toward the three-strikes law, with 16 (19%) coded pro-passage (containing references to positive effects of passage only), 26 (30%) coded anti-three strikes (containing references to negative effects only), 34 (39%) coded as balanced (containing references to both positive and negative effects), and 10 (12%) coded as neutral (no references to effects; containing factual information only). The negative effects most frequently mentioned were costs (23 stories), prison crowding (12), and taxes (11). The most common positive effect mentioned was crime reduction, cited in 11 stories. The single element found most frequently was a reference to political campaigns, candidates, or general politics, found in 49, or 57%, of the stories.

Regarding the amount of coverage over time, over the entire 322 days between the first and last story, a story on either three strikes or the U.S. crime bill ran on average every 3.7 days. However, coverage is relatively sparse prior to January 1994, with most of the stories appearing after the passage of the California law on March 7, 1994. Fifty seven, or two thirds, of the stories appear following the enactment of the three-strikes law. The construction of reality theoretical perspective suggests that the coverage prior to enactment to be more significant in the construction process than coverage following enactment. The signing of the three-strikes bill into law is a construction breakpoint.

At that point, the claims-makers who have worked to construct a positive view of the law have succeeded in getting the law created, a major construction victory (the final step would occur 8 months later with the passage of Proposition 184 in the November election by 77% of the voters). With that in mind, the coverage prior to and following enactment is compared. Table 8.1 provides the descriptive details of the 86 stories and details differences in the preenactment and postenactment coverage.

As Table 8.1 indicates, prior to enactment there were fewer stories, and the tone of the stories was seldom positive toward three strikes but was equally distributed among anti, balanced, and neutral stories. Following enactment, total coverage increased from a preenactment average of a story every 4.5 days to one every 3.4 days. The proportion of positive stories regarding the three-strikes issue also increased significantly after the enactment of the California law, doubling from 11% to 22%. Even larger shifts are shown in the proportional decline in neutral stories and increase in balanced stories. These shifts in the tone of the coverage are even greater when news reports are examined separately from editorials. The proportion of news stories critical to three strikes increased from 22% to 29% following enactment. In sum, news reports after enactment were much less likely to be neutral, substantively more likely to be positive or balanced, and slightly more likely to be critical.

A further comparison of the pre- and postenactment coverage was conducted via a set of *t*-test comparisons. The two groups of stories were compared on their length and on the proportion mentioning the following issues (all coded as 1/0 dichotomies): cost, taxes, prison crowding, court crowding, crime reduction, and politics. For the pre- and postenactment comparisons, Table 8.2 reveals that postenactment stories were about 25% longer than preenactment stories and were significantly more likely to discuss the law's effect on taxes. Other factors were not significantly different.

A second area of interest in the social construction process involved distinctions between the coverage of the U.S. crime bill backed by President Clinton and the California three-strikes bill. Although the two bills overlapped in philosophy, due to the potential influence of local claims-makers it was hypothesized that construction efforts and media coverage for the California bill might be distinct from the

TABLE 8.1 *Los Angeles Times* Three-Strikes Reports, November 4, 1993-September 22, 1994						
	Total (N = 86) 322 Days		Preenactment (N = 27) 123 Days		Postenactment (N = 59) 199 Days	
	N	%	N	%	N	%
Type of report						
News report	75	87	23	85	52	88
Editorial	11	13	4	15	7	12
Coverage						
U.S. bill	34	39	6	22	28	47
California bill	52	61	21	78	31	53
Story features						
Front page	34	39	8	30	20	44
Pictures used	17	20	3	11	14	24
Graphs used	2	2	0	—	2	3
Tables used	7	8	0	—	7	12
Story tone						
Pro-three strikes	16	19	3	11	13	22
Anti-three strikes	26	30	8	30	18	31
Balanced	34	39	8	30	26	44
Neutral	10	12	8	30	2	3
Story content						
Increased cost	23	27	5	18	18	31
Increased taxes	11	13	0	—	11	19
Prison crowding	12	14	5	18	7	12
Court crowding	5	6	1	4	4	7
Reduced crime	11	13	3	11	8	14
Politics	49	57	18	67	31	53
Column inches	23		21		24	

federal bill. To test for differences, a set of *t*-test comparisons was run on the U.S. crime bill and California three-strikes story groups (see Table 8.3). Although the coverage of the California bill approaches statistical significance regarding its discussion of prison crowding, no significant differences emerged in the *t* tests comparing the coverage of the U.S. and California bills.

TABLE 8.2   Selected *t*-Test Comparisons, Pre- and Post-California
            Three-Strikes Enactment

Variable	N	Mean	t	df	Two-Tailed Probability
Length					
Pre	59	25.8	2.09	81.96	.039
Post	26	20.8			
Cost					
Pre	59	.305	1.23	58.64	.223
Post	27	.185			
Taxes					
Pre	59	.186	3.65	58.00	.001
Post	27	.000			
Prison crowding					
Pre	59	.118	−.76	42.81	.450
Post	27	.185			
Court crowding					
Pre	59	.067	.62	65.25	.537
Post	27	.037			
Crime reduction					
Pre	59	.135	.32	54.15	.750
Post	27	.111			
Politics					
Pre	59	.525	−1.25	52.75	.218
Post	27	.666			

However, when the tone of the stories prior to and following enactment were examined while controlling for whether a story was about the U.S. crime bill or the California three-strikes bill, some differences did emerge. Focusing on positive or negative stories, Table 8.4 reveals that the U.S. crime bill was much more likely to receive favorable coverage than the California crime bill. Of all the critical stories, nearly 81% of them were about the California bill.[5] Breaking out the tone of coverage of the U.S. crime bill and the California three-strikes law by pre- and postenactment coverage, the U.S. crime bill received significantly more positive coverage following enactment of the California three-strikes law. Indeed, there are no stories critical of the U.S. crime

TABLE 8.3 Selected *t*-test Comparisons, California Three-Strikes and
U.S. Crime Bill Stories

Variable	N	Mean	t	df	Two-Tailed Probability
Length					
U.S.	34	23.4	−.55	82.99	.587
California	51	24.8			
Cost					
U.S.	34	.323	.92	65.12	.360
California	52	.230			
Taxes					
U.S.	34	.176	1.03	57.87	.308
California	52	.096			
Prison crowding					
U.S.	34	.058	−.194	83.50	.055
California	52	.192			
Court crowding					
U.S.	34	.058	.02	69.98	.983
California	52	.057			
Crime reduction					
U.S.	34	.117	−.23	73.31	.819
California	52	.134			
Politics					
U.S.	34	.617	.72	71.72	.473
California	52	.538			

bill until after the signing into law of the California bill. On the other hand, the proportion of positive and negative coverage of the California three-strikes bill is similar prior to and following its March 1994 enactment. Last, the average length of time between stories about the U.S. crime bill was significantly longer prior to the enactment of the California three-strikes law, averaging a story every 20.5 days prior to enactment and a story every 7.1 days following. Comparatively, the time between stories focusing on the California three-strikes bill did not alter, averaging 5.9 days prior to and 6.4 days following enactment. The finding suggests that claims opposed to the California three-strikes law were more often reported, and in comparison, the federal crime bill fared better in the California media during this period.

TABLE 8.4 Cross-Tabulation Three-Strikes Bill by Report Tone

	Report Tone				
	Pro-Three Strikes	*Anti-Three Strikes*	*Balanced*	*Neutral*	*Row Total*
U.S. crime bill					
n	10	5	13	6	34
Row percentage	29.4	14.7	38.2	17.6	39.5
Column percentage	62.5	19.2	38.2	60.0	
California three strikes					
n	6	21	21	4	52
Row percentage	11.5	40.4	40.4	7.7	60.5
Column percentage	37.5	80.8	61.8	40.0	
Column total	16	26	34	10	86
Percentage	18.6	30.2	39.5	11.6	100.0

Chi-square value = 9.79; *df* = 3; significance = .02044.
Contingency coefficient = 3.19; significance = .020.
Cells with expected frequency <5: 1 of 8.

A final issue regarding the coverage is whether news reports, which are normally thought of as objective and factual, differed from editorials, which by definition are expressions of opinion. Although 44% of the news reports were either pro- or anti-three strikes, not surprisingly, the editorials were more partisan, with 82% either for or against three strikes. Only one editorial was found to be neutral, and just one was coded as balanced. And although more than half of the editorials (54%) were found to be critical of three strikes, whereas only 27% of the news stories were, this difference in proportions is not statistically significant for this sample due to the limited number of editorials. This difference does further support the general observation, however, that negative claims regarding three strikes outnumber positive claims, at least in quantity if not in effect. Reflecting the approaching state elections, news stories, however, were more likely to include a discussion of politics after enactment, increasing from 39% to 61% of the reports.

In summary, this initial content review suggests that total coverage increased as enactment approached. As the reality of three strikes neared, a flurry of critical, analytical stories appeared. This trend increased after the California three-strikes bill was enacted as stories containing graphs and tables were for the first time published (see Table 8.1). Coverage is also seen to be less critical of the U.S. crime bill than the California bill. In addition, attention to the California bill in terms of the amount of coverage actually dropped slightly from every 5.9 days to a story every 6.4 days on average after enactment, with a suggested shift of attention to the U.S. crime bill. Last, the analysis reveals that although there were some early stories critical of the three-strikes idea, the bulk of coverage (59%) prior to passage was neutral or balanced in nature. Most of the negative coverage immediately preceded and followed enactment (a few stories did appear just before the November vote on three strikes' Proposition 184). By the time of enactment, most observers felt that the issue was a fait accompli and that the social construction of three strikes as a needed response to violent crime was already assured (Gillam, 1994; Morain, 1994a).

Discussion

Three strikes is a prime example of the social construction of reality in criminal justice. Using the preexisting social construction of predator criminals in the entertainment and news media, three strikes demonstrates the role of claims-makers, competing claims, and symbolic campaigns in contemporary criminal justice policy formations. The three-strikes symbolic campaign was capped by the murder-kidnapping of Polly Klaas. Sadly, the passage of three strikes was assured the day Polly Klaas was kidnaped. Noting the effect of the Polly Klaas murder and other highly publicized violent crimes, it was said: "Last year, a similar bill could not get out of committee. But after several highly publicized crimes, and the onset of the election year, legislators are acting with unusual haste to show their support for tough crime laws" (Morain, 1994a, p. A1). The Polly Klaas murder became the reference event that was used to show that three strikes was needed, that its underlying model of relentless predatory criminality was valid, and that its message of out-of-control crime was true. Various claims-makers, most notably Governor Pete Wilson, advanced their construction of crime and justice reality on the foundation of the Polly Klaas murder. Eventually, the prison guard union also become a strong claims-maker group touting positive effects of the passage of the law on crime. The law's effect on the correctional systems would be a massive infusion of public money and a greatly expanded number of correctional personnel (Morain & Jacobs, 1994). Similar to the FBI and serial murder, the prison guard union thus stood to be the big winner from the creation of three strikes.[6] A second symbolic event was later created by Governor Wilson, who called an anticrime summit for February 1994. In the spirit of Daniel Boorstin (1961), this symbolic pseudo-event was an effort by Wilson to exert ownership over three strikes and the other punitive legislation that was racing toward passage.

Claims-makers involved in the three-strikes law, both for and against its passage, covered the political spectrum and involved a number of citizen groups, criminal justice professionals, and national experts. Examples of claims-makers included citizen groups such as Mad About Rising Crime—a nonprofit group founded by a couple whose 15-year-old son was killed in 1990 in a dispute over an electronic beeper. In addition, private citizens such as Mike Reynolds, a photographer whose 18-year-old daughter was murdered by a parolee outside a Fresno restaurant, led the drive to have three strikes placed on the ballot as a referendum. Reflecting the fact that critical coverage was more common than positive coverage, the claims of negative effects from the three-strikes law are numerous. Note, however, that the claims are published just before or after enactment and that many originate from claims-makers outside of California.

Positive claims are less numerous but have the advantage of aligning with the preexisting cultural view of predator crime. Ironically, the basic positive claim of a reduction in crime from three strikes was often left unstated, attesting to the powerful match between three strikes and the preexisting public conception of crime, its causes, and its solutions.

Of the three effect models derived from communication research (see the earlier section in this chapter), the model of simultaneous influence from external events and the news media is proposed as the most explanatory for the three-strikes phenomenon. In Washington and California, a series of horrible crimes by ex-offenders set the stage for the media coverage of both the crimes and the three-strikes initiatives. The media cannot be forwarded as the main cause of three strikes as the direct influence model would suggest. The critical coverage

1. The mandates result in irrationality, disparity and discrimination in the enforcement of criminal laws, and decrease certainty and deterrence in sentencing.

   American Bar Association spokesperson (Eaton, 1994, p. A3)

2. Three time loser laws eventually would make prisons look like nursing homes. We're going to have a nation with geriatric prisoners—comatose guys in oxygen tents—and nobody will be able to turn those guys loose until they die.

   Special counsel to National Legal and Defender Association (Eaton, 1994, p. A3)

3. Legal experts say harsh sentencing as urged by the governor could backfire and increase leniency in courts, judges would lack flexibility and jurors might balk at severe penalties.

   Unattributed (Dolan, 1994, p. A3)

4. There would be 17,000 additional jury trials a year, requiring 322 more judges at a cost of $276 million annually.

   Placer County superior court judge on behalf of the State Judicial Council (Morain, 1994b, p. A1)

5. Those charged with serious crimes will be far less likely to plead guilty because it would mean being that much closer to a life sentence. The consequences of pleading guilty are much greater.

   Assistant district attorney, Los Angeles County (Morain & Jacobs, 1994, p. A20)

6. Three strikes will almost certainly worsen the crime rate by forcing cuts to programs that help prevent crime, such as Head Start, medical care and job development.

   Executive vice president of the National Council on Crime and Delinquency (Morain & Jacobs, 1994, p. A18)

7. Another possible outcome is that younger and more violent prisoners who have not accrued "strikes" may be released more readily than older criminals who may be locked up for life. That possibility would actually result in a higher rate of serious crime.

   RAND (Colvin, 1994, p. A23)

Figure 8.1. Selected Claims Against Three Strikes

1. Wilson said similar fears have been voiced before the passage of other major crackdowns on crime and have been unfounded. Costs have been exaggerated because the estimates do not consider savings from a reduction in crime. Those behind bars cannot commit more crimes, and others on the streets might be deterred by fear of the longer sentences.

   Governor Pete Wilson (Morain & Jacobs, 1994, p. A1)

2. This is impacting the repeat offender—and that is the key, the guy who won't learn to adjust his behavior.

   Lobbyist, California Prison Guards Union (Morain & Jacobs, 1994, p. A20)

3. The new "three-strikes" law will provide five times more in savings than it will cost.

Figure 8.2. Selected Claims in Favor of Three Strikes

belies that conclusion, and the initial failed effort in Washington State showed that media attention alone could not trigger enactment. In Washington and California, galvanizing, highly publicized, external events were necessary for three strikes' success. What is important in the three-strikes case is that the events were amplified beyond regional effects throughout the nation by the media. In addition, the passage of three strikes generated the echo and anticipatory effects described earlier. Beginning with the Polly Klaas murder, an echo effect of close scrutiny of violent offenders in the California criminal justice system is indicated. There is also evidence of a three-strikes announcement effect whereby decision makers in the system began to alter their case-processing decisions immediately following the enactment of the law (Morain, 1994c; Weinstein, 1994).

The construction of three strikes also demonstrates the important role that the public sometimes plays in criminal justice policy and suggests a linear relationship between the public, the press, and policymakers. Doppelt and Manikas (1990), however, report that the public is often aroused by the media concerning a crime or justice issue, but legislators and criminal justice professionals will simply wait out the period of public arousal without instituting any policy changes. The 1991-1992 period in Washington State in which there was little legislative or criminal justice interest in the idea of three strikes despite public support exemplifies this more common, nonlinear relationship. The fact that the public was ignored for a number of years indicates that the additional goad of elections was needed. Within California, however, the public and particularly citizen-based claims-maker groups played a crucial role in the eventual passage of three strikes although a simple linear relationship between the three groups is again not an adequate model.

Three strikes appears like a lightning strike in the political world of criminal justice policy. Apparently unanticipated by criminal justice professionals, the supportive reasoning for three strikes is found in the historical arguments for the justice model in the 1970s and subsequent policies regarding the violent repeat offender (cf. Cavender, 1984). Three strikes and its boot camp and shock incarceration predecessors recycle similar rhetoric—a rhetoric and imagery of predatory criminality that originated largely in the entertainment media and now appears heavily in the news media (Surette, 1994). The increase in critical media coverage of three strikes just prior to enactment is impotent against the historic tide of violent, predatory media imagery, imagery that could not be counteracted at the last moment by analytical coverage. The California citizens simply ignored and discredited the negative claims. They would have none of it. The citizens of California (and likely the United States in general) are not willing to credit negative cost analysis, forecasts of nil or counterproductive effects, or arguments that such laws are unnecessary. In an electronic-dominated, visual media society, the massive emotional coverage of heinous crimes overwhelms any analytical coverage of legislation (Meyrowitz, 1985). In California, one immediate effect was a reported surge of crime-busting legislation even as figures showed that the number of reported crimes, including homicides, dropped 7.5% during the first 6 months of 1994 (Gladstone & Weintraub, 1994).

The concern is that the visual, visceral, electronic media have sped up the development, deliberation, and consideration process for policy to such an extent that criminal justice policy is formed and passed before the implications and ramifications are known, must less considered. This was not unrecognized in California. "The Legislature did not get into gear until a couple of tragedies that were well-covered in the press. It's a shame to have to be motivated by anecdotal, disparate events, but that seems to be the way they operate" (assistant attorney general, quoted in Gladstone & Weintraub, 1994, p. A1). And as the media have become more intrusive and encompassing, the policy-generating crimes will more often be distant but media-amplified crimes, crimes that are packaged by the media as representative of the local crime problem, eventually expanding to become part of our national policy. As one observer of the three-strikes phenomenon concluded: "In the predominant pattern of modern crime fighting in America, an idea from the grass roots that would do little about the nation's real crime problems nevertheless had captured the fancy of the nation's political leadership" (Gest, 1994, p. 9). We now have news and policy from nowhere.

In the end, three strikes marks what very likely will be the modern process of criminal justice policymaking. One California politician stated: "There is so much public pressure that proposed 'three strikes and you're out' anti-crime legislation will be passed and enacted without rational dialogue. The people are frightened, really frightened. Those kinds of horror stories wipe away rationality" (Assembly Speaker Willie Brown, quoted in Gillam, 1994, p. A3). If the three-strikes model persists and there is no reason to expect otherwise, contemporary criminal justice policy will more often be based on raw, emotionally driven opinion. Three strikes will stand as a harbinger of a new type of electronic criminal justice policy. The significance of this change lies in the distinction between raw opinion in the early stages of public debate on an issue, and later, responsible "public judgment" where the public has the opportunity to consider alternatives and payoffs (Yankelovich, 1994). Massive coverage of emotion-rending, horrible crimes spawns policy based solely on raw opinion. Laws like three strikes will be more often created and passed on a foundation of raw opinion, rather than public judgment, erupting into existence following tragic, heavily publicized crimes. Unthinkable crimes will procreate thoughtless policies.

Notes

1. These world models are analogous to the worldviews of George Gerbner and his colleagues (Gerbner & Gross, 1976; Gerbner, Gross, Jackson-Beech, Jeffries-Fox, & Signorielli, 1978; Gerbner, Gross, Morgan, & Signorielli, 1980; Gerbner, Gross, Signorielli, Morgan, & Jackson-Beech, 1979) or the cognitive maps referred to by Doris Graber (1980).

2. Lichter and Lichter (1983) found in a representative content study of television entertainment programming that murder, robbery, kidnapping, and aggravated assault make up 87% of all television crimes. Crime news is similarly composed largely of violent personal street crimes such as murder, rape, and assault, whereas more common offenses are notably underplayed (Best, 1989; Cavender & Bond-Maupin, 1993; Graber, 1980; Sheley & Ashkins, 1981).

3. Cavender and Bond-Maupin (1993) discuss similar ideas in terms of reality crime programming.

4. Jenkins (1994) contends that the FBI sought and received funding for its Behavioral Science Unit due to its ability to present itself as the best source to deal with a "new" serial homicide problem.

5. The difference also holds when only the news reports are compared. Of the news reports that were coded as either pro or anti the bills, 38% of the news reports of the U.S. crime bill were critical, whereas 75% of the reports about the California three-strikes law were (χ^2 is significant at the .035 level).

6. A final sad comment on this process is the eventual recognition of the symbolic use of Polly Klaas's murder by her father (Wilkie, 1994).

References

Adoni, H., & Mane, S. (1984). Media and the social construction of reality. *Communication Research, 11,* 323-340.

Austin, J., Jones, M., & Bolyard, M. (1993). *The growing use of jail boot camps: The current state of the art* (Research in Brief). Washington, DC: National Institute of Justice.

Barber, S. (1987). *News cameras in the courtroom.* Norwood, NJ: Ablex.

Becker, H. (1963). *Outsiders.* New York: Free Press.

Best, J. (Ed.). (1989). *Images of issues: Typifying contemporary social problems.* New York: Aldine de Gruyter.

Boorstin, D. (1961). *The image.* New York: Harper & Row.

Cavender, G. (1981). "Scared Straight": Ideology and the media. *Journal of Criminal Justice, 9,* 430-441.

Cavender, G. (1984). Justice, sanctioning, and the justice model. *Criminology, 22,* 203-213.

Cavender, G., & Bond-Maupin, L. (1993). Fear and loathing on reality television: An analysis of "America's Most Wanted" and "Unsolved Mysteries." *Sociological Inquiry, 63,* 305-317.

Cohen, A., Adoni, T., & Bantz, C. (1990). *Social conflict and television news.* Newbury Park, CA: Sage.

Colvin, R. (1994, September 22). 3 strikes found hobbled by enormous prison costs. *Los Angeles Times,* pp. A1, A23.

Cook, T., Kendzierski, D., & Thomas, S. (1983). The implicit assumptions of television research: An analysis of the 1982 NIMH report on television and behavior. *Public Opinion Quarterly, 47,* 161-201.

Cook, T., Tyler, T., Goetz, E., Gordon, M., Protess, D., Leff, D., & Molotch, H. (1983). Media and agenda-setting: Effects on the public, interest group leaders, policy makers, and policy. *Public Opinion Quarterly, 47,* 16-35.

Cromer, G. (1978). Character assassination in the press. In C. Winick (Ed.), *Deviance and the mass media* (pp. 225-241). Beverly Hills, CA: Sage.

Dolan, M. (1994, January 7). Critics dissect Wilson anti-crime plan. *Los Angeles Times,* p. A3.

Doppelt, J., & Manikas, P. (1990). Mass media and criminal justice decision making. In R. Surette (Ed.), *The media and criminal justice policy* (pp. 129-142). Springfield, IL: Charles C Thomas.

Duffee, D. (1980). *Explaining criminal justice.* Cambridge, MA: Oelgeschlager, Gunn & Hain.

Eaton, W. (1994, January 25). 3-time loser bill a political winner, but critics abound. *Los Angeles Times,* p. A3.

Egan, T. (1994, February 15). A 3-strike penal law shows it's not as simple as it seems. *New York Times,* p. A1.

Elias, R. (1986). *The politics of victimization.* New York: Oxford University Press.

Gans, H. (1988). *Middle American individualism.* New York: Free Press.

Gerbner, G., & Gross, L. (1976). Living with television: The violence profile. *Journal of Communication, 26,* 173-199.

Gerbner, G., Gross, L., Jackson-Beech, M., Jeffries-Fox, S., & Signorielli, N. (1978). Cultural indicators: Violence profile no. 9. *Journal of Communication, 29,* 176-207.

Gerbner, G., Gross, L., Morgan, M., & Signorielli, N. (1980). The mainstreaming of America: Violence profile no. 11. *Journal of Communication, 30,* 10-29.

Gerbner, G., Gross, L., Signorielli, N., Morgan, M., & Jackson-Beech, M. (1979). The demonstration of power: Violence profile no. 10. *Journal of Communication, 29,* 177-196.

Gergen, K. (1985). Social constructionist inquiry: Context and implications. In K. Gergen & K. Davis (Eds.), *The social construction of the person* (pp. 1-18). New York: Springer-Verlag.

Gest, T. (1994, February 7). Reaching for a new fix to an old problem. *U.S. News & World Report,* p. 9.

Gillam, J. (1994, March 2). Legislators fear public on "3 strikes," Brown says. *Los Angeles Times,* p. A3.

Gladstone, M., & Weintraub, D. (1994, September 6). Flood of anti-crime bills unprecedented, state officials say. *Los Angeles Times,* pp. A1, A14.

Gordon, M., & Heath, L. (1981). The news business, crime and fear. In D. Lewis (Ed.), *Reaction to crime* (pp. 227-250). Beverly Hills, CA: Sage.

Graber, D. (1980). *Crime news and the public.* New York: Praeger.

Jenkins, P. (1988). Myth and murder: The serial killer panic of 1983-85. *Criminal Justice Research Bulletin, 3*(11), 1-3.

Jenkins, P. (1994). *Using murder: The social construction of serial homicide.* New York: Aldine.

Kappeler, V., Blumberg, M., & Potter, G. (1993). *The mythology of crime and criminal justice.* Prospect Heights, IL: Waveland.

Lichter, L., & Lichter, S. (1983). *Prime time crime.* Washington, DC: Media Institute.

Meyrowitz, J. (1985). *No sense of place.* New York: Oxford University Press.

Morain, D. (1994a, February 1). Three strikes bills sweep state assembly. *Los Angeles Times,* pp. A1, A18.

Morain, D. (1994b, March 1). Costs to soar under 3 strikes plan, study says. *Los Angeles Times,* pp. A1, A16.

Morain, D. (1994c, March 9). Citing "3 strikes," lawyers to shun plea bargains. *Los Angeles Times,* pp. A1, A15.

Morain, D. (1994d, April 3). Wilson adviser says "3 strikes" will save money. *Los Angeles Times,* pp. A1, A18.

Morain, D., & Jacobs, P. (1994, March 8). Measure is no guarantee of cut in violence. *Los Angeles Times,* pp. A1, A20.

Page, B., Shapiro, R., & Dempsey, G. (1987). What moves public opinion? *American Political Science Review, 81,* 23-43.

Pritchard, D. (1986). Homicide and bargained justice: The agenda-setting effect of crime news on prosecutors. *Public Opinion Quarterly, 50,* 143-159.

Pritchard, D., Dilts, J., & Berkowitz, D. (1987). Prosecutors' use of external agendas in prosecuting pornography cases. *Journalism Quarterly, 64,* 392-398.

Scheingold, S. (1984). *The politics of law and order.* New York: Longman.

Schneider, J. (1985). Social problems theory: The constructionist view. *Annual Review of Sociology, 11,* 209-229.

Sechrest, D. (1994). Prison "boot camps" do not measure up. *Federal Probation, 53*(3), 15-20.

Sheley, J., & Ashkins, C. (1981). Crime, crime news, and crime views. *Public Opinion Quarterly, 45,* 492-506.

Skolnick, J. (1995). What not to do about crime. *Criminology, 33*(1), 1-14.

Stroman, C., & Seltzer, R. (1985). Media use and perceptions of crime. *Journalism Quarterly, 62,* 340-345.

Surette, R. (1989). Media trials. *Journal of Criminal Justice, 17,* 293-308.

Surette, R. (1992a). *Media crime and criminal justice: Images and realities.* Pacific Grove, CA: Brooks/Cole.

Surette, R. (1992b). Methodological problems in determining media effects on criminal justice: A review and suggestions for the future. *Criminal Justice Policy Review, 6,* 311-332.

Surette, R. (1994). Predator criminals as media icons. In G. Barak (Ed.), *Media, process, and the social construction of crime* (pp. 131-158). New York: Garland.

Weinstein, H. (1994, November 11). 3 strikes-spawned crush of cases crowds out civil suits. *Los Angeles Times,* pp. A1, A30, A31.

Wilkie, D. (1994, October 21). Polly's slaying now just politics? *San Diego Union-Tribune,* pp. A1, A25.

Yankelovich, D. (1994, September 17). What polls say—and what they mean. *New York Times,* pp. B1, B3.

Zucker, H. (1978). The variable nature of news media influence. In B. Ruben (Ed.), *Communication yearbook* (pp. 225-240). New Brunswick, NJ: Transaction Books.

Chapter Nine

Street Gangs and Deterrence Legislation

MALCOLM W. KLEIN

As events turned out, I think we must assume that the victim was not very bright and certainly not very sophisticated about gang matters despite his age (32) and his membership in the Varrio Segundo street gang.[1] On the rough border of two rival gangs, he was found alone, drunk, on foot, by several members of the Latins gang cruising in their van. Two of the Latins left the van and battered the Varrio Segundo member, and it should have been enough to send him scurrying back to protected surroundings. But unfortunately, it was not.

The Latins youth next went to a large barrio party where the booze was plentiful, as were other Latins members. The story of the beating of the lone Varrio Segundo boy took on the character of a brazen territorial invasion as it was retold several times. This time, a truck pulled out from the party in search of the victim. And there he was, still unaccountably available although by now, in V. S. territory. This

AUTHOR'S NOTE: I am grateful to Michael Genelin, Cheryl Maxson, and the editors of this volume for their comments on an early draft.

time, the Latins identified themselves as fellow Varrio Segundo members, concerned that the victim should not be wandering about on party night. "C'mon, *ese,* we're Varrio Segundo like you—we'll take you home." The victim likely had never seen these *carnales* before, because Varrio Segundo numbered in the hundreds and had many subgroups as is common among traditional Hispanic gangs, so he readily joined his new friends—after all, they had the right look about them, and they flashed the Varrio Segundo hand signs readily.

He had less than a half hour to reconsider. They drove around briefly, cruised by the party, where the victim was beaten again, and then headed out of the area and pulled over to the curb near an alley. While the driver remained by the truck, the three other suspects led the victim into the alley and beat him severely. Then they doused him with gasoline and lit it. The autopsy revealed that it was the conflagration, not the beating, that was the immediate cause of death.

The three alley assailants found themselves in a capital case, later reduced to life without possibility of parole, and the prosecution had a good case against them. But the attorney who approached me for expert testimony had the driver of the truck as his sole client. It was stipulated by all concerned that he had not been in the alley, nor could he see the event as it took place; he remained behind the wheel. The prosecution wanted the life sentence for him as well; the defense attorney, new to gang cases, turned to the author for help.

Before going further, I urge the reader to close this book for a moment to consider the situation of the driver/client. Is he guilty of first-degree murder?

There are two elements to the case of direct importance to this essay. The first is legal; the second, social psychological. The legal issue was posed by the prosecution with the backing of case law: If the driver knew that a "natural and probable consequence" of a gang assault is a homicide, then he can share full responsibility for the homicide. The phrase "natural and probable consequence" comes from a 1979 case, *People v. Montano,* and a 1992 opposite finding in *People v. Godinez.* The issue is specific to gang cases and opens the door to enhanced sentencing available to gang members under California law.

The social psychological issue has to do with group processes in the gang setting—gang dynamics, if you will. First, how common is it for a gang to kidnap a rival member from outside its own territory, bring him back into that territory, "display" him openly to partying friends, and then kill him? Are the gang dynamics sufficiently strong and predictable in such cases? Second, how likely is it that an assault by gang members will result in death? Is this "typical" gang behavior? Should the driver have known the outcome ahead of time?

The prosecution's expert witness testified with an unequivocal yes to both questions—such incidents were known to him, and the driver should have known that the natural and probable consequence would be the death of the victim. The expert witness was a member of a police gang unit and had familiarity with both Varrio Segundo and the Latins. His opinion, as is commonly true of police gang unit members, would carry much weight in a gang trial.

The defense expert witness, this author, provided contrary evidence. Based on intimate contact with a number of traditional gangs in prior years, but not with the Varrio Segundo or the Latins, I reported the incident to be so rare as to defy prediction. As to the "natural and probable consequence" argument, I presented data showing that *reported* gang assaults resulted in death in about 6% of cases, and of course the percentage would be far smaller if one considered nonreported assaults as well; that is, the resultant homicide was empirically neither natural nor probable.

It is not the outcome, but the issues, that I emphasize here. They are relevant to the effect of three-strikes laws on street gangs because three strikes is but one among many new pieces of suppressive legislation being brought to bear on gang members. The California Legislative Analyst's Office has provided a preliminary assessment of the effects of the state's three-strikes law (Esparza, 1995). In reviewing it, I am impressed by how little it is likely to add to the current deterrent and suppressive approach to street gangs. Indeed, it is likely to have less effect on gang offenders than on perhaps any other category of persons.

The reasons have to do with (a) the nature of deterrence as enacted in suppressive laws like three strikes, (b) the nature of group dynamics as played out in the gang setting, and (c) the interaction between these. In the case cited above of the Latins's attack on the Varrio Segundo victim, it is difficult to see how deterrence legislation was somehow going to penetrate into the dynamics of the event sequence that led to the homicide. The rationality underlying a suspect's perceiving the natural and probable consequence of any one early act in the escalating sequence of acts is hard to accept: It requires deliberate planning and intent not common to many gang assaults and on which deterrence propositions depend. Thus, the remainder of this chapter reviews the issues of deterrence and of gang dynamics, and then illustrates the problems of both in a series of additional court cases where, after all, the utility of criminal legislation finally is tested.

Deterrence

Various chapters in this book speak to the components of deterrence theory, the notions that presumably underlie the three-strikes laws and others similarly designed both to incapacitate charged offenders and to deter criminal acts by would-be offenders.[2] If certainty, severity, and swiftness of punishment are the three best known prongs of deterrence, it is clear that most suppressive legislation adds little to these. Severity is increased for second and third strikes, as is certainty that the severity will be applied. But the severity principally takes the form of belated incapacitation, which applies only weakly to *general* deterrence, the effect on would-be offenders: Incapacitation is an event of the distant future, seldom salient in the gang offender's mind at the point of an assault. Certainty of punishment is only slightly increased, because these laws do nothing to affect the likelihood of detection, apprehension, and court conviction, which precede punishment. Nor is swiftness of punishment materially altered.

Another aspect of effective punishment, long recognized by psychologists but seldom acknowledged by proponents of deterrence, is the provision or encouragement of alternative behavior. If the experimental rat is punished for going down the wrong path but not rewarded for choosing a preferred path, it learns poorly what is expected of it. If the student is punished for habitual truancy from school but not shown ways in which regular attendance can be rewarding, he or she is not likely to reform. No suppressive legislation known to me combines punishment or its threat with any form of swift or certain and equally rewarding alternatives, positively valued behavior, or situations to compete with the rewards of crime. The law taketh away, but giveth naught.

There are yet more subtle aspects of deterrence theory and research. Studies suggest that certainty, severity, and swiftness are of unequal value, with severity of far less value—yet severity is the component most stressed by the new suppressive legislation. It also appears to be the most visible and politically rewarding of these three components. Studies also suggest that it is the would-be offender's *perception* of certainty, severity, and swiftness that is more effective than the absolute level of each.[3] Again, I know of almost no deterrence legislation that specifically attempts to increase offenders' awareness of increased certainty, severity, and swiftness. The publicity attendant on three-strikes legislation has that effect, of course, but it was hardly planned that way; the publicity was more politically inspired. Similarly, federal and state RICO (Racketeer Influenced and Corrupt Organizations [Act]) statutes have become well known to professional drug traffickers through some deliberate publicity, but this probably fails to reach the bulk of the street-dealing offenders.

An explicit exception to this absence of attention to perceived deterrence comes in the case of California's Street Terrorism Enforcement and Prevention (STEP) act to which I will refer a bit later. This attention resulted from legal necessities rather than deterrence reasoning, but it exists nonetheless and is worth specification.

There are still other subtleties. These apply with particular relevance to the gang members whose situation I address in this chapter. For instance, the source or applier of sanctions must be seen as *credible* by the would-be offender. Many criminals, and most street gang members, seriously question the integrity and believability of the police who promise to crack down on them, or the courts who promise to commit them. Similarly, the source must have perceived legitimacy. For many offenders and most gang members, police and prosecutors and courts are suspect as bureaucratic, ineffective, unfair, and racist. The message of deterrence is weakened when it comes from perceptually tarnished sources.

Finally, of critical importance in the gang setting is the issue of countermessages. The promise of deterrence, if unchallenged, may yield some measurable effect. But if it is countered by credible alternative messages, then by inoculation or rebuttal, it is weakened. Much of the banter that features gang member interaction results from what Moore and Vigil (1989) call the "oppositional culture" of the gang.

Police are ridiculed, probation and parole officers demeaned, and laws denigrated in the self-reinforcing peer culture of the gang. Bravado replaces rationality, and exploits in escaping the reach of the law are emphasized far more than the occasional (noncertain), slow (nonswift) sanctions, which are then used in the distorting gang culture to build personal "rep" in the group. The gang dynamic manipulates messages of attack by the law and the justice system to feed the special gang culture and reinforce gang cohesiveness. Effective antigang legislation must come to grips with this self-protective, discounting process within the street gang; increased levels of suppression are counterproductive.

A recent interim report on three-strikes effects in California (from the Legislative Analyst's Office, January 6, 1995) emphasizes five trends seen to date: (a) already, thousands of offenders have been charged; (b) system overload is increasing due to refusals to plead guilty; (c) financial resources are being drained and civil cases postponed; (d) various actors in the justice system are finding ways to circumvent the law's intent; and (e) most offenders are being handled for "nonviolent, nonserious offenses." This is not a picture of effective general deterrence in action. Certainty, severity, and swiftness are not being potentiated; credibility of the system is being undermined; the legitimacy of the system is open to corrosion—the opportunity for countermessages becomes obvious.

However, three strikes was not aimed specifically at street gangs, so we can look at other suppression laws that were, to see if they are more likely to yield deterrence. They fall under three general headings.

The first of these are statutes aimed at behavior said (usually correctly) to be more associated with gang than nongang offenders. These include witness intimidation, victim intimidation, use of "rock" or crack houses, graffiti writing, and drive-by shootings. More questionably related to gangs and subjected to special attention are possession or use of automatic weapons and drug sale or distribution. In most of these laws, only severity of punishment is increased, either by turning misdemeanors into felonies or by increasing sentences following conviction (Jackson & Rudman, 1993).

Other statutes are more often but not exclusively civil in nature. Some strengthen existing civic codes to apply more directly to gangs' use of real estate, cars, and other elements of the drug trade. Others take the form of specific injunctions against a wide variety of behaviors in which gang members may engage—carrying certain tools, beepers, items with both illegal and legal applications (marbles, "slim jims"); gang-related dress styles; hand signals; and so on. Often included as well are special curfews, forbidden associates, and presence at specified public spaces such as parks, playgrounds, and malls. Notorious instances in southern California (injunctions against the Playboy Gangster Crips and the Blythe Street Gang) and others have generally beaten off court appeals, although one in Orange County failed on constitutional grounds and another in San Jose is on its way to the state supreme court as this is written.

The third category of suppressive laws is based more directly on one's membership in a gang. Several decades ago, a criminal charge of "gang membership" or "gang activity" was generally ruled to be unconstitutionally vague. New legislation of this sort, such as the STEP acts to be described, are more careful to avoid this vagueness, but at a cost to the empirical facts of gang membership. Constitutional and civil rights issues remain alive.

A comprehensive view of defense issues in gang-related court cases has been provided by Burrell (1990). The Los Angeles District Attorney has, with others, completed a guide for the successful prosecution of gang cases (Genelin & Naiman, 1988). Destro (1993) has offered a review and critique of the civil rights issues involved in antigang legislation. Thus, the legal issues are well articulated and available to scholar and practitioner alike. My own take on all this is different because the legislative, defense, and prosecutorial views are framed for the court case, not the street. As I understand gangs, these legalistic views are oddly at variance with gang life, with what leads to or is involved in gang crime.

This is why I led off this chapter with the case of the Latins versus Varrio Segundo. I was called in as an expert witness by the defense. But with the jury out of the courtroom, and following extensive testimony about my expertise and reputation, the judge ruled that my testimony was inadmissible. Acknowledging my *generic* expertise, he ruled that whereas the prosecution's expert—a police gang unit officer—had specific knowledge of the two gangs involved, I did not because I had never studied them. The logic is striking, being as I read it contrary to both the Evidence Code (720a) and the Kelly-Frye test (Burrell, 1990, p. 772). In any city with gang units in the police force, the judge's view would allow expert witness testimony to the prosecution, but not to the defense. That, at least, is the unanimous view of attorneys with whom I have discussed this case. Again, legalistic evidence is divorced from empirical evidence.

Gang Dynamics

This disparity between legal and social science evidence is nicely raised by the best known piece of antigang legislation, the STEP act. Later copied in other states, the STEP act (a) carefully defines a "criminal street gang," (b) specifies a set of serious criminal behaviors to be invoked in its application, (c) specifies a procedure by which the court may declare a group to be a "criminal street gang," and (d) spells out how a member, properly notified beforehand, may be subjected to enhanced sentencing (i.e., increased severity) on conviction for a new crime following such notification. It is a neat package that studiously avoids social science knowledge about gangs; I know this because I spelled it out for the act's principal framer during the initial stages of bringing the proposed legislation to the state capital. Major concerns include the following:

- The term *criminal street gang* was invented to avoid the ambiguity that exists in reality about the definition of many gangs for whom criminal activity may not be a major focus.
- Such a group is defined as three or more persons, whereas no self-respecting criminologist would apply the term so broadly.
- The act refers to people joining a gang because of their knowledge of its criminal nature, whereas many young joiners are engaged primarily for needs of status, identity, and peer companionship, as well as in many instances for the perceived protection a gang offers.
- The set of crimes specified, although serious, is the minority of crimes actually committed by gang members, who are far more versatile in their behaviors than prosecutors ever see (Klein, 1984).
- The gang has "as one of its primary activities" the commission of the listed serious felonies, whereas in fact group commission of such serious felonies is rarely *if ever* a primary activity of street gangs.

These and other disjunctures between legal provisions and behavioral realities mean (a) law enforcement will often miss its mark in applying the law; (b) inaccurate depictions of gangs will become widespread, further decreasing deterrent credibility; and (c) numerous defense challenges will needlessly be upheld, once defense attorneys cotton to the inaccuracies in the law.

The STEP act does, however, contain one element directly related to deterrence propositions. When the court approves a proposed injunction and a specific gang is STEPped (as the phrase now goes), deputy attorneys and police then personally give written notice to named members of the gang, acknowledging their specific membership and indicating the consequences of future specified behaviors. Here, severity is combined with increased certainty, and the notification, it is hoped, penetrates the perceptual world of that gang member. He now becomes at risk, not just through the diffuse maze of gang membership but at a most direct, individual level. With all the gangs that have been STEPped over the past few years, the pity is that no independent research has been undertaken to assess the effect. Prosecutors' testimony of effectiveness is simply not adequate. If STEP has found a way to individuate gang members for deterrence purposes, then such a crack in dynamics might help the social scientist to educate the lawyer about the street-level character of the street gang.

Perhaps we can further that process by explicating some of the misconceptions about gangs that can mislead well-meaning and other attempts at gang control. In general, these misconceptions follow the stereotypes of fictional or media accounts of gang nature—strong, tough leadership, hierarchical structure, monolithic form, high cohesiveness, codes of loyalty to group and community, commitment to violence, and a secret culture of dress and argot. Such characteristics, if common, would indeed justify special investigative techniques and special laws (such as RICO statutes) and would confirm the view of many enforcement officials that street gangs are perfect mechanisms for the distribution and control of large quantities of street drugs. But with relatively few exceptions, most street gangs in most cities are a far cry from this depiction. In fact, there are only two major generalizations that may fairly describe the majority of street gangs (see Klein, 1995, chap. 2):

■ Street gangs are generally distinguishable *as a category* from most other associated groups, including drug gangs, prison gangs, hate gangs, and numerous peer groups that dabble in crime and delinquency.

■ Street gangs nonetheless manifest a wide degree of variability in structure and behavior, making a clear definition and depiction highly suspect.

Leadership in street gangs tends to be age related. Thus, if a street gang is of the "traditional" form with several age-graded subgroups, each subgroup will contain its own leadership. In many gangs, older leaders do not or cannot call the shots for their younger brethren.

Furthermore, group leadership may reflect a number of valued characteristics. Toughness is certainly one of these, but only one. Members may also gain leadership status (formal or informal) via verbal acuity, athletic prowess, criminal daring or skill, or social skills. An excess of violent talk or behavior can, in fact, cause loss of respect.

Finally, gang leadership is often short term due to member turnover, group instability, and challenges from other members. The commonly held notion that arresting and incarcerating gang "leaders" will eviscerate the gang structure has seldom been supported in practice. Gang leadership is as much functional as it is structural: Bust me, and my "homie" steps in. Suppressive laws and practices that do successfully put away leaders will have little effect on overall gang structures. One of my prosecution colleagues points out that the three-strikes law applied to violent gang leaders is of little use because the severity of the offense alone is generally enough to do the trick; most of his cases, he reports, are first or second felonies with long sentences in any case.

The monolithic form of gangs portrayed in the media is highly misleading. Several researchers (Fagan, 1989; Skolnick, 1991; Taylor, 1989) have recently offered typologies of street gangs based on typical behavior patterns and structures. Research with my own colleagues, based on data from more than 200 cities, suggests a rather comprehensive structural package of five street gang forms, ranging from the traditional, age-graded subgroup cluster described by Miller and by Short and Strodtbeck in the 1960s to the entrepreneurial gangs proposed by Skolnick and others in the 1980s. These five forms are loosely but not predictably related to such factors as ethnicity, internal (subgroup) structure, crime pattern, size, recency of formation, and characteristics of the host city. Legislation and practice that assume homogeneity of gang structures cannot help but be inefficiently applied at best.

Cohesiveness of gangs, similarly, is generally thought to be high. In fact, however, it is quite variable across gangs and seldom high for any sustained period. Because intermember bonding is terribly important to many gang members, attempts at gang suppression will often have a boomerang effect. Gang members under pressure will turn that pressure into cohesion-building material: Increase the pressure, increase the cohesion. Thus, the most effective legislative approach is to target the individual, not the group. The laws for this are already on the books.

Codes of loyalty to gang or neighborhood do indeed exist, in rhetoric and in fact. But they tend to be overstated, often dissipating under individual threat. Most police gang officers, for instance, find that they can "turn" individual members (i.e., get them to serve as informants on fellow gang members) to avoid police or court sanctions. The kind of loyalty required for successful drug distribution rings is less often found in the street gang, making statutes such as RICO superfluous in the street gang setting.

Commitment to violence, taken literally, is characteristic of few gang members. Commitment to *claims* of violence, to *talking* about violence, even to a *belief* in the legitimacy of violence, are common. But it is a long step from attitude to act. Most gang behavior, like that of most police, lawyers, and criminologists, is pro-social and inconsequential. Gang member crime and delinquency is important but occupies relatively little time. And within that time, violent behavior is far less common than theft, vandalism, public disorder, status offenses, and so on. Many gang members, more than most of us, become oriented to violent activity, but seldom committed to it; "the violent gang" is generally a misnomer although there are plenty of gang members whose violent acts merit individual law enforcement responses.

Gang culture in earlier decades was quite observable and distinctive. Special dress, body adornments, street slang, hand signals, graffiti, and the like rather clearly signaled "gang" to the persistent or even casual observer. Nowadays, however, gang culture is inextricably intermixed with more widespread youth culture—rap, hip-hop, all the manifestations of dress in the Gap or on MTV. Special legislation and court injunctions aimed at baggy pants, high-top shoes, Raiders caps, belt buckles, colors, and hand signals cast a wide net over a host of gang and nongang youth. My next-door neighbor's boy "looks gang," but is on his way to play basketball at the University of Oregon.

Federal law enforcement officials, and selected local police (but by no means all), share with me a fascination with the emergence of drug gangs. But whereas their interest is in the equation of drug gang with street gang, mine has been just the opposite, in the differentiation between the two. Fueled by a few academic writers (Skolnick, 1991; Taylor, 1989), many in law enforcement see drug and street gang as inseparable, as being a single category and therefore properly the subject of state and interstate statutes based on conspiracy theories. Street gangs involve themselves in a wide variety of crimes; drug gangs are far more focused in their criminal pursuits.

Yet every bit of independent evidence my colleagues and I have been able to adduce suggests that (a) drug gangs are but one form of crime specialty gangs, (b) they comprise a small percentage of all gangs and are not found in most gang-involved cities, and (c) structurally they differ enough from other gang forms that they should call forth special control efforts. Those efforts, of the sort well within the repertoire of federal agents and local narcotics officers, are not usefully applied, however, to most forms of street gangs and may instead increase the cohesiveness of street gangs. Caveat emptor (Klein, 1995, chap. 1; also see Decker's 1995 review).

One point of amplification is important: I agree with writers like Skolnick and Taylor that drug distribution gangs are more rationally oriented than street gangs. They are in the marketplace and tend to adopt reasoned practices to protect and expand those markets. A good ethnographic depiction of such a group is provided by Padilla (1992). But this level of rationality, also assumed in most antigang legislation and civil injunctions, applies far less readily to the informal interpersonal dynamics of most street gangs (whether members sell drugs or not). Street gang crime tends to be more impulsive, poorly planned, and based on very short-term goals and assessments of risk. Street gangs normally are not up to the sustained, rational planning and conspiracy demanded of them by deterrence adherents. Furthermore, many street gang members are not committed to the same mores as those on which our rational legislation is based.

Gang Issues in Court Cases

I turn now to a series of court cases, a context in which the "gang relatedness" of events has direct, practical significance. The cases I use as illustration are of two general sorts, those that show antigang deterrence legislation at work and those that involve some aspect of gang dynamics. Most of these are homicide cases, the ones so serious that defense attorneys are desperate enough to turn to an academic for help, usually after they have decided the weight of evidence against their clients is overwhelming. Homicide cases are also the ones with the greatest concentration of prosecutorial expertise and commitment to gang suppression capacities; this in turn brings the defense to the academic door to counter the mounting armament against their gang member clients.

As noted in the Varrio Segundo versus Latins case, prosecutors have effective expert witnesses, usually in the form of police officers who are members of special gang units or, failing that, have nonetheless become streetwise about particular gangs. In most courts, it is not difficult to get the judge to stipulate that these gang cops are experts in the gang arena. Once accepted as experts, these officers then carry considerable weight with juries and judges. How does the defense counter such expertise?

Until recently, with the publication of Susan Burrell's (1990) treatise on gang case defense, they had no decent literature to use. And most of the "experts" are wearing police uniforms. Thus, defense attorneys had at their disposal little information to forestall the consequences of new gang suppression legislation. Increasingly, attorneys have turned to research scholars to counter the effect of the prosecution's witnesses. In my own case, I have been approached in the past few years to consult in several dozen cases. Two dozen of these have never made more use of me than one phone call or visit because my testimony would have been harmful to the defense. In most of these cases, attorneys were looking for someone to say that growing up in a gang neighborhood *compelled* one to join the local gang. Or they wanted testimony that being a gang member *compelled* one to participate in the criminal incidents at hand. But such is simply not the case. Most neighborhood youths do not join their local gangs, and those who do can often opt out of an impending incident. Group *pressure,* often strong, is still not *necessity.* Free will is still to be found in the gang.

Most of my other case involvements have led to plea bargains, sometimes because of my advice but usually for more compelling reasons. In these cases, what I have been able to do is help the defense prepare its questioning of the prosecution's expert witness, the gang cop: For example, what gang literature has he read? What differences can he describe between black, Hispanic, and Asian gangs? How does he distinguish between core and fringe membership? What does he know of gang leadership? In several cases, this has been enough to bargain out the case because the prosecution's expert turns out to be rather limited.

Gang Suppression Cases

An arson case following a drug sales homicide of two buyers. Did the arsonist's act in the later torching of the victims' car emanate from an affiliation with the gang members who committed the killings, and thereby justify an enhanced sentence for the arsonist?

Conspiracy in homicide. Following a schoolground fight, two rival gangs agreed to meet at a local park to continue the action. The defendant, a fringe gang member and a spectator in both events, was present when the continuation at the park ended in mutual gunfire and a death. Although cleared of active involvement, could he legitimately be charged with conspiracy to commit murder because he had foreknowledge of the event and its violent implications due to his gang membership? Note the similarity to the Varrio Segundo/Latins case.

A federal drug case. Following extensive undercover work, a group of drug dealers was arrested under federal statutes. The prosecution wished to demonstrate that the dealers were members of a long-standing street gang, and thus subject to more serious charges of complicity, conspiracy, and violence. The defense was attempting to separate any evidence of prior gang membership as an issue immaterial to current and different criminal activity. This was to be a test case of new conspiracy statutes making gang membership a key ingredient of both adjudication and penalty decisions.

A codefendant in the Reginald Denny beating that resulted from the not-guilty verdicts given to the officers who beat Rodney King. The issue here was not motive, but simply whether this man could be certified as a gang member, thereby increasing the severity of the sentence options. The reader may recall in this case that the principal police expert was revealed to be under internal investigation, leading to his withdrawal from the case and reduced interest in pursuing the gang angle.

The shooter in a robbery of auto parts. The issue was not guilt, but penalty as affected by gang membership; that is, is being a gang member pertinent to the likelihood of murder resulting from an otherwise normal robbery? If so, a more severe sentence was available.

Gang Dynamics Cases

The shooter in a drive-by killing. A fringe member of an out-of-state gang, he was enticed into the incident by local gang members even though he had only very recently moved in. He readily and shamefully admitted his role. The issue was whether to try him in juvenile court or remand him to adult court. My reading of the case materials strongly suggested his best hope for straightening out—he had some marketable skills—was in the juvenile system, but he was remanded to adult court because he was within months of his 18th birthday. All other personal characteristics and gang relationship were deemed immaterial by the judge, including my conclusions about his fringe relationship to the gang.

A double homicide by knife attack. In the adjudication phase, the question was whether gang affiliation of the assailants contributed to what seemed like a simple escalation of an argument over purchasing liquor for the juvenile attackers. Does gang membership contribute to escalation and therefore to culpability?

A drive-by shooting between two cars, resulting in death. For the fringe member juvenile (age 16) who was driving and felt threatened by the other driver, was there a reasonable self-defense claim based on a gang-related assessment of imminent threat because of his under-standing of drive-by challenge norms?

A drive-by shouting (not shooting) that in time did lead to an escalated argument. In this setting of a verbal confrontation between four mem-bers of one gang and three of another, a one-on-one fistfight ended when a fringe gang member pulled a gun from his shoe and killed his prone and beaten antagonist. The gang issue had to do with conflicting evidence about the level of gang membership of the defendant, because this related to the presence of other gang members at the scene. Was the presence of his homies a contributor to his state of mind that led to the killing?

A one-on-one fistfight that ended when a gang member witness went to the aid of his homeboy and fatally shot the other fighter. The defense attorney in this instance wanted to show that the shooter's actions derived from his emotional commitment to his gang peers. In this case, the shooter's mother reported that her 17-year-old son had all but abandoned his family home. The argument was that the gang had become the sub-stitute family.

A carjacking in which gang members shot and paralyzed a 21-year-old car club member. This was a civil case in which the plaintiff sued the management of the emporium and its parking lot in which the event took place, claiming they were in a known gang area and should have provided adequate security measures. At issue was whether the nature of gang activity would have prevented the event in the presence of security guards; it is not merely the presence of guards, but how this might *interact* with the nature of gang behavior.

The motiveless gang killing. This was an odd case in which a fringe member well known to his gang peers was accused of shooting and killing a "retired" core member of the same gang following a party. Identification of the purported shooter was inconclusive; events at the party provided no clear motive, nor did anything else. Forensic evidence also was inconclusive. The defense argument was that there was no reason, in the nature of gang dynamics, for a well-known fringe member to kill a *veterano* of his own gang, and that in fact such an act would be highly irrational, even suicidal. Thus, the prosecution countered that because this was not an instance of one gang versus another, it should not be handled as a gang case, and the issue of gang dynamics was irrelevant. The judge accepted the prosecution's argument, in effect ruling that "gang conflict" refers to intergang, but not intragang, matters. An arbitrary legal definition overrides social science knowledge. Here, we come full circle to the Varrio Segundo versus Latins case and the dismissal of the relevance of social science or criminological expertise via narrow legal interpretation.

What these cases illustrate is that issues of definition are no longer, if ever they were, only matters of scholarly interest. How one defines *and* determines what is a gang, who is a gang member, and what is a gang-related event have very important consequence for both prosecution and defense. Locus of jurisdiction, charges filed, guilt, and penalty will readily be affected by definitional issues.

Furthermore, legal and criminological definitions, having different purposes to serve, often diverge at precisely the point when decisions about guilt and sentence severity—even death—may hang in the balance. In an era of political conservatism, suppressive laws like three strikes and STEP acts place special emphasis on legal definitions that favor prosecutorial interests. Criminological definitions, which may favor either the defense or the prosecution, are at risk of being ruled nonprobative.

Finally, legalistic knowledge of street gangs, that is, knowledge in the hands of attorneys and judges, is minuscule (and I do not exaggerate). Criminological knowledge, although far from achieving consensus among all gang scholars, is nonetheless highly relevant to a limited but important set of issues about legislative validity and court applicability.

It would seem appropriate for criminologists to adopt one of two approaches. The first would argue that gang *members,* not gangs, commit criminal acts; therefore, special gang issues should be eliminated from legislation and case law. There are plenty of laws applicable to individual perpetrators. Of course, the defense, too, would have to forgo gang-related mitigations.

The second approach would argue that there is now sufficient generic knowledge about gangs that this should be brought to bear both to the framing of legislation and to the issues of individual court cases and thereby to case law. Let the criminology gang expert contribute to legislative enactments and to individual court cases.

Finally, I note one anomaly: In all the dozens of court cases in which I have been involved, not once has it been at the request of the prosecution even though expertise is neutral; it works both ways. No, I am not looking for more hours in court. I am looking for more balance in the consideration of gang issues. They are complex issues, but our new laws and too many decisions by the players in court treat them simplistically. This, of course, has also been the history of the three-strikes laws to date.

Notes

1. All references in the court cases cited are pseudonyms.
2. The deterrence literature is by now massive. The best discussions nonetheless remain the two volumes published in the mid-1970s by Gibbs (1975) and by Zimring and Hawkins (1973). Deterrence principles applied to the gang setting have been explicated in Klein (1993, 1995).
3. For details on these studies, see Klein (1993).

References

Burrell, S. Z. (1990). Gang evidence: Issues for criminal defense. *Santa Clara Law Review, 30,* 739-790.
Decker, S. H. (1995). *Gangs, gang members and drug sales* (Draft paper). St. Louis: University of Missouri at St. Louis, Department of Criminology and Criminal Justice.
Destro, R. A. (1993). Gangs and civil rights. In S. Cummings & D. J. Monti (Eds.), *Gangs: The origin and impact of contemporary youth gangs in the United States* (pp. 277-304). Albany: State University of New York Press.
Esparza, D. (1995). *The "three strikes and you're out" law–a preliminary assessment.* Sacramento, CA: Legislative Analyst's Office.
Fagan, J. (1989). The social organization of drug use and drug dealing among urban gangs. *Criminology, 27,* 633-669.
Genelin, M., & Naiman, L. (1988). Prosecuting gang homicides. In *Prosecutor's Notebook, Vol. X.* Los Angeles: Los Angeles County District Attorney's Office.
Gibbs, J. P. (1975). *Crime, punishment, and deterrence.* New York: Elsevier.
Jackson, P., & Rudman, C. (1993). Moral panic and the response to gangs in California. In S. Cummings & D. J. Monti (Eds.), *Gangs: The origin and impact of contemporary youth gangs in the United States* (pp. 257-276). Albany: State University of New York Press.

Klein, M. W. (1984). Offense specialization and versatility among juveniles. *British Journal of Criminology, 24,* 185-194.

Klein, M. W. (1993). Attempting gang control by suppression: The misuse of deterrence principles. *Studies in Crime and Crime Prevention, 2,* 88-111.

Klein, M. W. (1995). *The American street gang: Its nature, prevalence and control.* New York: Oxford University Press.

Moore, J., & Vigil, J. D. (1989). Chicano gangs: Group norms and individual factors related to adult criminality. *Aztlan, 18,* 31.

Padilla, F. M. (1992). *The gang as an American enterprise.* New Brunswick, NJ: Rutgers University Press.

Skolnick, J. (1991). Gangs and crime old as time: But drugs change gang culture. In *Crime and Delinquency in California, 1980-1989* (pp. 171-179). Sacramento, CA: Department of Justice.

Taylor, C. S. (1989). *Dangerous society.* East Lansing: Michigan State University Press.

Zimring, F. E., & Hawkins, G. J. (1973). *Deterrence: The legal threat in crime control.* Chicago: Chicago University Press.

⤬⤬⤬
Chapter Ten

Women Offenders and
"Three Strikes and You're Out"

KAREN A. CASEY
MICHAEL D. WIATROWSKI

In the past decade, legislatures have passed mandatory minimum statutes, repeat offender statutes, and most recently, "three strikes and you're out" legislation in response to the perceived threat of violent crime. Three-strikes legislation has been passed in California and Washington State and is under consideration in 30 other states (Greenwood et al., 1994). This type of legislation typically targets males, who most often fit in the category of repeat violent offender.

The intended goal of revising sentencing structures is to provide rational sentencing policy and reduce class and race disparity in sentencing. However, reform efforts have focused on male offenders and have virtually ignored the effect of new sentencing schemes on female offenders (Daly, 1994). Mandatory policies that equate men's and women's crimes as deserving the same punishment ignore the gendered nature of female criminality and the different family responsibilities of men and women (Raeder, 1993). The question then becomes, can justice be accomplished when a sentencing policy fails to consider the differential effect of implementation on women?

This chapter discusses the potential effect of three-strikes legislation on women and presents several substantive arguments opposing the use of this legislation against women. First, women are not the type of offender to which the legislation is geared. Women are, to a significant degree, property and drug offenders; they are not violent, predatory repeat offenders (Bureau of Justice Statistics, 1994a, 1994b). Moreover, women commit property and drug crimes for reasons that are not addressed by legislators. The "feminization of poverty" has been used to explain women's participation in crime. Women lack meaningful employment opportunities, and their criminal involvement is often linked to their gendered role in society. This is reflected in the commission of sex-role-specific crimes: Women shoplift and write bad checks; they do not rob liquor stores with sawed-off shotguns (Merlo, 1995).

In addition, women tend to have less extensive and less violent criminal histories. Involvement in serious crimes for women often means dealing in drugs or acting as an accomplice to males. However, women could be subject to sentencing under a three-strikes scheme if their prior crimes are serious felonies. Although some legislation requires prior violent crimes, others do not (Greenwood et al., 1994). Again, women could be incarcerated for long periods of time when they are not violent, predatory offenders.

Furthermore, von Hirsch (1985) has pointed out the moral and ethical dilemma inherent in punishing offenders based on future conduct. Overprediction of criminal behavior occurs because we are unable to accurately predict who will commit crimes (Doerner & Wright, 1989). Three-strikes legislation incarcerates offenders who are considered likely to commit further violent crimes. Consequently, many offenders who would not commit violent felonies are imprisoned. These types of laws would overestimate the likelihood of future conduct for females and would incarcerate women who are not deserving of such punishment.

Moreover, the incarceration of women has a substantial negative effect on children. The majority of female offenders are mothers of minor children (Bloom & Steinhart, 1993; Bureau of Justice Statistics, 1994a; Casey, 1993). Furthermore, women are primary caretakers of children, and when they go to prison, children are left in the care of relatives or placed in institutions. Incarcerating women for 25-year sentences can have devastating consequences for children who are left behind.

Historical Perspective of Female Offenders

Little has been written about female criminals or female criminality in early colonial America (Pollock, 1995). Feinman's (1984) review of this time period indicates that men and women were basically egalitarian and were considered equal partners. Both sexes were likely to receive physical punishments and were treated similarly by the courts. However, beginning in the 19th century, women were relegated to the "separate sphere" of domestic life, and their behavior was controlled by what has been referred to as the "cult of true womanhood" (Feinman, 1994; Pollock, 1995; Rafter, 1990). Women were expected to be pious, pure, and submissive, and proper women were revered and respected. Those who dared to break out of this role were considered immoral, a threat to family and social order, and were perceived to be more evil than their male counterparts. Punishment of women was based on this madonna/whore duality, and women who were convicted were not considered capable of reform (Feinman, 1984).

In the late 19th century and early 20th century, vice commissions were established to control the behavior of prostitutes and, by the 1920s, what were called flappers—young, working-class ethnic/minority girls who were sexually active. The goal of the commissions was to reform young women, and special courts were established for treatment of girls. Reformatories were used to rehabilitate young women and girls from their immoral ways (Messerschmidt, 1993). White middle-class women took up the cause of their "fallen sisters" and were determined to provide role models for prostitutes and sexually promiscuous women. Houses of refuge for homeless and destitute women were established so that reformers could fulfill their goals of rehabilitating their charges through moral and religious teachings (Feinman, 1994).

Reformatories were reserved for those women who were thought to be redeemable: white, young, unhardened moral offenders (Rafter, 1990). Reformatories provided girls with programs that focused on womanly duties, such as sewing, cooking, laundering, dressmaking, and beauty culture (Messerschmidt, 1993). Custodial institutions, on the other hand, held black women between the ages of 31 and 50, who were considered to be hardened offenders. The majority of prisoners were housed in these institutions, and black women were disproportionately represented in the population (Rafter, 1990). Conditions for women in prison were typically unsanitary and crowded. They were typically confined in separate quarters of men's institutions and were kept in small, poorly ventilated, dangerous conditions. Women of all ages, races, and charges were housed together. Moreover, female prisoners were often subjected to sexual assault and abuse by their male keepers.

In the mid-1800s, women accounted for only 3.6% of the prison population in 34 states (Pollock-Byrne, 1990). Middle-class reformers were instrumental in promoting and establishing separate institutions for women, but it was not until 1840 that a woman headed the first all-female wing at Sing Sing prison in New York. The first female reformatory opened in Indiana in 1873. Other institutions soon opened in Framingham, Massachusetts (1877), and Bedford Hills, New York (1901). Between 1860 and 1900, a total of 22 new reformatories were created, and between 1900 and 1927, 27 new state-run reformatories were built. Institutions for women continued to be built throughout the 1900s. Rafter (1990) reports that between 1930 and 1950, two to three prisons per decade were created. Between 1960 and 1980, 17 prisons opened, and in the 1980s, 34 women's prisons were established. By 1994, most states had separate institutions for women (Pollock-Byrne, 1990), representing approximately 4.4% of the total number of correctional facilities in the United States (Maguire & Pastore, 1994).

Today, women comprise approximately 5.8% of the total incarcerated population in the United States (Bureau of Justice Statistics, 1994b). The number of women has tripled since the late 1970s. The number of incarcerated women rose from 12,746 (4.2%) in 1978 to 47,691 (5.8%) in 1991. The dramatic rise in female commitments to prison has been explained as the result of many factors. As pointed out by Feinman (1994), the increase since 1983 is attributed at least partly to the war on drugs. Women are increasingly involved in the sale and possession of drugs, especially crack, and they are more likely to be punished for their behavior. Chesney-Lind and Pollock (1995) suggest that women have been affected by the societal attitude to "get tough on crime," and officials are more likely to incarcerate women than they were in the past. Steffensmeier and Streifel (1992) have suggested that more aggressive policing techniques have led to increased arrests of women. Consequently, today more women are processed through the system and end up confined in jails and prisons. Mandatory sentencing for drug offenses and second-felony offenders has also increased the number of women in prison (Feinman, 1994).

In both federal and state jurisdictions, incarceration of female drug offenders has increased significantly. Of all women admitted to the federal system, the proportion of women committed for drug offenses increased from 26% in 1981 to almost 64% in 1991 (Bureau of Justice Statistics, 1994b). The percentage of drug offenders in state prisons also grew considerably. Nearly a third of the women were serving time for a drug offense in 1991. According to the Bureau of Justice Statistics (1994a), this increase in drug offenders accounted for 55% of the increase in female prisoners since 1986. In New York and New Jersey, more than half of female commitments in 1991 were for drug offenses (Feinman, 1994). Additionally, in New York, women committed to prison under second-felony-offender legislation rose from 41% to 51% (New York State Department of Correctional Services, 1992).

The proportion of women imprisoned for violent offenses declined during the 1980s. In 1979, 48.9% of women in prison were incarcerated for a violent offense. In 1986, the percentage had dropped to 41%, and by 1991 only 32.8% were committed for a violent offense (Bureau of Justice Statistics, 1994b). Of the women incarcerated for a violent offense, it is estimated that half of them killed their abusive mates. Women incarcerated for property offenses also declined. In 1986, the percentage was 41% and dropped to 29% in 1991. In the federal system, only 8% of the women were incarcerated for a violent offense, and 17% were imprisoned for a property offense (Bureau of Justice Statistics, 1994a). Interestingly, in the early 1980s the most frequent incarceration offense for both state and federal inmates was property offenses. The trend in both jurisdictions is a decline in property offenses and an enormous increase in commitments for drug offenses.

The Bureau of Justice Statistics (1994b) also collected prior-record data on women in state prisons. Twenty-eight percent of the women had no prior convictions. Nearly half the women were serving time for nonviolent offenses and had only nonviolent prior convictions. Fifty-one percent of the women had only one or no prior offenses, and 66% had two or fewer offenses. In the federal system, 58% of the women were serving their first sentence for a nonviolent offense. Additionally, only 11% of the women had current or past violent sentences (Bureau of Justice Statistics, 1994a).

The demographic characteristics of women in prison have not changed significantly over the years. An American Correctional Association (1990) survey and recent data from the Bureau of Justice Statistics (1994a, 1994b) on federal and state prisoners portray prison inmates as disproportionately young, from racial/ethnic minority groups, and mothers of minor children. According to the American Correctional Association study, about half the women had run away from home, and a quarter had attempted suicide. Many of the women had serious drug problems. One third never completed high school, and 23% of the dropouts were pregnant. Twenty-two percent of the women had been unemployed in the 3 years prior to their incarceration.

The Bureau of Justice Statistics (1994b) data report that nearly half of the women in state prisons grew up in single-parent households, and 17% had lived in a foster home, agency, or other institution while growing up. In addition, 47% of the women had a family member who had been incarcerated. Moreover, a third of the women reported that a parent or guardian abused alcohol while the inmate was growing up. An estimated 34% of female inmates reported being physically abused, and 34% reported being sexually abused. Furthermore, 32% indicated the abuse occurred before the inmate was 18. More than three quarters of the abused women said they were raped. Women in federal prison were half as likely as women in state prisons to report being physically or sexually abused. However, in both the federal and state jurisdictions, women were 3 to 4 times as likely as males to report abuse (Bureau of Justice Statistics, 1994a). Several other studies have found that incarcerated women were victims of physical and sexual abuse (Chesney-Lind & Pollock, 1995; Daly, 1994).

An estimated 75% of the women in prison are mothers and are the sole caretakers of their children. Approximately 25,700 inmates had more than 56,000 children under the age of 18 (Bureau of Justice Statistics, 1994b). Children are most likely to be placed with grandparents while their mother is incarcerated. Nearly 10% of children are placed in foster care or other institutions (Bloom & Steinhart, 1993; Bureau of Justice Statistics, 1994a; Casey, 1993).

Clearly, women are not predatory, violent offenders who would be suitable candidates for mandatory 25-year sentences. Women are typically mothers of small children who commit drug or property offenses and have two or fewer prior convictions. Furthermore, most women involved in drug and property crimes lack meaningful employment opportunities. Raeder (1993) reports that the average monthly income of a federally sentenced female defendant is $687. As stated previously, women commit property crimes that are related to their gendered status in society, such as writing bad checks and forging credit card purchases (Merlo, 1995). Lack of employment options may also partially explain women's involvement in the drug business. Although still relegated to subordinate positions in the drug hierarchy, women are at least able to support themselves and their families with the money gained through illicit drug deals (Merlo, 1995). Still other women are linked to the drug business through their relationships with men (Raeder, 1993). Living with a drug dealer is enough to implicate a women in the business even if she has a minimal role in the actual dealing. A woman in this position is economically dependent on her mate for support, and yet is at great risk for arrest, conviction, and subsequent incarceration.

Moreover, female offenders are likely to have come from abusive childhoods, which may at least partially explain their involvement in a criminal lifestyle. Many women in prison ran away from home at an early age to escape from sexual and physical abuse (Bureau of Justice Statistics, 1994a; Chesney-Lind, 1995; Daly, 1994; Raeder, 1993). Options for the survival of these young women were limited to engaging in petty theft and/or prostitution. Consequently, women end up involved with criminal men whom they depend on for economic and emotional support. Again, many women are codefendants with men who are the primary instigators in the crime (Raeder, 1993).

In addition, as mentioned previously, the majority of female offenders are single mothers who bear the sole responsibility for child care (Bloom & Steinhart, 1993; Bureau of Justice Statistics, 1994a; Casey, 1993). Single mothers are quickly becoming the most impoverished group in America. Thirty-five percent of single-female households fall below the poverty line. The rate for minority women is more disheartening. Fifty-two percent of black female-headed households live in poverty; the rate is 49.7% for Hispanics and 28.4% for white mothers (Raeder, 1993). Additionally, in 1993, 22.4% of children under the age of 6 lived with their mothers only. Of these, 57.5% lived below the poverty line (Merlo, 1995). Incarcerating women for 25 years who are responsible for children can further disadvantage an already impoverished group of youngsters. Furthermore, many female offenders had relatives who were incarcerated during their childhoods. The effect on a child of a mother being incarcerated could continue the cycle of incarceration in the family (Raeder, 1993).

Rationale for Sentencing of Women

Throughout the late 1800s and well into the 1900s, the sentencing of female offenders was based on the philosophy of rehabilitation. Women were punished for failing to live up to the standard of "true womanhood" and were sent to institutions to be resocialized into "ladies" (Feinman, 1994; Rafter, 1990). It was believed that with the proper training and guidance, women could learn to become proper and respected ladies. Women were taught how to be ladies by exposure to training that was limited to basic domestic skills, such as cooking, sewing, cleaning, and beauty care. The rehabilitative model is still strong in prisons for women, even though over the past 20 years, there has been a general shift from rehabilitation to incarceration and punishment as a penal philosophy (Blumstein, Cohen, Martin, & Tonry, 1983; Feeley & Simon, 1992; Zimring & Hawkins, 1995). The "get tough" attitude has been used to explain the increased incarceration of women (Chesney-Lind, 1995); however, many prisons for women still have sex-role-stereotyped programming, such as cosmetology, typing, cooking, and child care. Rehabilitation as a justification for sentencing has been generally discounted, but it still permeates the correctional treatment of women (Pollock-Byrne, 1990).

In the past, differential sentencing of men and women had been justified on the basis of the distinct natures of men and women. Women were thought to be more amenable to change. This, however, justified longer periods of confinement to achieve reformation. At one time, women were subject to indeterminate sentences in situations where men were not, to provide ample time for their rehabilitation (Feinman, 1994). Women are no longer subjected to harsher legislative treatment, and there is evidence to suggest that women are actually receiving more lenient treatment than men in sentencing today (Daly, 1994; Steffensmeier, Kramer, & Streifel, 1993).

Steffensmeier et al. (1993) have conducted an extensive review of previous studies on gender disparity in sentencing. Their review suggests that studies have failed to control for important variables, including seriousness of offense, the defendant's prior convictions, and the race of the defendant. Some studies failed to analyze different sentencing outcomes, such as the decision to incarcerate and the length of sentence. Other problems identified include small sample size and lack of generalizability.

Steffensmeier et al. (1993) examined records of male and female offenders sentenced in Pennsylvania from 1985 to 1987. The authors incorporated controls for offense seriousness and prior record. The findings indicate that the primary determinants of judges' imprisonment decisions are the type or seriousness of the crimes committed and the defendants' prior records, not the defendants' gender or other background characteristics (age, race, etc.). Gender was found to have a small to moderate effect on the decision to incarcerate, yet had no effect on the length of sentence decision. Judges' reasons for not incarcerating women were based on legally relevant variables (nonviolent offense/accomplice) or social variables (child care responsibilities, physical or mental problems, defendant showed remorse). Overall, judges viewed female defendants as less culpable than male codefendants and as having more responsibilities and connections to the community. Furthermore, judges viewed their decisions not to incarcerate as warranted disparity.

Daly's (1987) research suggests that it may be family variables that act as a mitigating factor in sentencing and not necessarily gender. She found that being "familied" (having dependents) resulted in a lesser penalty regardless of gender. However, women who were familied were treated more leniently than men who were familied, suggesting that women are perceived to be more important to the family unit in terms of their responsibilities for child care. Probation officials also thought some women were more threatened by the thought of jail and therefore were more easily deterred. Other research by Daly (1994) indicates that women are perceived to be more reformable, which may explain the gender differences found in her research of felony sentencing in New Haven, Connecticut. Women received shorter sentence lengths than men, and court officials were more were likely to connect prior victimization of the women with their criminal behavior. Consequently, they felt women were less blameworthy and therefore deserving of leniency.

Other research also suggests that leniency toward women is accounted for by gender-related differences in informal controls operating in women's lives. Various studies indicate that women who are economically dependent, married, and have child care responsibilities are treated more leniently than single, independent, childless women. Moreover, married women are treated more leniently than married men (Bortich, 1992; Daly, 1987; Kruttschnitt, 1982, 1984).

Throughout the early part of this century, women were treated more harshly then men because it was felt their inherent biological differences required longer periods of confinement for reformation. Paradoxically, prior to 1970 women's reformation potential justified longer periods of incarceration, and today the same rationale is being used to excuse women from harsher sentencing. Today, it appears women may be treated more leniently due to their rehabilitative potential. An additional factor considered in sentencing women today is the unique position of women as caretakers of children. Although sentencing disparity is always suspect, differences in sentencing women may be justified because of the profound effect incarceration has on children. In a three-strikes sentencing scheme, it is possible that family responsibility will be considered a viable reason not to charge a woman with a third felony.

Sentencing Reform

As noted, the past two decades have witnessed a major shift from rehabilitation to incapacitation as primary justification for imprisonment (Blumstein et al., 1983; Feeley & Simon, 1992; Zimring & Hawkins, 1995). Prior to 1970, the majority of states relied on indeterminate-sentencing schemes and parole boards, which were predicated on the rehabilitation of the offender (Blumstein et al., 1983). Since the mid-1970s, roughly one half of the states have engaged in sentencing reform. Fourteen states and the federal government have created sentencing commissions whose goals are to write sentencing guidelines (Steffensmeier et al., 1993). Many other states have legislatively written guidelines. Several states have abolished parole, and more than 30 states have passed mandatory minimum sentence laws.

Feeley and Simon (1992) have advanced the proposition that there is a "new penology" based on incapacitation. They describe the new discourse emerging as being concerned with managing large groups of dangerous individuals who have not responded to other forms of offender treatment. Traditional concerns with the individual have shifted to concerns about public safety and surveillance of dangerous classes of individuals. Incapacitation is the clearest example of the new penology. Incapacitation strategies rearrange the distribution of offenders in society, with the goal of reducing the crime rate. However, the effect on individual offenders is questionable.

Feeley and Simon (1992) posit that the shift in thinking has led to the formulation of new objectives and new techniques for achieving incapacitation objectives. Included in this strategy is increasing reliance on imprisonment, prediction tables, and population projections to manage dangerous groups. Discussions of sentencing schemes involve talk of "high-rate offenders," and "career criminals," who are typically male offenders. Three-strikes legislation can be viewed as part of the new penology at work. The goal of three strikes is to target certain categories of individuals (repeat felony offenders) in an effort to ensure public safety through incapacitation. Generally, three-strikes legislation requires a mandatory prison term on conviction of a third felony offense.

One of the major problems of this approach is the inability to predict with precision who is deserving of such restraint (Doerner & Wright, 1989). Research (Blumstein et al., 1983) has indicated that there is typically a small group of criminals who could be considered at high risk to become repeat offenders. A strategy of selective incapacitation that targets repeat offenders is therefore likely to incarcerate people who are low-risk offenders, not likely to commit a high number of crimes if left in the community. In a system of selective incapacitation, overprediction of dangerousness or future criminal activity is bound to occur (Zimring & Hawkins, 1995). Three-strikes legislation reflects an effort to predict behavior for specific categories of offenders. All offenders who have three felony convictions are treated alike. In California, for instance, a third felony conviction results in a prison sentence of 25 years (Greenwood et al., 1994), regardless of the nature of the third conviction. However, the first two convictions must be serious offenses. Therefore, an offender who is convicted for grand larceny is situated similarly to someone who is convicted of strong-arm robbery. The larceny offender may not necessarily have a violent prior record, yet is considered to be as threatening to the community as a violent robber. Under the new federal crime law, the possibility of overprediction is lessened because the law is limited to those who have three convictions involving serious injuries to their victims (Greenwood et al., 1994). The rhetoric of politicians leads the public to believe that this legislation will take violent offenders off the street to ensure public safety. This may or may not be the case. The likely result is an overprediction of future crime, at least for some offenders. As noted previously, this is especially true for female offenders.

This has been the case under mandatory minimum statutes in the federal system. More than 60 federal crimes contain mandatory minimum penalties. If a defendant commits a crime with a weapon, possesses a certain amount of drugs, or has a certain number of convictions, a judge must impose a prison term of 5, 10, or 30 years or life without the possibility of parole. Every year, thousands of low-level offenders are sentenced to lengthy incarceration. The legislation does not target violent criminals or major drug traffickers, and yet the intention of the legislation was to target the most serious offenders (Vincent & Hofer, 1994). A similar result was found in Florida under the Habitual Offender Statute. The statute mandates a prison sentence for an offender convicted of two or more prior felony convictions within a 5-year period. The prosecutor retains discretion whether to charge an offender under the Habitual Offender Statute. Evaluation of the law indicates that it has been applied most frequently to less serious offenders (Florida Legislature, 1992).

Another issue with legislation mandating prison on a third conviction is the prosecutors' discretion on whether to charge a person with a felony that would invoke the possibility of a 25-year sentence (Greenwood et al., 1994). If a prosecutor determines that a third felony conviction would punish an offender too harshly, he maintains the discretion to charge with a misdemeanor. Such discretion is often hidden and unsystematic and replaces the discretion of judges with the hidden discretion of prosecutors. Schulhofer (1993) evaluated the effect of New York State's mandatory drug laws. In New York, the volume of arrests, rates of indictment on arrest, and rates of conviction on indictment all declined after the law was enacted. The result was that the overall probability of imprisonment was lower than before the enactment of the law. As suggested by Cohen and Tonry (1983), efforts to reduce sentencing disparity result in shifting discretion rather than eliminating it.

In the case of three-strikes legislation and female offenders, it is likely that prosecutors will not charge an offender with a felony if it is possible she would be convicted of a third felony. It is reasonable to expect that many of the same considerations that judges weigh when sentencing women will be factored in at the charging stage. Given that women have been viewed as less culpable than men, as having more child care responsibilities, and as having suffered from prior victimization, prosecutors may be hesitant to invoke a penalty that would carry a 25-year to life sentence. Women may be perceived as less blameworthy and more deserving of leniency. This practice is evident in Florida, where women are less likely to be habitualized under the Habitual Offender Statute (Florida Legislature, 1992).

Disparity in the implementation of mandatory minimum sentences has also had a negative effect on nonwhite offenders in the federal system (Vincent & Hofer, 1994). White offenders are less likely than both black and Hispanic offenders to receive a mandatory minimum term. Furthermore, since the enactment of mandatory minimum statutes, the gap between the average sentences of white and black offenders has grown wider. The disparity may be a result of different sentences for the use and sale of crack versus cocaine. Blacks are more likely to use crack; whites prefer powder cocaine. Blacks are also less likely to plead guilty or cooperate with authorities, which may explain some of the differences in sentencing. A similar result has been found in Florida. Seventy-eight percent of offenders sentenced under the Habitual Offender Statute were black, but only 66% of offenders who were eligible for habitualization under the statute were black (Florida Legislature, 1992).

Additionally, gender also has an effect on the imposition of mandatory minimums in the federal system. In 1984, women received sentences that were, on the average, 38% lower than those for men for the same offense. Furthermore, women were 69% less likely to receive a sentence at the prescribed minimum term. In 1990, the sentences for women were 42% lower than men. However, women are now only 20% less likely to receive a sentence below the mandatory minimum term. This pattern indicates that mandatory minimums have had a greater influence on the sentencing of females than of males (Meierhoefer, 1992). As suggested by the author, sentencing disparity may reflect factors related to gender not considered in the analysis such as child care responsibilities. Although not documented, it is likely some of the same factors are considered in determining not to invoke the Habitual Offender Statute against women in Florida (Florida Legislature, 1992).

Another concern with three-strikes legislation is the overreliance on imprisonment to achieve the goal of incapacitation. Zimring and Hawkins (1995) have pointed out that prisons are uniquely suited for the incapacitative function. No other penal sanction (other than death) can guarantee that offenders will not commit crime in the community while serving their sentence. This has led politicians to urge their constituents to support the building of more prisons. They claim that without more prisons, there will be more crime. Although their contention that building more prisons will reduce crime is appealing to voters, the only thing that can be said with certainty about prison construction is that it will result in more people being imprisoned.

The move to build more prisons for women is apparent. As mentioned previously, more than 40 new prisons have been established since the 1970s (Rafter, 1990). The growth in women's prisons occurred with little thought or planning and appears to be a response to the rapid increase in incarcerated women in recent decades. Authorities have converted abandoned hotels and motels, mental hospitals, nurses dormitories, and youth training schools into prisons for women (Chesney-Lind, 1995). In the late 1980s, many states were planning to expand their facilities to hold more women (Rafter, 1990).

Incapacitation as a goal in sentencing can also cause dramatic increases in prison populations, with subsequent overcrowding (Florida Legislature, 1992). Florida has experienced greatly increased sentence lengths and a rapid increase in admissions to the prison system since the enactment of the Habitual Offender Statute. It is projected that by fiscal year 1995-1996, 47% of the prison population in Florida will be composed of offenders sentenced under the Habitual Offender Statute (Florida Legislature, 1992). Low-risk offenders are taking up prison space that should be reserved for the most serious offenders. Despite the intention of legislators, prisons are occupied by less serious offenders. The federal system is also projecting population increases. The U.S. Sentencing Commission anticipated a doubling of the prison population in the first 10 years of operation under sentencing guidelines that require longer terms of imprisonment (Zimring & Hawkins, 1991). Under New York State's second-felony-offender law, the probability of imprisonment rose from 70% to 92%, subsequently increasing the prison population (Cohen & Tonry, 1983).

The implicit assumption of three-strikes legislation is that locking up offenders will decrease crime. The basic argument about reducing crimes is simple. Incapacitation is achieved by incarcerating offenders and preventing them from committing crimes in the community. It follows that if more convicted criminals were sent to prison, or sentenced to longer terms, more crimes would be prevented. However, such an argument has not been empirically supported (Zimring & Hawkins, 1995). It has been suggested that although those in prison will not commit crimes, there are plenty of offenders left on the street who continue to commit crime. Furthermore, as pointed out in the RAND study (Greenwood et al., 1994), three-strikes legislation does nothing to address the fact that children under the age of 10 will be positioned to become felons in the next 10 years, and many of them will be repeat felony offenders. Those who are subjected to three strikes now will also age out of crime, leaving states to spend money on offenders who would desist from crime on their own.

The question whether the reduction in crime can justify the expense of incarcerating so many offenders for long periods of time has been raised. According to an evaluation conducted by the RAND Corporation (Greenwood et al., 1994), serious felonies in California will be reduced by 22% to 34% over what would have occurred under previous laws. However, the reduction in crime will occur at a cost of $4.5 to $6.5 billion per year. Furthermore, although savings may be found in police and court budgets, to lock up so many offenders will require the construction and operation of 15 more prisons by the end of the century (Legislative Analyst's Office, 1995). The anticipated reduction in serious crimes for women would be less than for males given that women do not commit the same volume of serious and violent crimes. Although states may not have to build new prisons for women, they would still be faced with accommodating long-term offenders who are not violent, predatory offenders threatening community safety. Community sentences for women have been advocated as an alternative to prison (Chesney-Lind & Pollock, 1995). Intermediate sanctions could apply the same effects at lower cost to taxpayers. The use of community alternatives would allow women to remain with their children, receive drug and alcohol treatment, and pursue employment opportunities at a much lower cost than prison.

Effect of Three-Strikes Legislation on Female Offenders

The effect of three-strikes legislation on female offenders is difficult to measure. The crimes that politicians are concerned with preventing by incarcerating offenders for long periods of time are typically crimes committed by males. It is possible that women will be affected, but there will be no generalizable effects on the crimes committed by women. Although women do commit serious felonies, they are not involved in violent, predatory crimes to the extent of males. In fact, women tend to commit drug and property crimes for reasons that legislators do not address. Furthermore, the violent crimes that women commit are usually in response to backgrounds characterized by physical and emotional abuse. Violent histories often lead women to abusive life situations. It is estimated that half of the women who commit homicide kill their abusive mates (Bureau of Justice Statistics 1994b). For women involved in robbery, there is support for the proposition that many were not active participants in the crime, but were possibly dependent accomplices to male partners (Chesney-Lind & Pollock, 1995). The image of the predatory, violent offender does not square with the reality of most women's situations.

Women are also less likely than men to have extensive prior conviction histories. According to the Bureau of Justice Statistics (1994b), the majority of women in state prison have fewer than two prior convictions (66%), and their previous convictions are nonviolent. In federal prison, the majority of women are serving their first prison sentence. Three-strikes legislation is not intended to incarcerate the nonviolent offender. In California, an offender must have committed two prior serious convictions before the third conviction invokes the 25-year to life sentence. The categories of serious offenses all include violence or intent to injure through violence. The only exception is burglary of an inhabited dwelling (Greenwood et al., 1994). Women's property offenses tend to be sex role specific, such as forgery and larceny without violence.

However, there will be situations in which women will be eligible for sentencing under a three-strikes sentencing scheme. The question then becomes, will women be treated the same as men? Or more significantly, should women be treated the same as men? Feminist scholars have pointed out the problem of conceptualizing the goal of sentencing women to be reaching equality with men (Chesney-Lind & Pollock, 1995; Daly, 1994). Because men are seen as the standard against which to measure female behavior, women end up getting treated more harshly on the basis of an equality model. Daly (1994) makes the excellent point that equality does not necessarily mean justice or fairness. In California, an attempt was made to address this issue. The legislature used a "split-difference" approach, which basically averaged men's and women's sentences to achieve a fair sentence for both. The unfortunate consequence of this scheme is that women's sentences were increased, and men's were decreased (Blumstein et al., 1983).

The countervailing argument holds that women are not the same as men and therefore should not be treated the same as men. This argument calls for recognizing the differential needs of women, similar to a separate but equal position. Women and men may receive different treatment, so long as women are not placed in an inferior position. However, some argue that a "special needs" approach always puts women at a disadvantage because the male standard is used to measure "needs" (Chesney-Lind & Pollock, 1995). For women to receive justice, there must be a recognition that women and men are affected differently by their social and economic situations. Women do not benefit by being treated the same as men.

For instance, there are many factors to consider when sentencing females that may not be relevant when sentencing males. As pointed out by Daly (1987), defendants who are familied (have dependents) receive some consideration at sentencing. However, women who are familied present a very different scenario than familied men. Women are often the sole caretakers of their children, and the majority of women have children under the age of 18 (Bureau of Justice Statistics, 1994). When men with children go to prison, the children's mother provides for them, but when women are incarcerated, children's lives can be completely dismantled. A sentencing scheme that permits the incarceration of a woman for 25 years to life effectively severs the mother-child bond for the rest of the child's young life. A child may be able to adjust to temporary absences in his or her life, but to completely dissolve the mother-child relationship is a consequence of three-strikes legislation that has not been considered. Raeder (1993) notes that the federal sentencing guidelines ordinarily do not allow for consideration of a defendant's employment, family ties, or family responsibilities to be used as factors in sentencing; however, it appears that in some instances these factors are considered at least informally. Consideration of these factors should be formalized given the responsibilities of women in caring for children.

A report issued by the California Senate in 1994 recommended that primary responsibility for child care be considered a mitigating factor in determinate-sentencing schemes affecting women. Although their recommendations are not binding, the report indicates that lawmakers are beginning to recognize the differential situations of male and female offenders. Their recommendations clearly state that males and females differ significantly in terms of their needs while incarcerated and that policies need to address these differences (California Senate, 1994).

Women who are sentenced to a 25-year sentence also suffer a more severe sanction than men for a number of reasons. Most states have only one prison for women located in a rural area far from the defendant's home (Pollock-Byrne, 1990). In the federal system, women may be incarcerated in another state. The distance families have to travel to visit can make it impossible for children to visit. Only half the women who are incarcerated receive visits from their children while incarcerated (Bloom & Steinhart, 1993; Casey, 1993). Because there are so many more facilities for males, men may eventually transfer closer to home and receive visits from their families. For women, this is not an option.

Moreover, programs in women's prisons are less adequate and accessible than in male prisons. Men sentenced to prison may transfer to a number of prisons within a state to have access to programming.

This is not the case for females. Furthermore, the rehabilitative ideal still permeates women's prison, with sex-typed vocational programming being the primary focus of reformation (Chesney-Lind & Pollock, 1995). Although some female prisons offer vocational programming, the quality and availability is limited. Several recommendations in the California Senate report called for gender-specific programs in prisons to address the unique problems of female inmates. Again, the report indicates a recognition by lawmakers that women have special needs that are not being addressed in the prison system (California Senate, 1994). Men and women may serve the same amount of time under a three-strikes scheme, but the conditions of confinement are substantially different.

Conclusion

Three-strikes legislation is gaining favor in many states (Greenwood et al., 1994). The implications of this legislation have not been well thought out, especially in reference to women. Women are not the type of offenders to which the legislation is geared, and there is evidence to suggest that these types of laws are not used against women as frequently as men (Florida Legislature, 1992; Meierhoefer, 1992). It is feasible that women will be less likely than men to be sentenced under these types of statutes.

One also has to question the purpose of three-strikes legislation when it is being applied to females. Does incarcerating a woman for 25 years whose crimes are a reflection of her gendered role in society serve justice? Just sentences need to reflect dissimilar patterns of criminality and distinct family backgrounds of women. Traditionally, women have been sentenced and incarcerated due to their rehabilitative potential. However, it is now politically expedient to discard the language of rehabilitation for the get-tough discourse of incapacitation. Unfortunately, women are bound to be brought into the net based on the equality model of sentencing.

A "different needs" approach may be more reasonable (Chesney-Lind & Pollock, 1995). Raeder (1993) has pointed out that damage has been inflicted on women under the "gender-neutral" federal sentencing guidelines. Many more women are serving time in prison rather than being sentenced to probation, and women are serving longer prison terms than in previous years. Furthermore, women's unique position in our society is ignored in a sentencing scheme whose goal is equality. Considering factors such as primary parenting responsibility may result in unequal sentences, but such disparity may be warranted to preserve the well-being of children in our society. Raeder (1993) supports a "totality of circumstances" approach to sentencing, which would account for a variety of factors in a woman's background that may justify leniency in sentencing.

Legislators who are responding to political pressure to get tough on crime need to consider the consequences of their actions on all offenders who will be affected. As argued above, female offenders do not present the same scenario as male offenders, and therefore do not deserve such excessive and punitive sentences. In fact, alternative sentences for women may be justified. What is clear is that in most situations, incarcerating women for 25 years based on a male model of sentencing is unnecessary and unproductive.

References

American Correctional Association. (1990). *The female offender: What does the future hold?* Washington, DC: St. Mary's.

Bloom, B., & Steinhart, D. (1993). *Why punish the children: A reappraisal of the children of incarcerated mothers in America.* San Francisco: National Council on Crime and Delinquency.

Blumstein, A., Cohen, J., Martin, S. E., & Tonry, M. H. (Eds.). (1983). *Research on sentencing: The search for reform* (Vols. 1, 2). Washington, DC: National Academy Press.

Bortich, H. (1992). Gender and criminal court outcomes: An historical analysis. *Criminology, 35,* 136-168.

Bureau of Justice Statistics. (1994a). *Comparing federal and state prison inmates, 1991.* Washington, DC: U.S. Department of Justice, Office of Justice Programs.

Bureau of Justice Statistics. (1994b). *Women in prison* (Special report). Washington, DC: U.S. Department of Justice, Office of Justice Programs.

California Senate. (1994, June). *Senate Concurrent Resolution 33 Commission Report on Female Inmates and Parole Issues* (Executive summary, final report). Sacramento: Author.

Casey, K. A. (1993). *The effect of visitation on the disciplinary adjustment of incarcerated females.* Ann Arbor, MI. (University Microfilms International No. 9403835)

Chesney-Lind, M. (1995). Rethinking women's imprisonment: A critical look at trends in women's incarceration. In B. Price & N. Sokoloff (Eds.), *The criminal justice system and women: Offender, victims and workers* (pp. 105-117). New York: McGraw-Hill.

Chesney-Lind, M., & Pollock, J. M. (1995). Women's prisons: Equality with a vengeance. In A. V. Merlo & J. M. Pollock (Eds.), *Women, law and social control* (pp. 155-175). Needham Heights, MA: Allyn & Bacon.

Cohen, J., & Tonry, M. H. (1983). Sentencing reforms and their impacts. In A. Blumstein, J. Cohen, S. E. Martin, & M. H. Tonry (Eds.), *Research on sentencing: The search for reform* (Vols. 1, 2, pp. 305-459). Washington, DC: National Academy Press.

Daly, K. (1987). Discrimination in criminal courts: Family, gender and the problem of equal treatment. *Social Forces, 66,* 152-175.

Daly, K. (1994). *Gender, crime and punishment.* New Haven, CT: Yale University Press.

Doerner, W. G., & Wright, B. S. (1989). Federal sentencing reform in light of incapacitation and recidivism. In D. Champion (Ed.), *The U.S. sentencing guidelines: Implications for criminal justice* (pp. 216-227). New York: Praeger.

Feeley, M., & Simon, J. (1992). The new penology: Notes on the emerging strategy of corrections and its implications. *Criminology, 30,* 449-474.

Feinman, C. (1984). An historical overview of the treatment of incarcerated women: Myths and realities of rehabilitation. *Prison Journal, 63*(2), 12-26.

Feinman, C. (1994). *Women in the criminal justice system* (3rd ed.). Westport, CT: Praeger.

Florida Legislature. (1992). *An empirical examination of the application of Florida's Habitual Offender Statute.* Tallahassee, FL: Economic and Demographic Research Division.

Greenwood, P. W., Rydell, C. P., Abrahamse, A. F., Caulkins, J. P., Chiesa, J., Model, K. E., & Klein, S. P. (1994). *Three strikes and you're out: Estimated benefits and costs of California's new mandatory-sentencing law* (Report No. MR-509-RC). Santa Monica, CA: RAND.

Kruttschnitt, C. (1982). Women, crime and dependency. *Criminology, 19,* 495-513.

Kruttschnitt, C. (1984). Sex and criminal court dispositions: The unresolved controversy. *Journal of Research in Crime and Delinquency, 21,* 213-232.

Legislative Analyst's Office. (1995, January 6). Status: The three strikes and you're out law—A preliminary assessment. Sacramento, CA: Author.

Maguire, K., & Pastore, A. (Eds.). (1994). *Sourcebook of criminal justice statistics, 1993* (U.S. Department of Justice, Bureau of Justice Statistics). Washington, DC: Government Printing Office.

Meierhoefer, B. (1992). *The general effect of mandatory minimum prison terms.* Washington, DC: Federal Judicial Center.

Merlo, A. (1995). Female criminality in the 1990s. In A. V. Merlo & J. M. Pollock (Eds.), *Women, law and social control* (pp. 119-134). Needham Heights, MA: Allyn & Bacon.

Messerschmidt, J. W. (1993). *Masculinities and crime.* Lanham, MD: Rowman & Littlefield.

New York State Department of Correctional Services. (1992). *Female offenders committed to state prison.* Albany, NY: Division of Program Planning, Research and Evaluation.

Pollock, J. (1995). Gender, justice and social control: An historical perspective. In A. V. Merlo & J. M. Pollock (Eds.), *Women, law and social control* (pp. 3-35). Needham Heights, MA: Allyn & Bacon.

Pollock-Byrne, J. (1990). *Women, prison and crime.* Pacific Grove, CA: Brooks/Cole.

Raeder, M. S. (1993). Gender and sentencing: Single moms, battered women, and other sex-based anomalies in the gender-free world of the federal sentencing guidelines. *Pepperdine Law Review, 20,* 905-990.

Rafter, N. (1990). *Partial justice: Women, prisons and social control* (2nd ed.). New Brunswick, NJ: Transaction Books.

Schulhofer, S. J. (1993). Rethinking mandatory minimums. *Wake Forest Law Review, 28,* 199-222.

Steffensmeier, D., Kramer, J., & Streifel, C. (1993). Gender and imprisonment decisions. *Criminology, 31,* 411-444.

Steffensmeier, D., & Streifel, C. (1992, March). Time-series analysis of the female percentage of arrests for property crimes, 1960-1985: A test of alternative explanations. *Justice Quarterly, 9,* 77-103.

Vincent, B. S., & Hofer, P. (1994). *The consequences of mandatory minimum prison terms: A summary of recent findings.* Washington, DC: Federal Judicial Center.

von Hirsch, A. (1985). *Past or future crimes: Deservedness and dangerousness in the sentencing of criminals.* New Brunswick, NJ: Rutgers University Press.

Zimring, F. E., & Hawkins, G. (1991). *The scale of imprisonment.* Chicago and London: University of Chicago Press.

Zimring, F. E., & Hawkins, G. (1995). *Incapacitation.* New York: Oxford University Press.

$$\times|\times|\times$$

Chapter Eleven

A Base on Balls for
White-Collar Criminals

GILBERT GEIS

||| The failure to extend the "three strikes and you're out" policy to white-collar offenders provides persuasive evidence of the class bias that fuels this viciously punitive policy. By common agreement, acts and omissions on the part of white-collar criminals account for a considerably higher percentage of people who lie in the gravesites in the nation's cemeteries than do the murders committed by so-called common criminals. Look at the brief roster of just a few of the many forms of lethal white-collar violence perpetrated by people who run the country's corporate giants:

> toxic chemical dumps that have poisoned drinking supplies, caused leukemia in children, and destroyed entire communities; cover-ups of asbestos-induced cancer, and the gradual suffocation of workers from inhaling cotton dust; radioactive water leaking from improperly maintained nuclear reactors; mangled bodies and lives snuffed out in unsafe coal mines and steel mills. (Hills, 1987, p. vii)

To these, add the roster of disabilities and deaths because of unsafe working conditions; dangerous food and drug products or additives; defective consumer goods; hazardous clothing materials and finishes; and the health effects of noise and the pollution of the air, water, and land by chemicals and radiation.

These acts, although they may be "silent violence," nonetheless involve the same kind of peril that lies behind the frustration and fear that produced the three-strikes laws. A federal judge sentencing a defendant charged with pollution insisted that we open our eyes and realize that violence takes many forms. Comparing the deliberate acts of pollution proven against the accused to common crimes, the judge noted of the polluters that "no defendants to come before this court have exhibited a more callous and flagrant disregard for the safety and lives of vast numbers of citizens than this defendant" (Carter, 1980, p. 607).

If monetary loss is taken to stand at the core of the three-strikes doctrine, it is more sensible to concentrate on constraining white-collar crooks, the people who produce the greatest fiscal deprivations. Edwin H. Sutherland, the sociologist who in 1939 coined the term *white-collar crime,* pointed out that just a few embezzlers or a couple of antitrust violators in any year will deprive the public of much more money than the total take of all the burglars, robbers, and the other street offenders during the same time period. Things have not changed in the more than half a century since Sutherland made his calculations of fiscal deprivations by different forms of crime. In 1992, for instance, the three biggest infant formula manufacturers, accounting for 90% of the market, were charged with rigging bids on prices charged to federal government programs, an offense that cost the government (and most particularly, its taxpayers) about $25 billion (Baucas, 1994). Federal Judge Henry J. Friendly summarized the fiscal harm of white-collar fraud aptly: "In our complex society," he pointed out, "the accountant's certificate and the lawyer's opinion can be instruments for inflicting pecuniary loss more potent than the chisel or the crowbar" (*U.S. v. Benjamin,* 1964, p. 863). A more blunt expression of the same sentiment has been offered by an attorney who, after the 1995 bombing of the federal building in Oklahoma City, was asked if he would—if requested—defend the accused. "If I want to represent right-wing murderers," he said, "I'd become a corporate lawyer" (Applebome, 1995, p. B10).

Braithwaite and Pettit (1990) point out that "in addition to causing greater economic losses, white-collar crimes also pose greater threat to relationships of trust which are vital to our political and economic systems" (p. 188). They note, as an example, that "a spate of securities scams or bankruptcy frauds can threaten investor confidence, thereby capital formation, and thereby employment." This effect of white-collar crime on the quality of our social life was highlighted in the report of the President's Commission on Law Enforcement and Administration of Justice (1967):

> White-collar crime affects the whole moral climate of our society. Derelictions by corporations and their managers, who usually occupy leadership positions in their communities, establish an example which tends to erode the moral base of the law and provide opportunity for other kinds of offenders to rationalize their misconduct. (p. 14)

Obviously, then, it is not the extent of the harm to the rest of us—the deaths, maimings, and fiscal losses—that has led to the exclusion of white-collar offenders and the inclusion of muggers, house breakers, rapists, and petty thieves on the roster of those who will be immured as a result of the three-strikes programs that have captured the fancy of politicians. If we honestly sought to locate the most effective means to protect our lives, health, and the contents of our pocketbooks, our efforts obviously would be better directed toward getting rid of the pharmacy company executives who falsify test results on drugs that they know to be dangerous but that they nonetheless will market to an unsuspecting public at great profit (Braithwaite, 1984) and the savings and loan gangsters who robbed us so mercilessly (Calavita & Pontell, 1990). Ninety-six percent of the loans by the Vernon Savings and Loan in north Dallas, for instance, were in default at the time of its failure in 1987; that particular S&L bankruptcy ultimately would cost the government $1.3 billion in bailout costs (Pizzo, Fricker, & Muolo, 1991). Don Dixon, owner of the Vernon Savings and Loan, had purchased a $1.9 million chalet in Colorado, a $1 million home in California, and a $2.6 million yacht docked in Florida (Poveda, 1994).

"Serious time for serious crime," the maxim underlying the three-strikes laws, ought to embrace convicted corporate executives such as Dixon if it seeks to be fair. Equal justice demands no less. Besides, it is easier to protect ourselves against street offenses than it is to guard against white-collar crimes. The 18th-century English satirist Jonathan Swift (1726) recognized this and located an ancient Hebrew tradition in a territory visited by Lemuel Gulliver:

> [The Lilliputians] look upon fraud as a greater crime than theft, and therefore seldom fail to punish it with death; for they allege that care and vigilance, with a very common understanding, may preserve a man's goods from theft, but honesty has no fence against superior cunning: and since it is necessary that there should be perpetual intercourse of buying and selling, and dealing upon credit, where fraud is permitted or connived at, or hath no law to punish it, the honest dealer is always undone, and the knave gets the advantage (Pt. 1, chap. 6, pp. 96-97; cf. Bellamy, 1992, p. 50)

Kepone and Ford Pinto

The Kepone case illustrates the vast and yet camouflaged nature of so many white-collar offenses and the threat they pose to all of us. The Allied Chemical Corporation set up a puppet business in Hopewell, Virginia—calling it the Life Sciences Products Corporation—to shield itself from lawsuits. Life Sciences produced Kepone, a deadly insecticide destined for use by banana growers in Latin America, Asia, and Africa. Workers were not told of Kepone's dangers when they began to produce it in an old building near the Allied Chemical plant. After Kepone poisoned the entire valley of the James River, Allied was made to pay heavy damages to remedy the environmental pollution it had caused. It also had to pay damages to former employees, many of whom suffered permanent bodily shaking and sterility (Berman, 1978).

The three-strikes doctrine could be fashioned to bring within its orbit both persons knowingly responsible for disasters such as the Kepone operation as well as those who merchandise automobiles such as the Ford Pinto, with a gas tank that the company knew would—as it did—produce dozens of unnecessary deaths. An internal company memorandum had concluded that it would be cheaper for Ford not to redesign the poorly placed tank but instead to go to court and fight suits and, if necessary, pay off in cases in which juries made awards to survivors of those who had been killed and to persons maimed in accidents caused by the faulty gas tank design (Cullen, Maakestad, & Cavender, 1987).

Ford presumed that there would be 180 burn deaths, 180 "serious" burn injuries, and 2,100 burned vehicles. A dead person, Ford calculated, would cost the company some $200,000 in settlements or jury verdicts, an injury $67,000, and a destroyed vehicle $700. The overall estimate was that if the company did nothing it would lose about $49.5 million as a consequence of the inadequate gas tank. Redesigning the tank for 11 million cars and 1.5 million trucks at a cost of $11 for each vehicle would cost $137 million. Obviously, any sensible corporate executive worth his salt could appreciate that saving $78.5 million was more sensible than saving 200 people from death and an equal number from terrible burns and other injuries.

Mark Dowie (1977), the investigative journalist who brought the Ford facts to light, ended his documentation of its cold-blooded cost-benefit calculations with a note directly applicable to the current debate: "One wonders," Dowie observed, "how long the Ford Motor Company would continue to market lethal cars were Henry Ford II and Lee Iacocca serving 20-year terms in Leavenworth for consumer homicide" (p. 55). Given the appearance since that time of the three-strikes laws, one wonders even more how long Ford or other companies would continue to treat human life and human well-being so indifferently if the consequence to those who did so was a hefty prison sentence that could involve life behind bars.

Public Opinion and White-Collar Crime

Because white-collar crimes—the most harmful kinds of crimes—are ignored in the three-strikes laws, we may conclude that it is not the protection of their constituents that compels the advocacy by legislators of this legislation. Lawmakers presumably are responding to what they perceive to be public opinion, that is, what the people who vote—they hope, for them—desire.

But the evidence on this point is at best mixed. Polls indicate a much greater public displeasure and unease in regard to many white-collar crimes than those offenses that, if they produce a third conviction, will land their perpetrator in prison for an extraordinarily long period of time. Surveys show that 65% of Americans believe that sentences for white-collar crimes are too lenient (Nagel & Swanson, 1993). More specifically, a poll has indicated that an offense such as "knowingly selling contaminated food which results in death" was regarded as much more serious by 200 randomly selected respondents than forcible rape after breaking into a home, assault with a gun on a stranger, armed robbery of a bank, killing someone in a barroom free-for-all, armed robbery of a company payroll, sexual advances to young children, selling heroin, and assault with a gun on a stranger. "Causing the death of an employee by neglecting to repair machinery" was, in the same survey, seen as more serious than the last four of the offenses noted above—the armed robbery, sexual advances to children, sale of heroin, and assault with a deadly weapon (Cullen, Link, & Polanzi, 1982).

Cullen and his colleagues also report that "over 80 percent [of the people they surveyed] stated that white-collar criminals have been treated too leniently and that they desire them to be punished just as severely as 'regular street criminals'" (Cullen, Mathers, Clark, & Cullen, 1983, p. 486). This survey discovered that public attitudes toward white-collar offenders seemed to have grown more punitive since a similar study (Rossi, Waite, Bose, & Berk, 1974) was conducted 8 years earlier. Summarizing the research, Braithwaite (1982) notes that "contrary to a widespread misconception, there is considerable evidence to support the view that ordinary people subjectively perceive many types of white-collar crime as more serious than traditional crime" (pp. 732-733; see also Grabosky, Braithwaite, & Wilson, 1987; Swigert & Farrell, 1980-1981).

This strong expression of public opinion hostile to white-collar crime exists despite the fact that the media tend to ignore or underplay such behavior. Complex commercial fraud cases are hard to convey on television because they are so complicated, involving events that do not lend themselves to vivid pictures and short catchy comments: White-collar crime stories, as one reporter has noted, fail the KIS (keep it simple) test that rules media news reporting. In addition, economic pressure can be brought to bear on media sources that threaten the image of powerful business enterprises (Lampe, 1992).

It would be disingenuous, however, to maintain that the results of the attitude surveys truly represent a popular will that is being ignored or thwarted by insensitive legislators perfervidly backing three-strikes positions. Surveys of crime seriousness collect responses to rather bloodless and cryptic phrases, such as "dumping toxic wastes," and not to full-blown criminal episodes. The respondents to the survey questions are not confronted with what they will see in the courtroom: the well-dressed, articulate, church-going, civic-minded white-collar crime defendants who stand in contrast to the less presentable (from a middle-class perspective) defendants in those kinds of cases that qualify for long-term imprisonment under three-strikes laws. And they do not take account of the cadre of high-priced, learned, clever, and articulate lawyers who defend the wealthy in contrast to the overworked and underpaid public defenders who use what limited resources they have to defend the street criminal (Mann, 1985).

Discrimination between crime in the streets and crime in the suites also is based on the fact that street crimes have a greater immediacy and visibility and appear to pose a more frightening threat than the distant and impersonal suite offenses. Industrial pollution and laxity regarding coal mine health conditions may take their toll in time, but that time tends to be somewhere vaguely in the future. Some people never succumb to asbestiosis while those who worked next to them die a slow and awful death; perhaps something else also contributed to their death. Besides, at least in theory, you have a choice about whether you will work under dangerous conditions (presuming you don't desperately need this particular job). That choice does not exist when you are confronted by an armed robber. Of course, in theory again, you could have stayed home, but most of us would regard that choice as obnoxiously restrictive.

It therefore is the terror of immediate and, especially, random infliction of hurt by the rapist and the mugger and the lessons that a drive-by shooting brings home so awfully regarding the lottery that is life that inculcate dread in people. This dread produces their support of the three-strikes approach for "violent" criminals and the exclusion of the white-collar crimes that in truth are more dangerous.

The Fear Factor

The striking disparity between the actual danger and fear of danger from street crime is continuously reflected, however, in the discrepancy between current crime statistics and surveys that ask about fear of crime. Suburban people are much more fearful of crime than inner-city slum residents, who have much more reason to be concerned. Old people are notoriously unnerved about being crime victims, although it is the young and the minority youths—who do not express nearly as much concern—who statistically are in greater peril (Hill, 1995). Particularly telling are the anomalous results of victimization surveys that have middle-class whites telling interviewers more often than inner-city blacks that they have been victims of assaults. Nobody believes this, but it provides powerful evidence about the differences between classes in the United States in their perceptions of criminal danger and harm. It also tells us in part why the heaviest support for such draconian measures as three strikes largely stems from people who are least susceptible to being victims of street offenses.

In time, citizens might come to appreciate the appalling harm visited on them and their fellows by white-collar crimes, and they may increasingly translate this understanding into votes for tougher sentences for those who perpetrate such crimes. But the legislators are not mistaken about how things stand right now: they understand very well that it is the street crimes by the dispossessed and the distasteful that offend the "respectable" people who will gather at the polls come the next election. Success in politics demands money. Campaign funds will not be forthcoming for incumbents or challengers who advocate embracing within the ambit of three-strikes laws acts that are committed by those very contributors and others like them.

Upgrading the Prisons

There could be substantial side benefits from enthusiastically embracing white-collar offenders within the three-strikes laws. Prison wardens tell us that what they most require to upgrade their wildly overcrowded and monstrously expensive institutions is a better class of clientele. Lester Maddox, onetime Georgia governor, made the point well: "What the Georgia penal system needs," he once intoned, "is a better grade of prisoners" (Grizzard, 1990, p. 154).

Recall, in this regard, what happened when a General Electric vice president and six other executives from various heavy electrical equipment companies were sentenced to 30 days in jail for the most notorious

price-fixing conspiracy in the long history of the Sherman Antitrust
Act. A few weeks into the brief time the executives were placed into
9-foot square cells at the century-old Montgomery County Prison in
Norristown, Pennsylvania, the *New York Times* heralded the fact that
they were "model" prisoners, had "adjusted easily to jail," and were
performing "clerical jobs ably." The warden at Norristown emphasized
that the executives were "the most intelligent prisoners" he had been
able to employ at the job of filing prison records (Weart, 1961, p. 72).
Just imagine what people like this could accomplish to becalm and
improve the boiling cauldrons that now make up the nation's penal
system if they were incarcerated for many more years.

Even more impressive testimony of the value and virtue of long-term
imprisonment for white-collar offenders comes from a review of the
career of Charles W. Colson, onetime special assistant to President
Nixon. Colson, according to Carl Bernstein and Bob Woodward (1974),
was "the resident White House practitioner of underhanded political
crafts" (p. 171). Leonard Garment, a Nixon attorney, found a "sadistic"
quality in Colson; his working philosophy, Garment said, was "to get a
man by the balls and his head and mind will follow" (Strober & Strober,
1994, p. 276). Herbert Klein, a longtime intimate friend of Nixon,
thought that Colson was "one of the meanest people I ever knew"
(Strober & Strober, 1994, p. 273).

Nixon's closest aides—Haldeman and Erlichmann—were overwhelmed by the president's demand for their time and attention as he
spun out political plots, some brilliant, some bizarre. In Colson, they
located a man who could sit endlessly and resonate to Nixon. Unfortunately, however, rather than dropping the president's nefarious
schemes at the door to the Oval Office, as others had learned to do,
Colson, the loyal soldier, often took action. Among other things, he
dispatched Howard Hunt, who would lead the Watergate break-in, to
a hospital bed in Denver to persuade Dita Beard to deny having written
a letter that incriminated her company, ITT, in bribery. ITT had
contributed $400,000 to Nixon's campaign war chest allegedly to
obtain his support for a favorable settlement of an antitrust case
involving the company.

Amid the debris of Watergate, Colson was able to negotiate a guilty
plea to one count of obstruction of justice, this in connection with the

burglary of the office of Daniel Ellsberg in an effort to defame and destroy Ellsberg, who had released the Pentagon Papers, which showed the falsity of government assertions about the progress of war in Vietnam. He was sentenced to 1 to 3 years in prison and fined $5,000 (Mankiewicz, 1975).

By this time, Colson had relocated God. In fact, it was Colson who, taking the title of his testament of faith (Colson, 1976) from the Book of John, rousingly resurrected the rather obscure words "born again" (Colson, 1979). Herbert Klein, Nixon's former press secretary, said he thought Colson "a tough son of a bitch," and that "as a Christian, I am gratified that he did have a conversion, because if there was ever a man that needed it, it was Chuck Colson" (Strober & Strober, 1994, p. 279).

For his part, Colson accepted the time he had to serve at the Maxwell federal prison in Alabama with equanimity. "I can work for the Lord in prison or out of prison," he proclaimed (Ambrose, 1991, p. 363). And work he did, with the same ferocity he had demonstrated in the White House, only now in a different venue. In 1976, he formed the Prison Fellowship, which sought to change the lives of convicts through "a combination of practical assistance and relentless evangelism" (Carlson, 1992). So successful was Colson's ministry that two decades later he was awarded the Templeton Prize for Progress in Religion, a prize that carried a stipend of more than $1 million. "Twenty years later I see how God has used my life," Colson noted when getting the award. "Sometimes the greatest adversities turn out to be the greatest blessings" ("Colson's Triumph," 1993, p. 16).

Two lessons might be drawn from the Colson saga. First is how valuable a prison experience might become for white-collar criminals, persons with the particular backgrounds and personalities to turn imprisonment into constructive and law-abiding paths. And second, how extraordinarily valuable it might have been had Colson and others like him been retained inside the walls for all or most of the rest of their lives. Inside, their intelligence, energy, and other talents could have been employed in an even more productive intramural manner than they were outside. Imagine how wondrous it would have been for a prison to have had President Nixon in its inmate population.

Rewriting the Law

But how can patterns of law-breaking such as Colson's be embraced within a three-strikes program? The essence of the programs is that they are designed to warn off two-time losers and to incapacitate severely those who fail to heed the warning. Although these are reasonable goals, they fail to take into account other and more important considerations. For one thing, the criminal law ought to seek to protect the most people in the most effective way against the most harm. Obviously, as has been shown, white-collar offenders are the most dangerous category of lawbreakers. For another thing, a statute such as the three-strikes law should seek to deter as best it can those who will otherwise commit crimes that inflict heavy doses of physical and fiscal injury. Those in positions of power, as we have indicated, will respond much better than street offenders to the prospect of a long stretch in the state prison.

The current three-strikes laws typically require a new conviction that follows two earlier convictions (or guilty or nolo contendere pleas) for any one of a roster of predatory offenses. The law is based on the reasonable premise that some street offenders persist in a career of crime. White-collar offenders, however, almost invariably cease their law-breaking once they are apprehended: For one thing, they often lose the job that had been an essential element in their criminal activity; for another, they may have reached an age where they can gracefully (and often with lucrative ease) retire. Therefore, they are not likely again to be in a position where they will carry out acts such as polluting the environment, fixing prices, or bribing those who can favor them.

That a scenario in which white-collar criminals are embraced within the claws of the three-strikes formula is not too far-fetched can be seen from a brief look at California's law, the prototype for the nation. Three strikes was built on a sentence enhancement program that was inaugurated after a favorable citizen vote in 1982 for Proposition 8, a so-called Victim's Bill of Rights. In 1994, the legislature grafted the three-strikes policy onto the earlier law. The enhancement provisions, the courts had found, were neither arbitrary nor oppressive, although a defendant twice convicted for murder would receive the same mandatory enhancement on a third offense as one twice convicted of selling narcotics to minors. Both crimes, the court noted disingenuously, were

"serious" behaviors (*People v. Villasenor,* 1984). Similarly, juvenile offenses—at-bats in the minor leagues—were thrown into the hopper
when compiling a roster of previous offenses. At the same time, the
earlier enhancement provision that offenses needed to be "brought
and tried separately [Calif. Penal Code sec. 667a(1)]" was dropped in
the three-strikes statute.

Because offenses need not be brought and tried separately in California, it would require only a small stretch to include statutory
language that would capture white-collar criminals in the snare of the
three-strikes provisions. As suggested earlier, that stretch might be
made in terms of harm, which is precisely what the statute seeks to
avoid.

It might be argued that altering the rules so that white-collar criminals can be brought within the perimeter of the three-strikes laws
denies equal justice. I would maintain that on the contrary, it presses
toward equal justice and would emphasize Eugen Ehrlich's (1936)
observation that "the more the rich and the poor are dealt with
according to the same legal propositions, the more the advantage of
the rich is increased" (p. 238). Recall George Bernard Shaw's (1946)
comment that although a poor person "snatches a loaf from the baker's
counter and is promptly run into jail," the white-collar criminal
"snatches bread from the tables of hundreds of widows and orphans
and simple credulous souls who do not know the ways of company
promoters; and, as likely as not, he is run into Parliament" (pp. 61,
69-70). The same point is made in a doggerel folk verse popular in the
East Anglia region of Britain:

> They hang the man and flog the woman
> Who steals the goose from off the Common;
> But let the greater criminal loose
> Who steals the Common from the goose.
>
>   (Wilson, 1982, p. 71)

What is required is the counting for three-strikes purposes of discrete
white-collar criminal acts. The General Electric bid-riggers, for example, violated the law on innumerable occasions over the years when
they orchestrated who should submit the lowest bid on this or that
contract. Colson was known to be responsible for any number of

distinct violations in addition to the one to which he pled guilty. The three-strikes laws could be extruded so that they would not require three separate offenses but rather three white-collar offenses that produced a particularly serious rent in the social fabric or, perhaps, a monstrous kind of injury or deprivation; say, 15 or perhaps 50 deaths or the loss of a million dollars or so.

Of course, street offenders such as burglars also commit a bevy of offenses besides the one for which they ultimately are apprehended (Wright & Decker, 1994), but only one will be counted in the three-strikes calculations. True enough, but if criminal justice is truly to be just it ought to acknowledge that status and class position overwhelmingly dictate forms of criminal activity: The rich who own several cars do not feel any impulse to steal cars. The crimes white-collar offenders commit should not be shielded from the reach of three-strikes laws simply because such offenders are in a position to commit a series of crimes that will be detected only once. Neal Shover (1976) has expressed particularly well the imperative relationship between class position and criminal activity that challenges the justice of the three-strikes laws:

> The members of the underclass command so few resources that, when engaging in criminality, they must rely upon stealth, guile or frontal assaults on property to attain their objectives. No so for elites, whose resources include the bureaucratized labor power of others: elites can, therefore, use bureaucracies as instruments for the perpetration of their criminal ends. Control over organizations, as resources, thus becomes a kind of functional equivalent of the underclass bandit's pistol. (p. 12)

A more direct and simple approach to tough treatment of white-collar criminals has been blueprinted in California. In October 1994, triggered by the rape and murder of Polly Klaas in northern California, the state legislature enacted a "one-strike" law (Cal. Penal Code sec. 667.61) that decrees life imprisonment (with possibility of parole only after 15 years) on conviction of any of seven sexual offenses, including forcible rape, forcible spousal rape, and rape in concert. All that needs to be done is to extend this list to matters such as unnecessary surgery that results in death or serious injury and to other kinds of illegal elite violence and infliction of serious harm.

Corporations as Criminals

In line with a reclassification of the screening mechanisms for three strikes, it would be well to eliminate criminal culpability for corporations and to address their law-breaking civilly, where the burden of proof is less and the penalties can be just as severe, except for the shame and humiliation, which probably have only a slight, if any, effect in changing corporate behavior (Geis & DiMento, 1995). Eliminating entity criminal liability would encourage more intense focus on the acts of corporate officials who should bear personal criminal responsibility for their law-breaking. Note, in this regard, that the brokerage firm of E. F. Hutton engaged in a fraudulent scheme in which its bank accounts were overdrawn by as much as $270 million a day. Approximately 400 banks were cheated of $8 million. The company pled guilty to 2,000 felony counts of mail and wire fraud and, under the plea agreement, paid a $2.75 million fine and reimbursed the banks. But not a single human being was prosecuted; this despite the statement of the Justice Department that two Hutton executives were responsible for the fraud "in a criminal sense" (Fisse & Braithwaite, 1993, pp. 2-3). The Subcommittee on Crime of the House of Representatives' Committee on the Judiciary observed that "the Hutton plea contributed to a decrease in public confidence in the fairness of the criminal justice system—a pervasive feeling that defendants with enough money and resources can 'buy' their way out of trouble" (U.S. House of Representatives, 1986, p. 161).

E. F. Hutton executives are hardly the only white-collar criminals who have escaped the consequences of their illegal behavior. Asbestos is estimated to have led to 170,000 deaths from lung cancer and other related diseases, yet not one of the corporate executives who deliberately concealed the dangers of asbestos has ever been criminally prosecuted (Calavita & Pontell, 1994).

In the Kepone case, a grand jury charged the company with 940 counts of violating the Refuse Water Pollution Control Act (Fisse & Braithwaite, 1983). Fines against Allied Chemical amounted to $9.5 million. The amount was spread over 28.5 million shares of stock, resulting in a loss of about 33 cents a share. Stone (1977) notes, however:

In the Kepone affair, no one went to prison. Not a single employee of Allied was fired. None, so far as is known, lost his or her job, was passed over for promotion, or suffered censure from any of the professional societies that might have exercised some voice in the matter. (p. 9)

Questions of Deterrence

The three-strikes approach has a greater likelihood of producing useful results if used with white-collar criminals than with street offenders (Braithwaite & Geis, 1982). That white-collar offenders would be exquisitely sensitive to the threat of a three-strikes provision is suggested by the fact that all of the corporate executives at the Norristown jail declared that they did not want members of their family to visit them, presumably because of the humiliation and shame they felt regarding where they were. Commonplace crooks, we know, are not so readily deterred; that is why we will catch so many of them in our three-strikes nets. They often show little patience with persistent law-abiding ways, perhaps because there is a good deal less satisfaction for them in such a way of life than there is for a corporate executive making a salary in the hundreds of thousands—or more. Street offenders addicted to drugs find the lure of a fix so compelling that they readily will risk a long prison haul to try to obtain the wherewithal to meet their daily drug requirement.

The moods that thrust large numbers of street offenders into lawbreaking are anger, desperation, and defiance (Shover, 1991). Whitecollar offenders, on the other hand, are shrewd calculators. Costbenefit ratios and bottom lines are prominent considerations in their way of life. They have acquired an education, built a career, obtained a reputation for virtue. They usually have a good deal more than their fair share of the world's goodies, and they will be reluctant to risk losing what they have.

That strong action against others of their ilk will particularly convince white-collar criminals to hew to the straight and narrow was demonstrated in the General Electric price-fixing case. In this example, participants often laid off their antitrust conspiracy when they observed that enforcement agencies were particularly active in matters close to their realm. When the government agents eased off, the corporate executives went back to fixing prices (Geis, 1967). Chester

Bowles (1971), on the basis of his experience as head of the Office of Price Administration during the second World War, noted that 20% of all businesspeople would comply unconditionally with any rule but 5% would attempt to evade it. The remaining 75%, he concluded, are likely to comply, but only if the punitive threat to the dishonest 5% is made credible. Three-strikes laws make punitive threats very credible.

Corporate executives are likely to be well aware of the jeopardy of breaking the law, although they know right now that the odds are good that they will not be caught or, if caught, that they will be treated very leniently. As Braithwaite (1984) observed, many corporations have a "vice president in charge of going to jail" (p. 308). Carrying a good-sized salary, such a position is not uncommonly difficult to fill these days, given the insignificant risks. But imagine the recruitment problem that would arise if the potential fall guys appreciated that under a three-strikes law they would face a whopping long term, perhaps life, in a prison cell.

Three-strikes sentences also can overcome the nonchalance with which many white-collar offenders view the usual slap-on-the-wrist penalties that nowadays are visited on them if they are caught. A *Wall Street Journal* writer, commenting on illegal insider trading, noted that "crooked businessmen who have made a lot of dirty money don't mind going to jail." White-collar crooks, he observed, "just sit in prison waiting for the day when they get out and can go get the hoard they stashed" (Winans, 1984, p. 270). A wait in prison of 25 years or more might dim considerably such amiable anticipatory attitudes.

Because of general deterrence considerations (i.e., the deterrence of others), we can anticipate that the addition of white-collar criminals to the list of those who will be immured for long periods and up to life under the three-strikes laws will not further overburden the prisons to any great degree. We will need to capture only a few to deter most others. Besides, one of the worst aspects of the three-strikes approach will be circumvented with white-collar offenders. Many street criminals are caught in their third qualifying offense at a relatively early age, and therefore they will run up enormous incarceration expenses. White-collar offenders, on the other hand, are preponderantly middle-aged or older, with a modal age of between 40 and 50 for those convicted of business crimes involving gains of $25,000 or more (Steffensmeier, Allan, Harer, & Streifel, 1989).

Conclusion

The three-strikes proposal gained virtually all of its support because its embrace falls only on those "other people," not on us, the decent folk. We might in a startlingly rare moment lash out violently at a sassy wife or husband or slap an obnoxious kid for the kid's own good. But we are sensible and calculating. Our crimes involve a pen not a pistol. That's how we got where we are. If we are caught once or twice at these domestic peccadilloes, we will have enough wit to cease and desist; after all, we have the den and the extra bedroom to which to retreat when things get overheated.

That white-collar offenders have never been given even the merest consideration in the formulation of three-strikes laws readily betrays the race and class bias, even hatred, that lies at their core. It is those other people who don't learn the lesson. We would like to store them somewhere out of our sight, forever. White-collar offenders who maim and kill hundreds, even thousands, of people are people like us: They share our values, our churches, our neighborhoods. Never mind that street criminals would much prefer to perpetrate their offenses in the cozy confines of the corporate boardroom rather than run such fearful risks. When burglars break into a house, for instance, someone may be standing there with a rifle and blow their head off. But those on the lower rungs of society have so many fewer opportunities to commit the classier kinds of offenses—the antitrust violations, insider trading, savings and loan manipulations, and the bigtime frauds. Lower-class people are restricted to lower-class crimes, and it is these crimes that the three-strikes law myopically focuses on.

Miles W. Lord, the chief judge of the federal district court in Minnesota, put the matter well when he had before him the president and chief executive officer of the A. H. Robins Company as well as the company's senior vice president for research and development and its general counsel. Robins had marketed the Dalkon Shield, a birth control device, in the full knowledge that it induced spontaneous abortions and caused a septic condition that led to death of at least 17 women (Mintz, 1985). This is what Judge Lord (1986) said:

> If one poor young man were by some act of his . . . to inflict such damage upon one woman, he would be jailed for a good portion of the rest of his

life. And yet your company, without warning to women, invaded their bodies by the millions and caused them injuries by the thousands. And when the time came for these women to make their claims against your company, you attacked their characters, you inquired into their sexual practices and into the identity of their sex partners. You exposed these women and ruined families and reputations and careers in order to intimidate those who would raise their voices against you. You introduced issues that had no relationship whatsoever to the fact that you planted in the bodies of these women instruments of death, of mutilation, and of disease. (p. 9)

Morton Mintz (1985), after examining details of the Dalkon Shield disaster, came to essentially the same conclusion: "Americans remain content," he wrote, "to live with the paradoxical proposition that harm knowingly and willfully inflicted on them is to be punished, even by death, if done for personal reasons, but is to be unpunished, not even by a day in jail, if done for corporate reasons" (p. 125).

I would conclude with a strong disclaimer. The truth is that I do not favor the three-strikes laws, neither for street offenders nor for white-collar criminals. The foregoing observations have not truly been made to persuade people that the three-strikes law ought to be extended to white-collar crime. Such a policy is far beyond any possibility in the foreseeable future. Besides, it is a rotten idea for any society to so isolate anybody from its midst for so long and under such stark, vengeance-driven, and absurdly expensive and unreasonable conditions, except the most heinous offenders who are totally beyond redemption.

What I have tried to do is to further demonstrate, in line with other contributions to this symposium, that the roots of the three-strikes doctrine are marked by knee-jerk nastiness. Three-strikes laws reflect an absence of calm and sensible consideration of all the issues involved, both human and economic. The failure of three-strikes laws to meet standards of equal justice for equivalent kinds of criminal wrongdoing—that is, to omit the offenses of white-collar criminals—indicates their logical deficiencies and, more important, demonstrates the strong and ugly strains of race, class, and ethnic bias that have produced these laws.

References

Ambrose, S. E. (1991). *Nixon: Ruin and recovery, 1973-1990*. New York: Simon & Schuster.

Applebome, P. (1995, April 28). The pariah as client: Bombing case rekindles debate for lawyers. *New York Times* (National edition), p. B10.

Baucas, M. S. (1994). Pressure, opportunity, and predisposition: A multivariate model of corporate illegality. *Journal of Management, 20,* 699-721.

Bellamy, L. (1992). *Jonathan Swift's* Gulliver's Travels. New York: St. Martin's.

Berman, D. M. (1978). *Death on the job: Occupational health and safety struggles in the United States*. New York: Monthly Review.

Bernstein, C., & Woodward, B. (1974). *All the president's men*. New York: Simon & Schuster.

Bowles, C. (1971). *Promises to keep: My years in public life, 1941-1969*. New York: Harper & Row.

Braithwaite, J. (1982). Challenging just deserts: Punishing white-collar criminals. *Journal of Criminal Law and Criminology, 73,* 723-763.

Braithwaite, J. (1984). *Corporate crime in the pharmaceutical industry*. London: Routledge & Kegan Paul.

Braithwaite, J., & Geis, G. (1982). On theory and action for corporate crime control. *Crime & Delinquency, 28,* 292-314.

Braithwaite, J., & Pettit, P. (1990). *Not just deserts: A Republican theory of criminal justice*. Oxford: Clarendon.

Calavita, K., & Pontell, H. N. (1990). "Heads I win, tails you lose": Deregulation, crime, and crisis in the savings and loan industry. *Crime & Delinquency, 36,* 309-341.

Calavita, K., & Pontell, H. N. (1994). The state and white-collar crime: Saving the savings and loans. *Law and Society Review, 28,* 297-324.

Carlson, T. (1992, Fall). Deliver us from evil: Prison fellowship's saving grace. *Policy Review, 62,* 72-77.

Carter, R. M. (1980). Federal enforcement of individual and corporate criminal liability for water pollution. *Memphis State University Law Review, 10,* 576-611.

Colson, C. W. (1976). *Born again*. Old Tappan, NJ: Chosen Books.

Colson, C. W. (1979). *Life sentence*. Minneapolis, MN: World Wide.

Colson's triumph. (1993, March 1). *Time, 141,* 16.

Cullen, F. T., Link, B. G., & Polanzi, C. W. (1982). The seriousness of crime revisited: Have attitudes toward white-collar crime changed? *Criminology, 20,* 83-102.

Cullen, F. T., Maakestad, W., & Cavender, G. (1987). *Corporate crime under attack: The Ford Pinto case and beyond*. Cincinnati, OH: Anderson.

Cullen, F. T., Mathers, R. A., Clark, G. A., & Cullen, J. B. (1983). Public support for punishing white-collar crime: Blaming the victim revisited? *Journal of Criminal Justice, 11,* 481-493.

Dowie, M. (1977). How Ford put two million firetraps on wheels. *Business and Society Review, 23,* 46-55.

Ehrlich, E. (1936). *Fundamental principles of the sociology of law* (W. Moll, Trans.). Cambridge, MA: Harvard University Press.

Fisse, B., & Braithwaite, J. (1983). *The impact of publicity on corporate offenders*. Albany: State University of New York Press.

Fisse, B., & Braithwaite, J. (1993). *Corporations, crime and accountability*. Cambridge, UK: Cambridge University Press.

Geis, G. (1967). The heavy electrical equipment antitrust cases of 1961. In M. B. Clinard & R. Quinney (Eds.), *Criminal behavior systems: A typology* (pp. 139-151). New York: Holt, Rinehart and Winston.

Geis, G., & DiMento, J. (1995). Should we prosecute corporations and/or individuals? In L. Snider & F. Pearce (Eds.), *Corporate crime: Contemporary debates* (pp. 72-86). Toronto: University of Toronto Press.

Grabosky, P. N., Braithwaite, J. B., & Wilson, P. R. (1987). The myth of community tolerance toward white-collar crime. *Australian and New Zealand Journal of Criminology, 20,* 33-44.

Grizzard, L. (1990). *If I ever get back to Georgia, I'm gonna nail my feet to the ground.* New York: Villard.

Hill, E. G. (1995). *Juvenile crime: Outlook for California.* Sacramento, CA: Legislative Analyst's Office.

Hills, S. (Ed.). (1987). *Corporate violence: Injury and death for profit.* Totowa, NJ: Rowman & Littlefield.

Lampe, A. (1992). Media coverage of complex commercial fraud. In P. N. Grabosky (Ed.), *Complex commercial fraud* (pp. 189-197). Canberra, ACT: Australian Institute of Criminology.

Lord, M. W. (1986). The Dalkon Shield litigation: Revised annotated reprimand by Chief Justice Miles W. Lord. *Hamline Law Review, 9,* 7-51.

Mankiewicz, F. (1975). U.S. v. Richard Nixon: *The final crisis.* New York: Quadrangle/New York Times Book.

Mann, K. (1985). *Defending white-collar crime: A portrait of attorneys at work.* New Haven, CT: Yale University Press.

Mintz, M. (1985). *At any cost: Corporate greed, women, and the Dalkon Shield.* New York: Pantheon.

Nagel, I. H., & Swanson, W. M. (1993). The federal sentencing guidelines for corporations: Theoretical underpinnings and some thoughts about their future. *Washington University Law Quarterly, 71,* 205-259.

People v. Villasenor, 199 Cal. Rptr. 349, 132 Cal App.3d 30 (1984).

Pizzo, S., Fricker, M., & Muolo, P. (1991). *Inside job: The looting of America's savings and loans.* New York: HarperPerennial.

Poveda, T. G. (1994). *Rethinking white-collar crime.* Westport, CT: Praeger.

President's Commission on Law Enforcement and Administration of Justice. (1967). *The challenge of crime in a free society.* Washington, DC: Government Printing Office.

Rossi, P. H., Waite, E., Bose, C. E., & Berk, R. E. (1974). The seriousness of crime: Normative structure and individual differences. *American Sociological Review, 39,* 224-237.

Shaw, G. B. (1946). *The crime of imprisonment.* New York: Philosophical Library.

Shover, N. (1976). *Organizations and interorganizational fields as criminogenic behavior settings: Notes on the concept of organizational crime.* Unpublished manuscript, University of Tennessee at Knoxville, Department of Sociology.

Shover, N. (1991). Burglary. In M. J. Tonry (Ed.), *Crime and justice* (Vol. 14, pp. 73-113). Chicago: University of Chicago Press.

Steffensmeier, D., Allan, E. A., Harer, M. D., & Streifel, C. (1989). Age and the distribution of crime. *American Journal of Sociology, 94,* 803-831.

Stone, C. D. (1977, Summer). A slap on the wrist for the Kepone mob. *Business and Society Review, 22,* 4-11.

Strober, G. S., & Strober, D. H. (1994). *Nixon: An oral history of his presidency.* New York: HarperCollins.

Swift, J. (1726). *Travels into several remote nations of the world.* London: Benj. Motte.

Swigert, V. L., & Farrell, R. (1980-1981). Corporate homicide: Definitional processes in the creation of deviance. *Law and Society Review, 15,* 161-182.

U.S. House of Representatives. (1986). *E. F. Hutton mail and wire fraud case, Part 1.* Committee on the Judiciary, Subcommittee on Crime, 99th Cong., 2nd Sess.

U.S. v. Benjamin, 328 F.2d 854 (2nd Cir. 1964).

Weart, W. G.. (1961, February 26). 7 trust violators model prisoners. *New York Times,* p. 72.

Wilson, A. (Ed.). (1982). *East Anglia in verse and prose.* London: Secker & Warburg.

Winans, R. F. (1984). *Trading secrets.* New York: St. Martin's.

Wright, R. T., & Decker, S. (1994). *Burglars on the job: Street life and residential break-ins.* Boston: Northeastern University Press.

Chapter Twelve

Three Strikes as Public Policy

Future Implications

DAVID SHICHOR
DALE K. SECHREST

"Three strikes and you're out" legislation receives wide-scale support from the American public, which is upset with the high level of crime in American society and with the apparent lack of success in curbing it. Fear of crime is seen as widespread, and millions say that they are afraid to walk the streets of their neighborhoods after dark, and in many cases, during daytime as well. This situation, fueled by selective reporting of crime news and by the saturation of films and television with violence, has created a sociopolitical climate in which any policy aimed at "fighting crime" can muster great public support. Obviously, politicians are well aware of this matter, and they know that the safest bet in waging a successful political campaign is to promise tough crime policies if they are elected. In this atmosphere, the enactment of three-strikes laws is neither surprising nor unexpected. It is, to a large degree, the continuation of a trend, which Irwin and Austin (1994) called the "imprisonment binge" that started in the late 1970s and led to a threefold increase of the U.S. prison population during the 1980s (see also Bureau of Justice Statistics, 1995). These increases have occurred in the face of decreasing overall crime rates nationally as well as stable violent crime victimization rates through the mid-1990s, which are showing some recent increases mainly for teenagers and minorities (Mauer, 1994a; Zawitz et al., 1993). Three-strikes laws, as mentioned in several chapters in this book, also have antecedents in various types of mandatory prison term statutes (see Simon, Chapter 2, this volume; Zeigler & del Carmen, Chapter 1, this volume). The recent increase in the use of habitual offender, career criminal, or recidivist laws raises several important issues that have been discussed in this book. These have included legal, penological, social, organizational, and economic issues.

Legal Issues

One question concerns the Eighth Amendment issue of whether application of the three-strikes law may be construed as leading to cruel and unusual punishment in some cases (Zeigler & del Carmen, Chapter 1, this volume). In the case of the California law, if an offender has two "serious" felonies, the third, which may evoke the three-strikes penalty, can be any felony. Thus, it may be questioned whether sentencing someone to prison for 25 years to life for stealing a piece of meat from a supermarket, as happened in California, constitutes a proportionate punishment or whether it is so disproportionate that it violates the spirit of the Eighth Amendment. Another constitutional question that emerges concerns the separation of powers. In the case of three strikes, like the case of other mandatory sentences, the judicial power is severely limited because the legislative branch determines the nature and extent of punishment. Thus, there seems to be a formal encroachment by the legislative branch on the domain of the judiciary.

Even though there were not any Supreme Court decisions concerning the constitutionality of the three-strikes law based on the above points, these decisions are relevant for the understanding of the effects of this legislation. The California three-strikes law has stipulated also that serious felonies committed by an individual while he or she was a juvenile can be counted as a strike. This is a sharp departure from the prevailing judicial philosophy and criminal justice practice, which make a clear distinction between juvenile and adult courts and advocates the sealing if not the complete expunging of juvenile records.

Penological Issues

Three-strikes laws are a part of the deterrence-incapacitation trend that became prevalent during the 1980s and early 1990s in the United States and, to a lesser degree, in several other modern industrialized countries. This measure abandons ideas of retributive justice and "the justice model" of punishment derived from the neoretributionist era of the 1970s (Fogel, 1975; Shichor, 1987; von Hirsch, 1976) and the built-in proportionality between the harm caused by the crime and the punishment prescribed. When this law is applied to offenders who have committed relatively minor property offenses and who can be sent to prison for 25 years to life, then the claim for proportionality is abandoned.

Similarly, three-strikes legislation negates the idea of rehabilitation, which was the major penal policy for dealing with offenders during the 1960s. This approach lost its appeal due to the changing sociopolitical atmosphere that started in the 1970s (see Shichor, 1992). It is questionable whether a society will be able to maintain its capacity for harsh punishments infinitely. In the spring of 1994, the U.S. prison population passed the 1 million mark. Since then, this number has continued to grow, as have concomitant correctional expenditures (Maguire & Pastore, 1994). The United States already has the highest incarceration rate in the world (Mauer, 1994b).[1] The three-strikes law, according to all projections, will further enhance this imprisonment binge (Irwin & Austin, 1994). However, as noted by Austin (Chapter 7, this volume) regarding the national scene and by Cushman (Chapter 4, this volume) relating to California, the major prison population growth in the future will come not so much from sentences for third strikes but for second-strike commitments. In California, for example, the new laws require that offenders convicted of second offenses that qualify as second strikes will have to serve a term of at least 80% of their sentences before release as opposed to the 50% that was required before the new laws (Austin, Chapter 7, this volume).

Three-strikes laws raise similar questions as to what the selective incapacitation strategy does, namely, to what degree is it justifiable to send some habitual or repeat offenders who commit nonviolent crimes to prison for a very long term to prevent them from committing subsequent crimes (von Hirsch, 1985)? How many false-positive cases will result in unnecessarily long years in prisons for potentially nonviolent offenders?

Also, a serious concern for law enforcement officers has been raised by some experts. It pertains to the potentially violent resistance of arrestees who are three-strikes "candidates" and may know that a possible life sentence is awaiting them if they are apprehended. Will this measure endanger law enforcement personnel (see Casey and Wiatrowski, Chapter 10, this volume)? So far, the picture regarding this issue is not clear. Preliminary figures from California indicate that justifiable homicides by police officers, which is an indirect measure of how many suspects shoot it out with police, declined 9% during the first 9 months of the new law, and assaults on police officers statewide also declined 3.3%. However, one California city showed an increase of 48% in the past year, and the feeling is that this may become a trend (Willis, 1995).

Another question deals with the punishment of non-three-strikes offenders. There are strong indications that a much larger percentage of offenders than ever before has chosen to go to trial since the three-strikes laws came into effect (Cushman, Chapter 4, this volume; Greenwood et al., Chapter 3, this volume). Previously, in urban areas more than 90% of the cases were settled by plea bargains. Obviously, cases that go to trial demand considerably more time to prepare, investigate, and dispose of than plea-negotiated cases. At the same time, most of the fiscal efforts to implement the new law are directed toward the correctional system whereas the judiciary by and large has to use the same resources as before. It is feasible that non-strike cases will be less investigated and less well prepared than previously and that an increasing number of them will even be closed because of the emphasis on three-strikes cases. It may lead to the early release of sentenced nonstrike felons to make room for three-strikes convicts (American Society of Criminology, 1995).

The question is whether the severe punishment of a portion of convicted offenders, some of whom (by no means all of them) are a threat to the community, will provide more protection for society than the lesser punishment of a larger number of offenders, some of them involved in minor crimes. Will it result in further crime prevention, reducing the fear of crime, and improving public attitudes toward the criminal justice system? This penal policy seems to be in line with the "bifurcation of punishment" (see Cohen, 1985), in which there is a trend to make punishments more severe for serious or violent crimes, whereas increasingly, minor crimes are handled in community-based programs. However, in the three-strikes trend the "softer" handling of minor offenders is not implemented on the basis of penological principles, judicial considerations, or well-established criminal justice planning, but as a result of fiscal and time constraints.

Issues Related to the Criminal Justice System

The handling of three-strikes cases by the criminal justice system and the courts raises many questions. As noted, mandatory sentences that increase the severity of punishment for serious crime and enhance the uniformity of punishment curtail the discretion of judges, who are the most visible actors in the criminal justice system and, therefore, the easiest targets for public criticism and discontent. On the other hand, the legislation of mandatory sentences, including the three-strikes laws, increases to a great extent the discretionary power of the prosecutors who decide how a crime will be charged. In many three-strikes cases, the prosecutor's decision may determine whether an offender will serve a short or a long prison term (see Cushman, Chapter 4, this volume). For example, in California, filing a department store refund scam worth $161 as a felony in the case of an offender who already had two previous convictions resulted in a 25-year to life sentence for a 53-year-old offender. Such a charge in a non-three-strikes case would typically carry a 16 months to 3 years prison sentence if filed as a felony (Cekola & Ellingwood, 1995); as a misdemeanor, it could have carried a jail sentence. In the first application of the federal three-strikes law, an offender got life plus 5 years for committing his fourth violent felony by robbing a food store in Iowa, in which he and his companions brandished (but did not use) weapons (Ostrow, 1995). He had been involved in several prior holdups using weapons. According to the U.S. Attorney, if this individual had been convicted in a state court he would have probably served 8 years with parole eligibility at $2\frac{1}{2}$ years, but "because of the crime bill, we were able to remove him from society for the rest of his life" (Ostrow, 1995, p. A15).

The shifting balance of power in the criminal justice system, from the visible and easily criticized judges to the less visible and politically motivated prosecutors, may have a lasting effect on the criminal justice process and may increase rather than decrease the disparity of sentences (indications of this are made by Cushman, Chapter 4, this volume). There are already instances in California where some judges try to circumvent this process by discounting previous strikes or altering new charges to parole violations rather than sentencing someone to 25 years to life for a nonviolent crime (Spiegel, 1994). There are also court rulings that may curb the effects of this legislation. For example, a California appellate court ruled that three-strikes defendants can seek to have prior convictions thrown out by claiming that they were not adequately defended in previous cases that resulted in strike convictions (Willis, 1995).

Previous mandatory-sentencing research has indicated that in certain cases, juries failed to convict defendants when violations did not seem to them to be serious enough to warrant the long term of incarceration prescribed by law. Whether this situation will occur in three-strikes cases remains to be seen. A related issue that was touched on earlier concerns society's capacity to punish. This capacity is not infinite (Pontell, 1984). As demonstrated in chapters in this book (e.g., Greenwood et al.'s and Cushman's), the implementation and operation of this policy will put a tremendous financial burden on state and county governments, many of which are already under severe economic strain. Even if the monies needed for the full application of the three-strikes law were available, it is going to be hard to cope with the projected growth of prison population. For example, according to the California independent Legislative Analyst's Office (1995) report, to abide by the new law the state will have to build 15 new prisons by the year 2000.

As Greenwood et al. (Chapter 3, this volume) have demonstrated, projected correctional expenditures will almost completely deplete all tax dollars that are not mandated in California, a concern shared by many citizens. For example, the state budget for higher education, which is unprotected by law, could easily be consumed by new prison construction. This will occur in the midst of the "computer revolution," when significant changes are taking place in needed employment skills, and the "information explosion" will require a better-educated workforce. Supplementing the budget by increased taxes seems unlikely in the prevailing political atmosphere. When one of the foremost concerns of every politician is to promise tax cuts, it is ironic that the most fervent advocates of three-strikes laws tend to be members of the fiscally most conservative segments of society. Many critics of such laws suggest that legislatures and the public will ultimately refuse to fund expansion of the criminal justice system sufficient to manage the projected increases in offenders.

Policy Issues

The major policy goal of the three-strikes law was to decrease the occurrence of serious crime. Theoretically, this goal would be achieved by the long-term incapacitation of hardcore serious offenders. As Simon has pointed out in this volume, various research found that a small percentage of offenders is responsible for a disproportionately large number of major crimes (e.g., Hamparian, Schuster, Dinitz, & Conrad, 1978; Wolfgang, Figlio, & Sellin, 1972). Logically, these offenders should be the targets of this penal policy. However, it was shown that a large percentage of the prison population, including three-strikes cases, is incarcerated for nonviolent property crimes.[2] Moreover, the three-strikes measure will keep many repeat offenders incarcerated beyond the criminally active age span. In these cases, the preventive function of this measure will diminish considerably or disappear completely. On the other hand, the cost of incarceration will increase substantially because of the growth in health care expenditures due to a large elderly prison population, the average health condition of which is below of that of the general population. The care for elderly inmates will have to be provided by specially trained personnel, who will cost additional sums of money.[3] According to prison population projections based on 1995 figures, inmates 50 years and older (an age limit that many consider for prisoners as "elderly") in California will grow from 4.2% of the total to 8.2% in the next 5 years and will reach 19.8% by 2020 (Austin, Chapter 7, this volume).

Some of the more difficult questions to address at this time relate to the effect of three-strikes laws on individual offenders and on the operation of jail and prison systems. How many more jails and maximum-security prisons will be needed? Will triple-bunking in cells and dormitories be necessary? Will the behavior of pretrial inmates change in relation to the new law, as suggested later in this chapter? Will the behavior of sentenced inmates change significantly because of the time to be served under the new law? How will jail and prison administrators react to the influx of three-strikes offenders with respect to management problems that require improved security procedures and improved methods to control crowding? To what extent will inmate management procedures require revision, including security classification, disciplinary procedures, transportation, inmate employment (e.g., regular work programs, industries, etc.), health services, and even feeding arrangements for these inmates? How will correctional officers unions, who were the major supporters of the legislation, react to the problems generated by implementation of the law? Will additional training and/or pay be needed and/or demanded for correctional officers in jails and prisons? How will parole policies be affected? Will court or professional standards be affected by the law?

There is an increased probability that prison violence, which already has reached a high level in America, will continue to rise in the wake of the growing numbers in prison and the percentage of convicts sentenced to long-term incarceration under three-strikes laws. Thus, this policy will affect not only the inmates who will have to serve longer sentences but prison administration and management as well. Evidence from a state-sponsored study of 18 California jails shows increased violence rates in local jails since the passage of the law. Assaults by inmates against jail staff have risen 26.7%, from 333 to 427 during the first 9 months of the three-strikes law (McConnell, 1995). The report indicates also that pretrial populations have increased 10% (51% to 61%), length of stay for three-strikers is quite high, and more high- and maximum-security housing is needed for these cases. Of greatest interest is the fact that the majority of three-strikes inmates held were not charged with a violent crime; only 32.7% of the three-strikes inmates were in jail for violent offenses. Sources citing this study and officials of the California Department of Corrections note that offenders are becoming very much aware of the law and that it may be changing their behavior in the institutions (see Furillo, 1995). There is danger that the frustration level in the prisons will grow and that the ability of the prison personnel to use "good time" and favorable recommendations to parole authorities as management techniques will diminish. As with jails, attacks on prison staff are likely to increase.

These types of potential consequences may explain the great concern about three-strikes legislation expressed by corrections officials who are concerned with problems of maintaining order in crowded correctional facilities. Solutions include converting lower-security prisons (or any prison or local jail space available) to handle three-strikes inmates, triple-bunking cells and dormitories, using program space for housing, and crowding community correctional facilities. As one California prison official notes, we cannot predict all the changes that will occur in the criminal justice system as a result of three-strikes and related legislation, but failure to react to impending problems will be "unconscionable." The interests of the California Correctional Peace Officers Association have been documented by Schiraldi (1994), who notes that this union contributed almost a million dollars to the current governor's reelection campaign and lobbied heavily for the three-strikes law. Because the law will increase the number of correctional officers, it will give them even more bargaining power and political clout for the future.

In summary, the three-strikes laws are handling fewer violent offenders than originally thought, who were the real target. Courts will become clogged with these cases, driving out less severe cases that require attention and moving civil cases to the bottom of the list of judicial priorities. Some judges are already resisting implementation of the new laws, as are some citizens who have refused to testify where a third strike is possible. Costs to incarcerate these offenders in jails or prisons may simply become prohibitive in time, and the resulting crowding may result in increased violence and general disturbances. Turner, Sundt, Applegate, and Cullen (1995) document these concerns over escalating costs as well as the related constitutional issues. They, as do we, express concern about the implications of "quick fix" legislation that may shift attention from the more fundamental issues of addressing the problems of serious, violent offenders.

Issues of Justice

Originally, the three-strikes law targeted offenders who are repeatedly involved in "serious" crimes. These crimes by definition are infractions committed, in the overwhelming majority of cases, by the poor and minorities (i.e., lower-class people). Offenses that are loosely defined as white-collar crimes, and usually committed by "respectable" middle- and upper-class people often in the name of powerful corporations, very seldom (if at all) qualify as one- or two-strike offenses; thus, the second- or third-strike punishment may be applied rarely for white-collar crimes. This situation reinforces the relative neglect of white-collar crime as a criminological, penological, or criminal justice concern. Geis (Chapter 11, this volume), in his provocative chapter, underscores this issue clearly. The existing disparity in the social response to crimes committed by poor people versus offenses committed by respectable rich people will not only prevail under the three-strikes policies but will even grow. The percentage of poor and minority inmates in prisons will continue to increase because they will be the ones who are sentenced for very long periods of incarceration. Mauer (1994b) cites a study by the Federal Judicial Center showing that "black offenders are 21 percent more likely and Hispanic offenders are 28 percent more likely than similar white offenders to receive a mandatory sentence" (p. 8). There is little doubt that this measure will not only increase actual social injustice but perceived injustice as well.

Turner et al. (1995) have documented 77 proposed habitual offender statutes in 37 jurisdictions that could be considered true three-strikes laws, with 15 of 37 states having enacted the legislation. The various mandatory and three-strikes laws enacted in these states very likely will maintain or probably even contribute to the disparity of sentencing and punishment policies throughout the country. These variations in the punishments imposed by three-strikes laws may reinforce the perception that it is more important where one commits a crime than the type of crime committed. Thus, the goal of reduction of disparities to decrease the perception of injustice that is pervasive in American society hardly will be served by three-strikes measures. Punishment policies do reflect on the nature and core values of a society. Although there is a tremendous pride in the democratic system and the individual freedom accorded to every citizen in American society, the United

States has the highest incarceration rate in the world (Mauer, 1994a). Not only is a higher percentage of the population in confinement but the periods of confinement tend to be longer than in most other countries (see Langan, 1991). The image of America reflected in three-strikes laws is that it is either (a) a seriously crime-ridden society in which the often-cited personal freedoms ran amok and created anarchy at a level that prompted a search for extreme and desperate crime control measures; (b) a very punitive and vengeful society; (c) an alienated and anomic society that is using the punishment of criminals as a rallying cry to reestablish some level of societal cohesion (Durkheim, 1933); or (d) some combination of the above. Any one of these images is not very complimentary of American society, to say the least; in fact, if there is a kernel of truth in them it should be very troubling.

The American Society of Criminology's (ASC, 1995) task force on three-strikes legislation made several policy recommendations that may become useful for the continuous reevaluation and reshaping of sentencing legislation. Among others, the task force recommended (a) an impact analysis to study the effects of this law on the courts and the correctional system; (b) informing the public of the true costs and consequences of the various mandatory sentences; (c) developing sentencing legislation to allow sufficient judicial discretion to give consideration to individual differences among offenders; (d) conducting research concerning the effects of this legislation on the civil court system and various social programs, such as education, health, welfare, and infrastructure; (e) encouraging the development of alternative sentencing policies that may result in the same crime reduction benefits at considerably less cost; and (f) emphasizing early youth intervention efforts because they may be more effective in terms of crime prevention than three-strikes laws.

It would be a good idea for legislators, administrators, and other policymakers to use the information and analyses presented in this volume as well as the ASC recommendations to formulate more flexible and less arbitrary sentencing policies than those dictated by the types of three-strikes legislation now in place.

Ultimately, the test for the effectiveness of any combination of these measures will be whether there is a substantial decline in the level of crime and whether people will be safe in the sanctity of their homes or walking the streets of their neighborhoods. If these results do not come about, then it will be another costly and failed attempt to deal with a major symptom of severe social ills without trying to address, in serious and fundamental ways, the underlying problems that are plaguing American society.

Notes

1. A recent publication of the U.S. Justice Department reports that as of June 30, 1995, there were 1,004,608 inmates in state prisons, up 9.1% from a year before, and there were 99,466 federal inmates, up 6.1%. This combined growth of 8.8% exceeded the average rate of growth of the past 5 years (Shogren, 1994).

2. Even the father (and grandfather) of Polly Klaas felt that the three-strikes law did not properly target repeat violent offenders, like the one who murdered his daughter. The net was cast too wide over 500 possible third-strike felonies ("Prop. 184," 1994).

3. It is conceivable that this population will be an attractive target for private health care concerns, and prison officials may find it beneficial to contract for health services for many elderly inmates under the new law.

References

American Society of Criminology. (1995, November/December). Task force reports, National Policy Committee. *The Criminologist, 20*(6), 4-16.

Bureau of Justice Statistics. (1995, April). *Correctional populations in the United States* (Executive summary). Washington, DC: U.S. Department of Justice.

Cekola, A., & Ellingwood, K. (1995, September 23). Two strike out as own lawyers. *Los Angeles Times,* p. B1.

Cohen, S. (1985). *Visions of social control.* Cambridge, UK: Polity.

Durkheim, E. (1933). *The division of labor in society.* (G. Simpson, Trans.). New York: Free Press.

Fogel, D. (1975). *We are the living proof: The justice model for corrections.* Cincinnati, OH: Anderson.

Furillo, A. (1995, March 19). "Three strikes" deterrent effect noted. *San Bernardino Sun,* p. B5.

Hamparian, D., Schuster, R., Dinitz, S., & Conrad, J. (1978). *The violent few.* Lexington, MA: Lexington Books.

Irwin, J., & Austin, J. (1994). *It's about time: America's imprisonment binge.* Belmont, CA: Wadsworth.

Langan, P. (1991). America's soaring prison population. *Science, 251,* 1568-1573.

Legislative Analyst's Office. (1995, January 6). *Status: The three strikes and you're out law--A preliminary assessment.* Sacramento, CA: Author.

Maguire, K., & Pastore, A. L. (1994). *Sourcebook of criminal justice statistics 1993.* Washington, DC: Bureau of Justice Statistics.

Mauer, M. (1994a). *Americans behind bars: The international use of incarceration, 1992-1993.* Washington, DC: Sentencing Project.

Mauer, M. (1994b). *Three strikes and you're out* (Testimony before the House Judiciary Committee, Subcommittee on Crime and Criminal Justice, March 1, 1994). Washington, DC: Sentencing Project.

McConnell, T. (1995, February). *Three strikes jail population report.* Sacramento, CA: State Sheriff's Association Detention and Corrections Committee and Board of Corrections.

Ostrow, R. J. (1995, August 15). First life sentence under U.S. "three strikes" law. *Los Angeles Times,* p. A15.8.

Pontell, H. N. (1984). *The capacity to punish.* Bloomington: Indiana University Press.

Prop. 184: Why even Polly Klaas' father says it's a big mistake [Editorial]. (1994, October 24). *Los Angeles Times,* p. B10.

Shichor, D. (1987). Penal policies: Some recent trends. *Legal Studies Forum, 11*(1), 55-78.

Shichor, D. (1992). Following the penological pendulum: The survival of rehabilitation. *Federal Probation, 56*(2), 19-25.

Schiraldi, V. (1994, October). *The undue influence of California's prison guards' union: California's correctional-industrial complex.* San Francisco: Center on Juvenile and Criminal Justice.

Shogren, E. (1994, December 4). U.S. prison population rises a record 8.8% in year. *Los Angeles Times,* p. A.3.

Spiegel, C. (1994, October 24). 3 strikes has escape loophole. *Los Angeles Times,* pp. A3, A14-A15.

Turner, M. G., Sundt, J. L., Applegate, B. K., & Cullen, F. (1995). "Three strikes and you're out" legislation: A national assessment. *Federal Probation, 59*(3), 16-35.

von Hirsch, A. (1976). *Doing justice.* New York: Hill and Wang.

von Hirsch, A. (1985). *Past or future crimes: Deservedness and dangerousness in the sentencing of criminals.* New Brunswick, NJ: Rutgers University Press.

Willis, D. (1995, October 25). Felons not taking third strike lightly. *San Bernardino Sun,* p. A3.

Wolfgang, M. E., Figlio, R. M., & Sellin, T. (1972). *Delinquency in a birth cohort.* Chicago: University of Chicago Press.

Zawitz, M. W., Klaus, P. A., Bachman, R., Bastian, L. D., DeBerry, Jr., M. M., Rand, M. R., & Taylor, B. M. (1993). *Highlights from 20 years of surveying crime victims: The National Crime Victimization Survey, 1973-1992.* Washington, DC: Bureau of Justice Statistics.

Index

About the Editors

David Shichor is Professor of Criminal Justice at California State University, San Bernardino, where he has taught since 1975. He coauthored two books and published more than 70 articles and book chapters on various criminological and sociological topics. Recent research completed includes studies in the areas of privatization, victimology, punishment, and youth institutions. Several current articles address the problems of privately owned prisons. His most recent book is *Punishment for Profit: Private Prisons/Public Concerns* (1995). He earned his Ph.D. in sociology at the University of Southern California (1970).

Dale K. Sechrest is Professor of Criminal Justice, California State University, San Bernardino. He developed national standards for corrections and developed procedures for their application in an accreditation program for the American Correctional Association from 1975 to 1984. He recently completed a study of performance review and internal audit in corrections for the National Institute of Corrections. He has completed studies on corrections management, privatization of prisons, substance abuse treatment, and juvenile diversion. He is coauthor of *Jail Management and Liability Issues* with William C. Collins (1989). He earned his D.Crim. (1974) at the University of California at Berkeley.

About the Contributors

Allan F. Abrahamse received his Ph.D. in mathematics in 1967 from the University of Michigan. He joined the RAND research staff in 1974 and has served as a policy analyst, mathematical modeler, and statistician. He began working in criminal justice research in 1982 with a study of selective incapacitation, in which he developed a widely discussed scale for detecting high-rate career criminals. He is currently directing an evaluation study of violence prevention programs in California and is also engaged in a study of the effects of demographic changes on future homicide rates. In addition to criminal justice, he also is engaged in an analysis of no-fault automobile insurance plans and a study of excess claiming by automobile accident victims.

James Austin is Executive Vice President for the National Council on Crime and Delinquency (NCCD). He received his bachelor's degree in sociology from Wheaton College, his master's degree in sociology from DePaul University in Chicago, and his doctorate, also in sociology, from the University of California at Davis. Dr. Austin directs NCCD's national Research and publication program. Currently, he serves as director for several programs, most notable the Evaluation of "Three Strikes and You're Out," National Evaluation of the Multi-State Correctional Options Program for the National Institute of Justice, and the National Assessment of Structured Sentencing Reforms.

Karen A. Casey is Assistant Professor of Criminal Justice at the University of Tennessee at Chattanooga. She formerly taught at Florida Atlantic University. She received her Ph.D. in criminal justice from State University of New York at Albany, where she was awarded the Distinguished Doctoral Dissertation Award for her research on incarcerated women and their children. She also worked for the New York State Department of Correctional Services while in New York. She is presently involved in a project evaluating the success of a local drug treatment facility for children.

Jonathan P. Caulkins is Associate Professor of Operations Research and Public Policy at Carnegie Mellon University's Heinz School of Public Policy and Codirector of RAND's Drug Policy Research Center. He received his B.A. degrees in systems science and engineering, computer science, and engineering and policy as well as an M.S. in systems science and mathematics from Washington University in St. Louis. He received his M.S. in electrical engineering and computer science and his Ph.D. in operations research from Massachusetts Institute of Technology. His research focuses on modeling and analyzing drug markets and their response to policy interventions.

James Chiesa, a communications analyst, has for the past 12 years assisted the RAND researchers in organizing, revising, and summarizing written reports and oral presentations for clear communication of findings to diverse audiences. In recent years, his principal efforts have been in criminal justice and in defense acquisition and technology policy. He is coauthor of *Diverting Children From a Life of Crime: Measuring Costs and Benefits.* He has an M.S. in environmental science and an M.A. in zoology from Indiana University.

Robert C. Cushman has experience as a practitioner, planner, consultant, trainer, facilitator, demonstration project director, researcher, evaluator, and writer in criminal justice. He is a Justice Systems Specialist in the Office of the County Executive, Santa Clara County, California, and consultant in the administration of justice. He leads Santa Clara County's intergovernmental program to transfer justice simulation modeling software and technology to other units of government, and he also assesses comparative county justice system policies, expenditures, and workload. He is a consultant for the U.S. Department of Justice, the National Institute of Justice, the National Institute of Corrections, and units of state and local governments. Most of these assignments are focused on justice-system-wide assessments to help communities more clearly diagnose their justice system problems and fashion more affordable, coordinated, and cost-effective approaches. He is a member of the Board of the Association for Criminal Justice Research (California), the American Justice Institute, the National Association of Criminal Justice Planners, and other justice-related academic and professional organizations. He has a B.A. in sociology-anthropology from Pomona College and an M.A. in government administration from the Claremont Graduate School.

Rolando V. del Carmen is Professor of Criminal Justice in the College of Criminal Justice, Sam Houston State University. He received his B.A. and LL.B. degrees in the Philippines, obtained an M.C.L. from Southern Methodist University, an LL.M. from the University of California at Berkeley, and a J.S.D. from the University of Illinois. He has published extensively in law and criminal justice. His recent books include *Criminal Procedure: Law and Practice* (4th ed., 1995), *Briefs of Leading Cases in Corrections* (1995), *Civil Liabilities in American Policing* (1991), and *Briefs of Leading Cases in Corrections* (1993). He served for 6 years as a member of the Texas Commission on Jail Standards and has worked as a consultant with state and federal agencies on various projects. In 1986, he won the Faculty Excellence in Research Award; in 1995, the Distinguished Professor Award at Sam Houston State University; and in 1991, he was given the Academy Fellow Award by the Academy of Criminal Justice Sciences.

Malcolm M. Feeley is Professor and Associate Dean in the School of Law at the University of California at Berkeley, where he is Chair of its program in Jurisprudence and Social Policy. He received his Ph.D. in political science from the University of Minnesota and taught at NYU, Yale, and Wisconsin before joining the Berkeley faculty in 1984. He is the author of numerous articles and several books, including *The Process Is the Punishment* (winner of the ABA's Silver Gavel Award), *The Policy Dilemma* (with Austin Sarat), and *Court Reform on Trial* (recipient of a Citation of Merit from the ABA). He is currently completing *Judicial Policymaking,* a book on how courts made policy in prison conditions cases. His current research focuses on women and crime in the 18th century and the historical origins of plea bargaining.

Gilbert Geis is Emeritus Professor in the Department of Criminology, Law and Society, University of California, Irvine. He is former president of the American Society of Criminology and recipient of its Edwin H. Sutherland Award for research. He also has received awards from the American Justice Institute, the Western Society of Criminology, the Association of Certified Fraud Examiners, and the National Organization for Victim Assistance. His most recent publication is as an editor of the third edition of *White-Collar Crime: Classic and Contemporary Views,* with Robert F. Meier and Lawrence M. Salinger (1995).

Peter Greenwood is the Director of RAND's Criminal Justice Program. His areas of research have included violence prevention strategies, police investigation practices, prosecution policy, criminal careers, selective incapacitation, juvenile justice, and corrections. He is currently directing several evaluations of preventive and correctional interventions for high-risk juveniles. He is a member of the American Society of Criminology and Homicide Research Working Group, the Los Angeles Violence Prevention Coalition, and is a past President of the California Association of Criminal Justice Research. He has a B.S. from the U.S. Naval Academy and M.S. and Ph.D. degrees in industrial engineering from Stanford University. He has served on the faculties of Caltech, the Claremont Graduate School, the RAND Graduate School, and the University of Southern California.

Sam Kamin is a doctoral candidate in the Jurisprudence and Social Policy Program and a law clerk to the Honorable D. Lowell Jensen, Federal District Court Judge, Northern District of California. He received his J.D. from the University of California, Berkeley School of Law (Boalt Hall) and his B.A. *summa cum laude* in physics from Amherst College. His article "Technology and the Fourth Amendment: The Case for a Smart Gun-Detector" is forthcoming in *Law and Contemporary Problems.*

Malcolm W. Klein is Professor of Sociology and Director of the Social Science Research Institute at the University of Southern California. He served as Chair of the USC Sociology Department for 13 years, founded USC's Social Science Research Institute, and has received the university's Raubenheimer Award. He earned his Ph.D. in social psychology at Boston University (1961). He has served on the Board of the American Society of Criminology, as Chair of the criminology section of ASA and SSSP, as President of the Association for Criminal Justice Research (California), as Chair of an NIMH crime and delinquency review committee, and on numerous panels and committees. In 1990, he received the ASC's Edwin H. Sutherland Award and has served as the Vice President of that association. He has been elected to Fellow status in four professional associations. In 1995, he received the Paul Tappan Award from the Western Society of Criminology. His most recent research involves the nature and control of street gang violence, gang involvement in illegal drug distribution systems, gang migration, and gang resistance. He has published extensively about the juvenile justice system in western Europe, Russia, and China. His latest book is *The American Street Gang* (1995).

Stephen P. Klein is Senior Research Scientist at RAND, where he has led policy studies on educational, health, and criminal justice issues. He has investigated racial/ethnic biases in sentencing in capital and noncapital cases, the correlates of recidivism, the characteristics of stranger and acquaintance rapes, witness and juror attitudes toward the criminal justice system, and the consistency of adjudication decisions and case processing across states. He has served as an expert witness in state and federal courts and at legislative hearings. He received his Ph.D. in industrial psychology from Purdue University. He was Associate Professor in Residence at University of California at Los Angeles before coming to RAND.

Karyn E. Model received her Ph.D. in economics from Harvard University in 1992 and is currently Associate Economist at RAND. She participated in an evaluative study of the Alcohol, Drug Abuse and Mental Health Treatment Services Block Grant formulae, for which she examined the financing systems associated with treatment services and estimated models of funding need. She also analyzed the cost-effectiveness of innovative drug prevention programs piloted by the Department of Defense. Recent projects include RAND's analysis of California's three-strikes initiative, and the cost-effectiveness of alternate strategies for reducing violent crime.

C. Peter Rydell is Senior Researcher at RAND. He received his B.A. from Harvard and his M.C.P. and Ph.D. degrees from the University of Pennsylvania. He builds and analyzes computer models of public policy issues. His experience in model-based policy analysis covers areas such as rent control, drug control, housing vouchers, school vouchers, military personnel, and criminal justice. He has taught policy analysis courses at Hunter College, Columbia University, University of California at Los Angeles, and the RAND Graduate School.

Jonathan Simon is Professor at the University of Miami, School of Law. He holds a JD and a PhD (Jurisprudence and Social Policy) from the University of California, Berkeley. His book *Poor Discipline: Parole and the Social Control of the Underclass 1890-1990* (1993) won the American Sociological Association, Sociology of Law section book prize in 1994. Professor Simon's most recent work concerns the emergence of risk as a central problem for the exercise of governmental power in modern society.

Ray Surette is Professor in the Department of Criminal Justice and Legal Studies at the University of Central Florida in Orlando. His research interests include the study of crime, criminal justice, and the mass media as well as drug use and policy and the media, and media technology and crime control. He is also involved in studying the impact of immigration and statistical and organizational criminology. He has published a number of articles in the areas of media, crime, and justice, and he is editor of *Justice and the Media* (1984) and *The Media and Criminal Justice Policy* (1990) and the author of *Media, Crime & Criminal Justice: Images and Realities* (1992). He is also a coauthor of *Immigration and Its Impact on American Cities* (forthcoming).

Michael D. Wiatrowski is presently Associate Professor of Criminal Justice at Florida Atlantic University. He received his Ph.D. in urban studies in 1978 from Portland State University. He has served as a military police officer with the U.S. Army in the Republic of Vietnam and is presently a Lieutenant Colonel in the U.S. Army Reserve. His research interests include community policing, juvenile delinquency, crime prevention, and criminal justice policy. He is concerned with integrating community policing with the larger field of community development and community theory.

Frank A. Zeigler is a doctoral student and Instructor in the College of Criminal Justice, Sam Houston State University. He obtained his B.A. at the State University of New Jersey at Glassboro and his J.D. from the University of Tulsa. He practiced law for 20 years, during which time he founded and directed the Public Defenders Office for the City of Tulsa. He has extensive experience as a criminal trial lawyer, and while in private practice argued before the U.S. Supreme Court. He has been Adjunct Professor in Criminal Justice in Tulsa and has taught various topics in law.